Transpacific Cartographies

Asian American Studies Today

This series publishes scholarship on cutting-edge themes and issues, including broadly based histories of both long-standing and more recent immigrant populations; focused investigations of ethnic enclaves and understudied subgroups; and examinations of relationships among various cultural, regional, and socioeconomic communities. Of particular interest are subject areas in need of further critical inquiry, including transnationalism, globalization, homeland polity, and other pertinent topics.

Series Editor: Huping Ling, Truman State University

Chien-Juh Gu, *The Resilient Self: Gender, Immigration, and Taiwanese Americans*

Stephanie Hinnershitz, *Race, Religion, and Civil Rights: Asian Students on the West Coast, 1900–1968*

Jennifer Ann Ho, *Racial Ambiguity in Asian American Culture*

Helene K. Lee, *Between Foreign and Family: Return Migration and Identity Construction among Korean Americans and Korean Chinese*

Melody Yunzi Li, *Transpacific Cartographies: Narrating the Contemporary Chinese Diaspora in the United States*

Huping Ling, *Asian American History*

Huping Ling, *Chinese Americans in the Heartland: Migration, Work, and Community*

Haiming Liu, *From Canton Restaurant to Panda Express: A History of Chinese Food in the United States*

Jun Okada, *Making Asian American Film and Video: History, Institutions, Movements*

Kim Park Nelson, *Invisible Asians: Korean American Adoptees, Asian American Experiences and Racial Exceptionalism*

Zelideth María Rivas and Debbie Lee-DiStefano, eds., *Imagining Asia in the Americas*

David S. Roh, Betsy Huang, and Greta A. Niu, eds., *Techno-Orientalism: Imagining Asia in Speculative Fiction, History, and Media*

Leslie Kim Wang, *Chasing the American Dream in China: Chinese Americans in the Ancestral Homeland*

Jane H. Yamashiro, *Redefining Japaneseness: Japanese Americans in the Ancestral Homeland*

Transpacific Cartographies

Narrating the Contemporary Chinese Diaspora in the United States

MELODY YUNZI LI

Rutgers University Press
New Brunswick, Camden, and Newark, New Jersey
London and Oxford

Second Printing, 2024

Library of Congress Cataloging-in-Publication Data
Names: Li, Melody Yunzi, author.
Title: Transpacific cartographies : narrating the contemporary Chinese
    diaspora in the United States / Melody Yunzi Li.
Description: New Brunswick : Rutgers University Press, [2023] |
    Series: Asian American studies today | Includes bibliographical
    references and index.
Identifiers: LCCN 2023017866 | ISBN 9781978829343 (hardcover) |
    ISBN 9781978829336 (paperback) | ISBN 9781978829350 (epub) |
    ISBN 9781978829367 (pdf)
Subjects: LCSH: Chinese literature—History and criticism. | Chinese
    diaspora in literature. | Chinese in literature. | United States—In literature.
Classification: LCC PL2275.C45 L5 2023 | DDC 895.109—dc23/eng/20230629
LC record available at https://lccn.loc.gov/2023017866

A British Cataloging-in-Publication record for this book is available from the British Library.

Copyright © 2024 by Melody Yunzi Li

All rights reserved

No part of this book may be reproduced or utilized in any form or by any means, electronic or
mechanical, or by any information storage and retrieval system, without written permission
from the publisher. Please contact Rutgers University Press, 106 Somerset Street, New
Brunswick, NJ 08901. The only exception to this prohibition is "fair use" as defined by U.S.
copyright law.

References to internet websites (URLs) were accurate at the time of writing. Neither the
author nor Rutgers University Press is responsible for URLs that may have expired or changed
since the manuscript was prepared.

www.rutgersuniversitypress.org

For my mom, Yuefen Li, and my grandparents,
Wenbin Li and Anyi Fang

Contents

	Introduction	1
1	Mapping Experiences of De/Reterritorialization: Ha Jin's *A Map of Betrayal*	24
2	Cartographing Carceral Dystopia in the Mao Era: Yan Geling's *The Criminal Lu Yanshi*	46
3	Affective Mapping of Touristic Diasporic Experience	65
4	Palimpsestic Map of the American and Chinese Dreams: Contested Sites in Overseas Chinese Immigrant Stories	90
	Coda: Charting an Online Chinese Diasporic Literary Map	117
	Acknowledgments	135
	Notes	139
	Bibliography	163
	Index	175

Transpacific Cartographies

Introduction

At the end of Ha Jin's novel *A Free Life* (2007), the protagonist, Nan, has found a way to anchor himself beyond geographical boundaries by mapping his own immigrant journey to find a home. In a poem, "Homework," the child literally sketches a map of an imaginary country: "Under his pencil a land is emerging. He says, 'I'm making a country.' / . . . On the same map he draws a chart—/ railroads crisscross the landscape; / highways, pipelines, canals / entwine; sea lanes curve / into the ocean, airports / raise a web of skyways."[1] The places that he describes draw on the America that Ha Jin has experienced but in a way that gives agency to an immigrant in mapping his reality rather than being a victim of a map, with the borders of the nation-states drawn. As he writes in a separate poem, "Another Country," Nan works to "build" his "home / out of garlands of words," a home that is in a "country without borders."

In fact, by beautifully employing this seeming paradox that an ideal home country could be mapped without any borders, that home itself could be unbound, Ha Jin indicates distrust in the reality of what currently defines a country or nation. A beautiful country created by a child would be one "unmarked by missiles and fleets," one that would not abuse its power "to issue visas and secret orders."[2] These forms of political abuse prevent people from ever achieving a sense of belonging. Nan proves the futility of territories entirely— that is why the homeland must be boundless; a country without missiles is only possible as a country without borders. Once the territory and the lines are drawn, it begs the question of what is included and what is excluded. It is the illusion that geographical locales and physical entities as currently constituted can truly become home that devastates Nan, as well as many other immigrants on their journeys.

In the novel, neither the nation-state of China nor Nan's adopted land of America provides him with a sense of home. Instead, Ha Jin refutes the idea that countries are where one finds a sense of shelter, a feeling of belonging, and a stable place called home by highlighting the affective power of the unbound homeland in one's imagination and modeling for readers and by showing readers how to draw borderless maps of their own home. The real paradise lives within, and only exists in the landscape of the immigrants' imagination—their sense of home is generated through the maps they create.

In his essay "Imaginary Homelands," Salman Rushdie explains how the immigrant writer may never be able to accurately "reflect" exactly what was left behind, but the writer's "broken mirror may actually be as valuable as the one that is supposedly unflawed."[3] Building on Rushdie's formulation, this book looks at the broken mirrors and imaginary maps of literary and TV productions of the contemporary Chinese diaspora to argue that the intensified loss, imagined or real, produces artistic interventions that help us understand the contemporary Chinese diasporic experiences, especially during the China–U.S. tensions in the post–Cold War era. *Transpacific Cartographies* examines the cultural products of the Chinese diaspora from the 1990s to the present, focusing on each work's unique map of what it means to be home through the lens of geocriticism and spatial literary theories. Intersecting Sinophone and Chinese American studies, this project consciously reads Chinese diasporic stories as anything but binary narratives that either uphold or debunk the American dream or the new Chinese dream, that either suggest a return to an original home in China or advocate trying to find a new one in a foreign land.

Specifically, the book examines the cartographic narratives mapped by Anglophone writer Ha Jin; Sinophone writers[4] Yan Geling (嚴歌苓), Shi Yu (施雨), Chen Qian (陳謙), and Rong Rong (融融); selected TV shows; and internet writings. Whether created by people who have left China for the United States at one point, or describing characters who have gone on diasporic journeys, the narratives engage readers in both China and the United States by constructing complex concepts of home. At the core of this project is an analysis of the way in which these novels and various media map the contemporary Chinese diaspora through the language and the imaginaries they create. As we saw in Ha Jin's writings at the start of this book, this sort of mapping is not just an academic, theoretical construct but an important part of how Chinese diasporic writers themselves conceive of their diasporic experience. This monograph will follow its traces across several works, moving from the national boundaries to the familial and then to the affective, personal sense of home, examining the at times subtler, more internal mapping of home that characters undergo as they navigate their own diasporic journeys.

As texts and media, these writings not only tell stories that allow their creators to establish a sense of home through the temporal process of narrating their aspects of their lives, but they also produce different visions of belonging for the people of the Chinese diaspora. They form cognitive maps that locate their creators within imaginary spatial constructions of home and abroad, and of China and the United States. The concepts that have been increasingly used in the scholarship of Chinese American and Chinese diaspora studies, "in-betweenness," "hybridity," and "Chineseness,"[5] can no longer fully capture the complexities and contradictions of the Chinese diasporic space, of trying to map a home that paradoxically contains the individual and is without borders. Highlighting the Chinese diasporic lived-imagined space allows us to reconsider the transpacific methodology as one that is not merely about displacement or attachment but also about U.S.-China and English-Chinese circulation and entanglements and tensions, as well as the psycho-geography of homemaking in an era of global precarity.

Charting Home Amid Rising Sino–U.S. Tensions

As we will see in analyzing the cultural products selected for this study, diasporic Chinese communities in America are often simultaneously welcoming and alienating, a contested site of belonging. In these works since China's geopolitical and economic rise about three decades ago, we have seen a shifting, complex, and conflicting sense of identity and belonging affecting the members of the contemporary Chinese diaspora.

This complexity has only increased as Sino-U.S. tensions reached a boiling point in 2022 as consequential events unfolded one after another. First, there was a U.S. diplomatic boycott of the Winter Olympics in Beijing in February 2022, followed by President Joe Biden giving Chinese president Xi Jinping a strict warning in March of that year not to provide materiel support to Russia in its invasion of Ukraine. In May, the speech by U.S. secretary of state Antony Blinken outlined President Biden's China strategy as one that positioned China as "the most serious long-term challenge to the international order," and as the United States's opponent in economic and political power.[6] Then, on August 2, 2022, U.S. Speaker of the House Nancy Pelosi visited Taiwan to show support for the island, which triggered a heated response from China with the Chinese military conducting large-scale exercises around the island. In February 2023 a surveillance balloon connected to China's global surveillance program flying over the United States was found and shot down by the U.S. military on Biden's orders. The incident has further heightened the Sino-U.S. tensions.

However, this conflict between China and the United States is nothing new—it has been increasing over the past few years and has only been exacerbated by the pandemic: anti-Chinese sentiment has emerged as one of the most serious side effects of COVID-19. Former U.S. president Donald Trump insisted on referring to COVID-19 as "the Chinese virus," blaming

China for being the origin of the virus. Xenophobia and anti-Asian racism related to the pandemic have erupted all over the world: between March 2020 and March 2022, there were nearly 11,500 such cases just in America reported to the Stop AAPI Hate initiative. This racism also targeted Chinese immigrants who were already naturalized or had been in the United States for a long time, as well as Americans of Chinese descent.[7] The "model minority" Asian American community was suddenly stigmatized again by the "Yellow Peril" stereotype, and was subjected to other forms of discrimination and abuse.[8]

Due to these Sino–U.S. political upheavals, diasporic Chinese communities were thrown into a state of shock and instability. In the first years of the pandemic many of us Chinese immigrants and Chinese Americans could not travel back to China and see our families because of the pandemic travel restrictions, nor could we feel at home in foreign countries because of the verbal and physical attacks.[9] Such aggression threatens the entire Asian American community; suddenly, many of the places we once frequented became haunted to us. Hearing stories about Asians being violently attacked in supermarkets, we were afraid of going out. Within one month of the start of the pandemic in March 2020, around 1,500 hate incidents against Asian American and Pacific Islanders had been reported to Stop AAPI Hate. We were in limbo—doors were closed to us, borders hardened, and we were both visible and invisible. The anti-Asian racism and exclusion that have existed since our ancestors arrived in the United States in the nineteenth century, disappearing and reappearing in different forms, has once again become visible. On the one hand, Asian Americans might be less prepared to deal with this because we have grown up under favorable economic conditions; on the other hand, we are definitely capable of dealing with it because in the current situation we can speak up and protect ourselves through social media and publishing, which is shown in some of the works examined in this manuscript.

Given the complicated and antagonistic if not phobic geopolitical relationships between the People's Republic of China, Hong Kong, Taiwan, and the United States that worsened during the anti-global Trump administration, as well as the global pandemic's impact on overseas Chinese communities and Asian Americans, we as scholars wonder how we can join forces in fighting this battle. Many contemporary Chinese diasporic writers have found a way by contributing to the public's understanding of human rights and humanitarianism through literature and the arts. For example, in my 2020 open-access article published in the *British Journal of Chinese Studies*, "Building Home around Hardened Borders," I point out the multiple roles that Chinese diasporic literature has played during the pandemic: overturning large-scale propagandizing by disrupting state narratives and politicians' claims, exposing the realities of pandemic lives, and giving the diasporic community a nonphysical homecoming.[10]

This historical period of increasing Sino–U.S. tensions and the concurrent rise of domestic xenophobic attitudes shows us the precarity in the sense of home that the Chinese diasporic community has experienced. These Chinese diasporic writers create a sense of home that is imagined and imaginary, and although they may not improve the situation of the diaspora in a practical sense, their works are significant because they evoke the collective experiences of the Chinese diaspora today. Their sense of home, like my own, has been severely disrupted by the U.S.–China rivalry. While claiming loyalty and belonging to both nations seemed more feasible previously, it is now much more fraught to do so. For example, China's totally different reactions to the three U.S.-born Chinese Olympians at the 2022 Beijing Winter Olympics and the heated debates over their choices of which country to represent in the games are part and parcel of the same complicated issue of national affiliation and loyalty that the Chinese diasporic communities and Chinese Americans in particular now face.

In such a volatile political situation between the two countries, it is worth studying the ways that contemporary Chinese diasporic writers map their sense of home as the political rivalries and turbulences create even stronger boundaries to overcome. As this book demonstrates, the maps created in these narratives reveal the tensions inherent to trying to create a home without boundaries in today's current climate—tensions that mirror the ambivalences felt by the storytellers themselves along their diasporic journeys. These contemporary Chinese diasporic cultural projects bring up unique questions about languages, locations, loyalties, and relationalities that overlap with yet are distinct from those of previous Chinese immigrants and the diasporas of other countries. The following section will introduce this particular group of immigrants and address how the study of this population and their works contributes to and intervenes in the Asian American, global Asia, Sinophone, and transpacific fields, among others.

The Chinese Diaspora Today

Though working in different cultural and linguistic settings, most of the writers I discuss in this book were born in China in and after the 1950s and went to the United States in and after 1989 when communism had disappointed many educated elites. Although they are immigrants, it is important to note that they are not all from the same background. Yan Geling is a more or less free cosmopolitan citizen, freely traveling between China and the United States, and has been embraced by readers on both shores up until 2022. In contrast, Ha Jin, who has been exiled from China and lives and writes mainly in the States, seems to feel a sense of abandonment due to the treatment by his homeland. Other less known writers, such as Chen Qian, Shi Yu, and Rong Rong, mainly live in the United States yet publish in Chinese in mainland China, using their experience abroad as cultural capital. The TV shows *Beijingren zai Niuyue* 北京人在紐約 (*Beijinger in New York*, 1994) and *Gui qu lai* 歸去來 (*The Way We Were*, 2018) were both produced in China but became popular and circulated both within China and in the diasporic Chinese communities. This book ends with an exploration of new media—internet literature, social media literary platforms, online magazines, and WeChat—that make up an even less settled site of home, but one that is also less circumscribed than traditional cultural products and can travel instantly around the globe. The cultural production and circulation of these new writings and media are therefore all inherently transpacific in nature.

The new Chinese immigrant writers are important to Chinese American literature not only because they represent a demographically "new" group that politically and culturally complicates the map and meaning of "Chinese American," but also because the narratives they produce suggest a bilingual, bicultural, and transpacific formation of Chinese America, which in the current political climate is doubly precarious due to subjection to the dual forces of racism and extraterritorial domination that Ling-chi Wang discussed in 1995, with the latter referring to using sites as entry point for social, political, and economic penetration.[11]

While the core of this project is to examine how these contemporary cultural projects help us to map the Chinese diaspora's quest for identity, we also need to understand the kind of identity labels that they bring into tension with each other. The protagonist of one episode of the TV show *Beijinger in New York* is a female immigrant who has lived in the States for over a decade and become a successful businesswoman. In episode 18 she summarizes the dilemma of her identity: "I find I am neither American nor Chinese. . . . It's like this dance hall—when the music is on the dance hall is crowded, but when the music is off it is empty." When the other protagonist, her lover Qiming, comes to her, she says, "Let's fill the dance hall, even though it's [only] temporary." Here she is mapping America as the physical space of a dance hall, providing a temporary home to immigrants, yet never offering a permanent sense of belonging. The immigrants are like the dancers in the crowd who momentarily feel welcomed in the United States as their home. Who they are and where they belong stands at the core of these diasporic narratives. Therefore, a discussion of identity labels and categories is needed.

I encountered great difficulty when trying to categorize the writers and creators for this monograph, which is due in part to the very tensions of identities that the cultural products themselves bring to the surface in their narratives. They are referred to as Chinese immigrants, overseas Chinese students, Chinese Americans, expatriates, sojourners, or exiles—or they might not be referred to by any of these labels. The term "Chinese immigrant" often refers to a Chinese person who comes to live permanently in another country. "Overseas

Chinese students" (*liuxuesheng* 留學生) refers to those who were born in China (including Hong Kong and Taiwan) and study abroad in other countries. In the literary scholarship of Chinese Americans, the study of *liuxuesheng* has largely focused on the Taiwanese students who lived in the United States in the 1960s and 1970s.[12] The term "Chinese American"[13] has undergone several changes, but, essentially, it implies a person's identity as an American of Chinese descent; unlike the hyphenated term "Chinese-American,"[14] Chinese American takes "Chinese" as an adjective modifying the subject "American." This term is Anglocentric, as "American" is at the center. "Expatriate" may be a good term to describe those who left China, Hong Kong, or Taiwan and are living and working in the United States, but it does not imply that they have necessarily renounced the identity of their birthplace. "Sojourner," similarly, refers to people who temporarily reside in a place. "Exile" is used for people who have been expelled from their country for political or punitive reasons, as well as those escaping from political and social oppression who have entered into self-imposed exile.

In Chinese literary scholarship, the writers I study are mostly referred to by Chinese scholars as "new immigrants" (*xinyimin* 新移民), a term that refers to the Chinese emigrants who began leaving China for the United States in the late 1970s,[15] followed by a wave of student migration from China to the United States. With the emergence of Deng Xiaoping's Reform and Opening Up policy in 1978 and the establishment of U.S.–China diplomatic relationships in 1979, China's attitude toward the United States became more positive, and the relationship significantly improved. Since the 1980s, Chinese popular culture has portrayed the United States as a land of promise and material abundance, resulting in a huge wave of "going abroad" (*chuguo re*, lit. "going abroad fever"). For example, Chinese films like *Be There or Be Square* (*Bujianbusan* 不見不散, 1998, directed by Feng Xiaogang) and *After Separation* (*Da sa ba* 大撒把, 1992, directed by Xia Gang) depict Chinese people's imagination of and desire for the world outside of China.

Over the time period, many Chinese students have come to the United States to pursue advanced degrees. The Chinese Student Protection Act of 1992 granted permanent residence status in the United States to over 54,000 Chinese nationals, many of whom were overseas Chinese students.[16] The past three decades have witnessed a dramatic increase in the number of Chinese emigrants to the United States. In 2017 the number of Chinese students studying abroad reached about 608,400, solidifying China as the world's largest source of international students. Overseas Chinese are enrolled in colleges and graduate schools at more than twice the rate of other international students (15 percent compared to 7 percent of other nationalities).[17] The United States and Western Europe have been the most popular destinations for international students. Besides overseas Chinese students, there are new immigrants coming for business opportunities, mothers coming abroad to accompany their children to their place of study (*peidu mama*), and those coming to join family members who had arrived earlier. Compared to previous immigrants, these newcomers are wealthier and better educated—they are the beneficiaries of China's market transformation and globalization.

No matter whether they come for study abroad or business opportunities, the new generation of the Chinese diaspora is more privileged and globally oriented; many of them see the world less as a collection of discrete nation-states since they have grown up in a much more globalized environment. Perhaps it is the privileged character of the new diaspora that allows it to ignore or to free itself from questions of national identity with which earlier Chinese diasporic writers were obsessed. For example, for the 1960s and 1970s overseas Chinese students (*liuxuesheng*) who had first moved to Taiwan from the mainland before relocating to the United States, the sense of home was largely determined by their national identity. This is reflected in their obsession with their imagined homeland, China, and is clearly seen in the stories of Pai Hsien-yung and Yu Lihua.[18] By comparison, the more cosmopolitan, free-spirited new diasporic writers have sought to define their sense of home and identity in part through their affectionate relationships and attachments that are not bound solely by nationality. Therefore, the maps that the earlier Chinese diasporic writers produced were delineated by nation-states, whereas the new generation of Chinese diasporic writers that are the focus of this book seek to transcend or at least challenge those boundaries.

The contemporary Chinese diaspora, though privileged, is simultaneously vulnerable. Even though the new Chinese diasporic writers chart more personal and affective maps beyond the nation-state boundaries, their own upbringing has been grounded in Chinese culture. Some of them, like Ha Jin, Yan Geling, and Shi Yu, chose to self-exile as overseas Chinese students in the United States and, in Belinda Kong's words, belong to "a distinctly *politicized* Chinese literary diaspora" brought about by Tiananmen.[19] To a certain extent, because they still have family and links to China, and thus vulnerabilities, dealing with political subjects is not an easy choice for them. The majority of this contemporary diasporic population and most of the writers discussed in this book were Chinese student migrants, who, according to Lei Zhang, "exemplified the neoliberal and transnational features of the model minority racialization."[20] America's acceptance of these overseas Chinese students—granting them permanent residence and mobility—further reinforced America's separation of these "good immigrants"[21] or model immigrants from the "undeserving, uneducated" refugees. They exemplify what Chih-ming Wang calls "a global model minoritizing project."[22] Wang critiques the author of the Chinese bestseller *Harvard Girl Liu Yiting: A Chronicle of Quality Education* (*Hafo nühai Liu Yiting*: *Suzhi peiyang jishi* 哈佛女孩劉亦婷: 素質培養紀實, 2000)

for being disdainful of the less educated rural migrants and rewriting the Ivy League story into a global model-minoritizing project. Such elitism has given rise to resentment and animosity toward this group in an era of global populism precisely because its global orientation is seen as a symbol of privilege.

The new immigrant culture products emerging with this wave of immigrants started in the 1980s, developed in the 1990s, and matured in the early 2000s. These works in the 1980s focused on the immigrants' lives in their adopted land, like Zhou Li's *Manhattan's China Lady* (*Manhadun de Zhongguo nüren* 曼哈頓的中國女人, 1992), Su Wei's *Traveler* (*Yuanxingren* 遠行人, 1988), and Xue Haixiang's *Morning, America* (*Zao'an, Meilijian* 早安, 美利堅, 1995). After the 2000s, immigrant works focused more on love and relationships. While the struggles of the earlier Chinese immigrants were often negotiated through an obsession with their homeland or a strong sense of national identity and belonging, recent immigrants have charted their struggles through a more individual and less collective viewpoint, navigating a balancing act between the privileges they enjoy (and experience as eroding) and the daily vulnerabilities they face in America. They discover on their diasporic journey that their privilege is tenuous and fragile. The works produced by this group of immigrants have focused on the personalized and romanticized spaces where they navigate the twists and turns in their immigrant lives.

Previous scholarship on these writings tends to be either Sinocentric or Western-centric. The writers in this study are largely categorized by Chinese critics as *lümei zuojia* (旅美作家, sojourning writers in the States), a term that imagines the Chinese writers as sojourners or travelers who do not fully belong in or to the United States. This thinking is very Sinocentric, whereas its closest equivalent term in the American context—"Chinese American," which mostly refers to those who have already earned U.S. citizenship—is similarly Anglocentric. These two nationalistic terms in two different cultures establish binaries in the field that limit the scope of scholarship on Chinese expatriate writings in the United States, bounding works that themselves seek to be unbound. Similarly, the terms *haiwai huaren wenxue* (海外華人文學, literature by overseas Chinese [writers]) and *haiwai huawen wenxue* (海外華文文學, overseas Chinese [language] literature)[23] have been used to refer to works produced by overseas Chinese writers and are based on the ethnicity of the writers or the language the authors write in, respectively, regardless of where the writers were living when they authored their works. Similar terms in the context of the United States are *Meiguo huaren wenxue* (美國華人文學, American Chinese [writers'] literature) and *Meiguo huawen wenxue* (美國華文文學, American Chinese [language] literature). Although the latter term is more commonly used and discussed in current scholarship, the former term, *Meiguo huaren wenxue*, is more inclusive because it also applies to works written in Chinese or any other language. Writers in this book all technically belong to the group of *Meiguo huaren zuojia* (美國華人作家, Chinese American writers), including those who write in Chinese like Yan Geling, Shi Yu, and Rong Rong, as well as Ha Jin, who writes in English. As Sau-ling Cynthia Wong points out, there are updated versions of these two terms: *haiwai huaren wenxue* and *haiwai huawen wenxue* (both translate as "overseas Chinese literature," with the former emphasizing the identity of the authors, and the latter highlighting the language); and *shijie huaren wenxue* (世界華人文學) and *shijie huawen wenxue* (世界華文文學), both translated as "global Chinese literature," which is a "re-valuation, a rebranding of sorts."[24] *Haiwai* (海外, overseas) suggests "the process of scattering" because understanding the Chinese outside China as being "overseas" defines China as the center.[25] By contrast, *shijie* (global) ignores the issue of center/origin and "connotes an ambition to make one's presence known and appreciated in the world."[26] Among these terms, *shijie huawen wenxue* may sound the most suitable in this transnational age; however, it could also fall into the Sinocentric category because it seeks to enhance the global power of the Sinophone community and privileges the centrality of the Chinese language.

I have chosen to use "Chinese diasporic writers" here for several reasons: first, in conversation with current discourse on the complication of identities in African and Caribbean diaspora studies, this monograph offers a unique model for considering how diaspora represents more than a migratory or exilic experience. It shows how these narratives actively claim diaspora as a site of creative production, a cartographic attempt that constantly challenges, revises, and refreshes the maps of global Asia and Sino–U.S. networks. Second, the writers discussed in this book have all had unique experiences and relationships to their homeland and their adopted land (for example, Yan Geling is well-known as a *lümei zuojia* and is sometimes even thought of as a Chinese writer because her biggest market is in mainland China, whereas Ha Jin is in exile, having been expelled from mainland China). Because of such diversity in their markets and identifications, "diasporic Chinese" is a more inclusive term. Third, calling them diasporic writers stresses the tension between the homeland and adopted land, as well as the movement between the two.[27] Fourth, the term "diaspora" has recently been defined as connected to the existential condition. Following Lingchei Letty Chen's definition of diaspora as "a state of being, an existential condition and an emotional and psychic disruption,"[28] this monograph seeks to examine that condition and the complicated cultural identities of the contemporary Chinese diaspora who attempt to transcend the Sino-U.S. tension. Lastly, in the current political situation under which choosing a national affiliation is complicated and risky, diaspora offers Chinese immigrants a temporary liberation or exemption from the obligation of patriotism, from the harassment of the state, and a site at which holding both nations dear to their hearts is possible.

The Chinese diasporic storytellers I cover in this book, of course, cannot represent all the genres in the field, yet their works are endowed with images and tropes of transpacific mapping, which can help us understand the constructions of home and the cultural identities of the contemporary Chinese diaspora. These texts, though written and circulated in different languages and in various media, actively explore notions of home, space, and maps that inherently affect the social formation of identities.

The Ideas and Ideals of Home/Homelessness

The growing China–U.S. rivalry creates further tension in the Chinese diaspora's quest for homemaking that is beholden to no borders. Unlike previously, when there was more freedom of cultural affiliation regardless of country of citizenship, now the sense of home is being severely delineated by the U.S.–China tensions. We are therefore forever seeking a map to help us find a home. The rhetoric of home in Chinese diasporic literature and media not only portrays the complexity of the Chinese diaspora's cultural identity but also indicates a desire to challenge the fixed identity labels they are assigned.

"Home" in this book first refers to specific physical spaces, including public and communal spaces where one feels a sense of belonging, such as restaurants, cafes, and schools, as well as domestic, intimate spaces, such as houses; however, it also refers to virtual spaces, including social media, blogs, and online magazines, as well as those only found in the imagination. "Home" is not just a space, however; it is the feeling of being part of and identifying with something or someone—it is a sense of belonging. The works considered in this book show home to be an extremely fluid, frequently shifting construct shaped by multiple variables. The sense of belonging, therefore, is not fixed, but can shift in relation to the nation, place, people, or community to which one has at some time felt close to. "Home" is generated through experience and emotions and develops and changes as the experiences and emotions change. In sum, "home" in this book primarily refers to the emotive constructs through which diasporic subjects experience a sense of belonging, whether to a place, a political regime, a culture, a literary creation, or personal relationships. In the writerly imagination, as we will see, home can be both a safe haven where one feels comfortable and also boundless.

Home in these Chinese diasporic narratives is constantly being remade, recreated, negotiated, and redefined. It may start off as a specific locale on the map, whether it is the mainland China homeland, the new land of the United States, or somewhere else along the route. Yet the tortuous diasporic trajectory, as well as the tensions between the departure and the arrival, constantly shift the locales of home. These shifts prove the impossibility of mapping a definite home—or rather the need to constantly remap where one feels at ease. For these contemporary Chinese diasporic authors, I argue, writing about home is their way of rejecting being defined or located in response to society's impulse to categorize them. By mapping their own diasporic journey and that of their immigrant characters, they portray arduous, complicated routes that are barely stable, and it is the constant search for home that makes the mapping process intriguing and complicated. Because home as a site of comfort and belonging is constantly shifting, examining the underlying paradoxes can help us navigate our own diasporic paths. While home is an emotional space through which immigrant subjects construct their identities in relation to different social, spatial, and historical circumstances, dislocating home hints at the flexibility and vulnerabilities of their identities, to a world without boundaries.

This project reaffirms and further complicates the multiplicity and fluidity of "home," as shown in previous scholarship on diaspora studies. Diaspora destabilizes fixed notions of home and identity. The state of diaspora, according to William Safran, is one in which diasporic subjects "regard their ancestral homeland as their true, ideal home and as the place to which they or their descendants would (or should) eventually return. . . . they continue to relate, personally or vicariously, to that homeland in one way or another."[29] Safran refers to the diasporic longing for the homeland as "pull" factors from the old world and to the "push" factors of the new world, but his fixed notion of homeland has been challenged by critics who conceptualize diasporic identity as based on fluidity and anti-essentialism.[30] Current scholarship in diaspora studies, postcolonial studies, and cultural geography interpret identity not as a fixed notion or "an already accomplished fact" but as constantly in flux and in the making. Stuart Hall argues that identity should be read as "never complete, always in process, and always constituted within, not outside, representation."[31] Home as an in-flux concept affirms the difficulty of mapping a fixed geographical locale as home in the diasporic journey, and it also makes the mapping of identity and home a more complicated, interesting process—and one that does not necessarily have an end.

In response to Safran's definition of diaspora, theorists including Paul Gilroy,[32] Avtar Brah, James Clifford,[33] and many others have raised the idea of a "routed identity" that implies the interplay of "push" and "pull" forces. The "routed" approach suggests that the dynamic is not simply a push from the new world and a pull from the old. Rather, the old world pushes and pulls, as does the new. The immigrants are pulled and pushed in multiple directions in multiple ways, and the process continually repeats itself. The push and pull forces from both worlds constitute a mechanism that causes the diasporic subjects to be always moving between the two and never arriving: they are always "en route."[34] In such a process, "home" is no longer equal to the homeland. Rather, it becomes a multiplicity on diasporic routes, and may actually consist of multiple homes. Wendy Walters claims that "the notion of diaspora can represent a multiple, plurilocal, constructed location of home, thus avoiding ideas of fixity, boundedness, and nostalgic exclusivity traditionally implied by the word home."[35] Since diasporic subjects can establish homes along their migratory routes, the original home they set off from is replaced by multiple homes, creating a map that consists of several stopping points. For Asian Americans in particular, Helena Grice associates the concept of "home" especially with diasporic identity. For this community, "home" is not a singular geographical location but "may be contested, lost, out of reach or exist simultaneously in different locations."[36] In other words, the sense of home to a person in a diaspora constantly goes through disruption, negotiation, reconstruction, and transformation on different sites on their diasporic routes. Home becomes a site where diasporic individuals' subjectivity is performed. As Rey Chow aptly states, "Home is here, in my migranthood."[37] This idea celebrates rather than laments always shifting identities.

Redefining home as a malleable concept that is constantly being constructed, more recent diasporic theorists have turned the focus from home seeking to homemaking. Cultural geography theorists Alison Blunt and Robyn Dowling summarize the themes around the relationship between diaspora and home as "the relationships between home and homeland, the existence of multiple homes, diverse home-making practices, and the intersections of home, memory, identity and belonging."[38] Reading this from the perspective of cultural cartography, we can see that the diasporic writers and directors are drawing a journey and mapping scattered home places all over the map, making multiple homes along their journey. This diasporic cartographic practice emphasizes their refusal to locate a fixed home and maps out the disturbances and contradictions in the process of relocating home and identity.

Rather than celebrate or lament the routed identities, this book redefines home in Chinese diaspora by mapping the diasporic experience in contemporary Chinese diasporic narratives. Previous scholarship, whether locating home in a specific physical and geographical place or celebrating multiple homes in migranthood, limits the concepts of home to geographical or nation-state boundaries and set up a binary of home as a specific locale versus home as a multiplicity along the way. However, this idea fails in terms of explaining the nuances of home and identity in the present Chinese diaspora as discussed earlier. Contemporary Chinese diasporic writings and media works place peripatetic homes on imaginative maps constructed against the diasporic subjects' relation to geographic and nation-state boundaries. This book reinterprets home as the creative integration of physical locales that we belong to on diasporic routes, a knocking down of borders rather than setting up multiple ones. By looking beyond the either-or binary, we can focus on the Chinese diaspora's innovative endeavors of seeking home.

In the cultural formation of home, the changing influence of the traditional Chinese ideals of home in different generations of the Chinese diaspora gives added importance to this study. Some of the writers discussed in this book were born in the 1950s and immersed in Chinese culture for about three decades before coming to the United States. In the culture of that time, there was a strong attachment to and obsession with the homeland. Many poems about departure, farewell, or exile evoke nostalgia for the homeland, and dying in a foreign land (*kesi taxiang*, 客死他鄉) is portrayed as a tragedy. Yet today the new immigrants no longer necessarily identify their homeland as home; instead, they can see home as a cultural construct and as a sense of belonging that is found in their hearts. As Chen Xuechao writes in his preface to Chen Ruilin's *Honeymoon Paris* ("蜜月"巴黎— 走在地球經緯線上, 2003), "Home exists in one's heart and is a fluid cultural space."[39] Besides reinforming fluidity as discussed earlier, this quote also highlights spatial construction in the concept of home. The cartographies of contemporary Chinese diasporic writings and media work are an active, conscious crafting of the new Sino–U.S. cultural space rather than simply a merging or reacting with an existing site of home. Finding home in one's heart instead of a physical place is grounded in earlier Chinese philosophy and literature, as seen in the famous lines by the great Tang poet Bai Juyi (白居易, 772–846): "Without having a home in my life to begin with, / I settle down where I find peace of mind" (吾生本無鄉, 心安是歸處).[40] However, poetry like this often laments over homesickness and homelessness, thus suggesting that the longing to reclaim the home that is lost, to find the home that is lost, or to connect to a new home are the goals of mapping the diasporic journey. By contrast, the new generation of the Chinese diaspora juxtaposes the seemingly opposite concepts of home and homelessness, and in that juxtaposition finds a creative integration that breaks down the binary.

In his introduction to Matsuo Bashō's *Narrow Road to the Interior and Other Writings* (2000), Sam Hamill states, "His journey is a pilgrimage; it is a journey into the interior of the self as much as a travelogue, a vision quest that concludes in insight. But there is no conclusion. The journey itself is home."[41] Hamill here points out that the quest for self-identity is essential in Bashō's travelogues, and the journey itself is more important than the destination. Similarly, in the contemporary Chinese diasporic works in this book, the authors are not necessarily leading us to a satisfying destination. Rather, they are guiding us on their journey. Their goal, like Bashō's, is to guide the readers to find their own home through the process of mapping—and the journeys these diasporic writers map are often not so much physical as affective and philosophical. They are often a quest for self-identity in the entanglement between homeland and adopted land, between home and homelessness. The relationalities produced from these mapping activities and the internal conflicts between homes and countries play an important role in our understanding of the contemporary Chinese diaspora. The readers who have shared a similar experience or who resonate with the diasporic experience in any way will most likely be pleased with the journeys that these works take them on.

The works in this book map out a productive tension between home as an idea of peace, security, and protection, and the many national dreams that either hijack or disrupt the idea of home. As I will now discuss, home as a dialogical, psychological construct necessitates the mapping methodology.

The Power of Mapping

I argue that the Chinese diasporic narratives discussed in this book represent cognitive maps that locate their characters within imaginary spatial constructions of home and abroad, of China and the United States. Why is mapping such a suitable metaphor when discussing this sort of imagined space with shifting borders? Robert J. Tally has built a definition of cartography upon the concepts of "transcendental homelessness" (György Lukács), the existential condition (Martin Heidegger, Jean-Paul Sartre, and others), and "cognitive mapping" (Fredric Jameson), connecting spatial representation and storytelling.[42] According to Tally, maps are used to deal with the existential angst that comes with the experience of homelessness or being an "alien." Heidegger points out that the sense of anxiety resembles the feeling of the "uncanny" (*unheimlich* in German), which suggests an "unhomeliness" (*nichts-zu-hause-sein*).[43] The experience of being away from home evokes feelings of alienation and anxiety, and therefore necessitates this mapping. Tally argues that the writer maps the world "coordinating the existential data of the individual writer's or protagonist's experience with the unknowable."[44] We can, therefore, see an author's cartographic impulse as a means of conquering the unknown and the accompanying experience of estrangement. Being in a strange place where we do not belong can be terrifying, and therefore the immigrant, diasporic, and exilic experiences necessitate finding ways to cope with it.

The cartographies of the works discussed here resonate with Jameson's conception of cognitive mapping as a strategy to situate oneself in a complex social space. "Cognitive mapping," frequently cited by Tally, is a framework that enables "a situational representation on the part of the individual subject to that vaster and properly unrepresentable totality which is the ensemble of society's structures as a whole."[45] Built on a phenomenological perspective, Jameson's mapping is a means of finding one's place in a broader social context, while narratives function as maps to give form to the world. Similarly, Tally has summarized Sartre's thoughts on how to deal with the sense of being lost—ideas that tell us to "develop projects by which to give our lives meaning, or to put it in a vernacular more suited to space and spatial relations, to re-establish our sense of place in the world."[46] Sartre's famous "existence precedes essence" gives us agency to determine our paths. The cartographic narratives of diasporic authors, therefore, can be read as a way of creating a path for their diasporic characters and themselves, making sense of the world and their place in it, which is even more significant when their being is threatened by the unfamiliar.

I argue that contemporary Chinese diasporic storytellers narrate their immigrant stories to those back home or in the Sinophone community around the world to make sense of their experience and establish their sense of place and belonging in the world. This is not through establishing one home or even one map; rather, at times they overlay their exotic maps of the United States on their nostalgic maps of their homeland, at times adding on affective maps of their personal immigrant experiences, and at other times drafting political maps between China and the States that fit over or beneath these others. As such, cartography is a useful tool for providing possible navigations for the diaspora in an unfamiliar land. In *Maps of the Imagination: The Writer as Cartographer* (2004), Peter Turchi compares writing, which he sees as a combination of exploration and presentation, to cartography, which maps and guides a voyage. "To ask for a map is to say, 'Tell me a story.'"[47] By telling stories of the diasporic experience, these storytellers give their audience the opportunity to explore a world they have never been to or ideas that they have not confronted or considered. Turchi has pointed out that readers are not afraid of and even take delight in being lost: "A prerequisite for finding our way through any story or novel is to be lost: the journey can't begin until we've set down a place somewhere unfamiliar."[48] Of course, Turchi's idea is not limited to the diasporic realm, yet going to a foreign land naturally fits into his "place somewhere unfamiliar," culturally and geographically. So regardless of whether the authors are telling about China or Chinese immigrants to an American audience as does Ha Jin, or telling about the immigrant experience in the United States to an audience in mainland China as do Shi Yu and Chen Qian, the audience is transported to an exotic land and culture in which they learn about the Chinese diasporic experience and the Sino–U.S. relationship.

In addition, migrant stories like this can serve as guides for the transpacific journey. Numerous scholars have pointed out the significant role of migrant narratives in shaping transmigrants' trajectory from Asia. For instance, Karen Kelsky's *Women on the Verge: Japanese Women, Western Dreams* (2001) dives into female internationalism in Japan and Japanese women's use of the West.[49] Its first chapter introduces Umeko Tsuda, a famous Japanese educator schooled in the United States between the 1870s and 1890s who founded an academy for English study for girls that promoted Western thoughts and ideas. Besides the influence of successful early migrants like Tsuda, the fetishized imagery of the West and Western men portrayed in Japanese popular women's fiction and commercials also stimulated Japanese women's attraction to the West. Kelsky's book ultimately proves that migrant stories, real or fictional, can become maps to guide the new contemporary diasporic communities on their transpacific routes.

Introduction • 17

What makes these narratives worthy of study is the way they seek to break down the very barriers that maps can represent. The contemporary Chinese diasporic narratives in this book offer an imagination of "global Asias" as an instance of a fluid, asymmetrical, and exterritorial structure of production and circulation in which the sense of belonging must necessarily be understood dialogically rather than territorially. The emergent field of global Asias disrupts the traditional idea/notion of "Asia" and "Asian American" in area studies, which is defined and limited by geographical national boundaries, and redefines "Asia" more broadly beyond geography and geographical boundaries. Tina Chen, a foremost scholar in this field and one of the founders of *Verge: Studies in Global Asias*, argues that the notion of "global Asias" is inspired by structural incoherence, defined as "the multiple, overlapping, and embedded contradictions undergirding the cultural, social, political, and economic dynamics of a 'place' both real and imagined."[50] The ways in which the new Chinese diasporic writers map their immigrant experiences help us understand the contradictions of the homeland and the new land, both real and imagined. Because these writers were brought up in China and then moved to the United States, they all carry with them a Chinese cultural makeup that contributes to their cartographic practices. The real and imagined geographies of diasporic Asia expand the map of Asia, disrupting the traditional boundaries defined by nations and geographies, and provide new mappings of spatial imagination of the global Asias through the contemporary Chinese diasporic experience.

The global Asias project is not only about maps in the geographical sense; it also charts a new terrain of linkage and meaning. The diasporic narratives discussed here create various maps that deal with a new sense of Chinese American being and belonging that is not bound by territories, loyalties, or identities. Whether a palimpsest that overlays the Chinese dream onto the American dream, a tourist map that manufactures the affects of homesickness and lovesickness, or a multilayered, local–global map, they all make up a cartographic practice that connects transpacific spatial and temporal sites. What these Chinese diasporic works capture is not a static map with fixed borders and national state system, but the complex flows across transnational and transpacific spaces. The flows of the people and cultures and the linkages of borders that this diasporic population brings are moving maps of convergences and divergences—an important part of global Asias.

Besides offering a case for a map of global Asias, this group of contemporary authors contributes to and challenges the map of the Sinophone. In contrast to earlier generations of the Chinese diaspora who grew up in a less globalized China, the current group of writers are globally oriented and competent in both Chinese and English. And yet, if the cultural products of this new generation cannot be labeled "ethnic" or "minority literature," neither can it be associated exclusively with the Sinophone sphere. The familiarity of these authors with English and with the Anglophone world complicates the category of Sinophone. Flair Donglai Shi's comprehensive research in Sinophone studies problematizes the institutionalization of the Sinophone insofar as he sees an inherent Orientalist logic in its origination, as Sinophone studies was initially an attempt to counteract Sinocentrism. This Sinocentrism, in Shi's view, is "palimpsetic and US-centric as it is primarily concerned with the strategic importance of 'China' for the United States."[51] This view of China as a threat has contributed to the rise of Chinese and Sinophone studies in American academia. Chih-ming Wang further holds that "The proposal and subsequent development of Sinophone Studies is actually based on the importance of China Studies in Western academia and has as its background the Western imagination of China's rise as a threat."[52]

While acknowledging that the rise of Sinophone studies has brought inclusion and diversification to the Chinese studies curricula in America, Shi also points out the relative invisibility of Chinese-language literatures in Asian American studies, and he cites Tsai Chien-hsin's explanation that the discipline excludes "Asian languages in favor of American English as the main language of critical studies."[53] Currently, Sinophone studies focuses on the areas of Southeast Asia, Taiwan, and Hong Kong, while Chinese American studies mainly examines works written in English by second- or later-generation Chinese Americans. The new Sinophone authors discussed in this book, therefore, fill in this gap on the Sinophone map by illuminating the unique diasporic experiences of the new generation of Chinese immigrants—experiences that have rarely been addressed in the existing scholarship on Sinophone or Chinese American studies. In addition, because these Sinophone writers and producers live and study in the United States, Europe, or inside mainland China, unlike the Sinophone writers in other areas that are more studied, they can indeed challenge the Sinocentric concerns of American academia instead of falling into the danger of equating "American" with "international" in Sino–U.S. relations.

The original Sinophone map that Shu-mei Shih drew set the marginalized Sinitic world apart from China and the Anglophone world. Defining the Sinophone as "a network of places of cultural production outside China and on the margins of China and Chineseness, where a historical process of heterogenizing and localizing of continental Chinese culture has been taking place for several centuries,"[54] Shih reterritorialized the Sinophone world apart from China (Zhongguo). But by making this divide, she establishes the PRC–Sinophone dichotomy in a cultural domain, which many mainland academics see as flawed. Flair Shi contends, "It is problematic to allocate an a priori conception of hegemonic Chineseness to PRC academic discourse and cultural production and view PRC–Sinophone relations in the cultural domain via an antagonist postcolonial framework without historical nuances."[55] Clearly, mainland academics and writers, as well as Sinophone writers, do not hold homogenous views politically and culturally; therefore, to set up such a PRC–Sinophone binary is indeed problematic. Most immigrant writers that this book discusses grew up in mainland China and have studied and lived in the United States, further complicating this issue. Because they now write from outside mainland China, their works belong to what Shih first defined as the realm of Sinophone writings, yet the circulation and the production of their works break down the PRC–Sinophone binary. Some, for example, try to reach readers in their homeland by either translating their works back into Chinese, like Ha Jin, or publishing their works in mainland China, like Chen Qian and Shi Yu. It is fair to say that they articulate a different space of being and belonging that is more "Chinese [language]" (Huawen 華文) than "China" (Zhongguo 中國), but yet, through this Sinophone circulation of cultural capital, they can reach the PRC—their homeland. While Shih's Sinophone concept is an oppositional term to Chineseness, these contemporary Chinese diasporic authors redefine Chineseness as a literary and linguistic belonging that lies beyond national boundaries, thereby refuting Shih's original Chineseness/China–Sinophone binary.

These authors contribute to and yet challenge the categories of Sinophone and Anglophone because their choice of written language does not necessarily match their ethnicity. Rob Wilson's notion of heteroglossia in his account of the transpacific can provide an alternative to the Anglophone and Sinophone. In his theorization of the American Pacific, he argues that "it is becoming clear, in attempts to map the dynamics of postmodern spatiality, that the motions and flights of transnational capital entail the *disinvention* of the bounded 'nation-state' as we know it into a less tangible, more fungible and heteroglossic entity,"[56] a cartographic challenge that exceeds the representational fixity long associated with mapping. In contrast to the "static map with fixed borders" of an international system of nation-states with their homogenous national languages, the transpacific geography mapped by these newer authors constitutes a "heteroglossic entity" made up of a complex series of flows across transnational, transpacific spaces, the land without borders that was discussed at the start of this introduction.

The transpacific paradigm focuses on the transnational networks and movements beyond national, linguistic, and ethnic boundaries. Differing from the Western-focused transatlantic networks, these transpacific networks reveal the significance of the Asia-Pacific region and situate the Sino–U.S. relationship in a fluid contact zone.[57] Lisa Lowe tells us that "transpacific Asian migration disrupts disciplinary practices for the study of 'Asia,' 'America,' and even the 'Asian American' that emerged in US universities in the 1970s."[58] The notion of the transpacific has been developed over the past two decades, with the scholarship in the field focused primarily on displacement, attachment, and articulation.[59] For example, Yunte Huang raised the term "transpacific displacement," which he refers to as "a historical process of textual migration of cultural meanings, meanings that include linguistic traits, poetics, philosophical ideas, myths, stories and so on."[60] Later, he developed this notion further and used "transpacific imagination" to signify "a host of literary and historical imaginations that have emerged under the tremendous geopolitical pressure of the Pacific encounters."[61] Chih-ming Wang looks at the "foreign student" and its literary and political articulations to push us to rethink the category of Asian American. His discussion of foreign students in the United States breaks down the dichotomy of Asian American as a one-way or two-way street, and instead demonstrates that becoming Asian American is "a messy triangulation among 'Asia,' 'America' and the conditions of US power and involvement in Asia, particularly during the long Cold War era."[62]

These scholars and many others have extended the earlier geographical categories of "Asia-Pacific" and "Pacific Rim"[63] and shaped the discourse of the transpacific into one that focalizes contacts, conflicts, and exchanges. I see "transpacific" as a critical cartographic term being drawn by the writers, artists, and cultural practitioners who transcend national, ethnic, and geographical boundaries. This idea draws not only on my interests in literary cartography and spatial literary studies but also on previous work in transpacific studies. Notably, Yunte Huang emphasizes the spatial and temporal dimensions of transpacific critiques by viewing the transpacific as a "critical terrain," which serves "both as a contact zone between competing geopolitical ambitions and a gap between literature and history that is riddled with distortions, half-truths, longings, and affective burdens never fully resolved in the unevenly temporalized space of the transpacific."[64] Huang also proposes reading the transpacific as an "unfathomable chasm."[65] Using geographical terms like "terrain" and "chasm," he pinpoints the complicated, multilayered topographic, geographical makeup of the transpacific that challenges the single-layered map that is national or local. While Huang's study is innovative in its use of geographical critiques in Asian American literature, Tina Chen's review of his book also points out that the oceanic space of exchange, projection, and conflict are too abstract to map.[66]

While acknowledging the abstract spaces and concepts in transpacific mapping, I do not intend to map out transpacific trends. Rather, this book will contribute to the journey and discovery of the transpacific discourse by examining some of the maps made up by contemporary Chinese diasporic narratives. These maps, regardless of their accuracy or literary beauty, contribute to our understanding of the contemporary Chinese diaspora, as well as the Sino–U.S. relationship in the current age. They help us examine how the Chinese diasporic narrative transforms, shifts, or reaffirms the existing transpacific paradigm. Moreover, the endeavor to understand these maps can help us navigate the transnational, transpacific networks between China and the United States.

Built on the existing transpacific paradigm, this work presents a transpacific project that is not just about displacement, attachment, or articulation but also about the U.S.–China / English–Chinese circulation, entanglement, and transaction, and, most importantly, the (im)possibility of homesteading in an era of global precarity and homelessness.

Structure of the Book

This book examines works of different genres, from traditional novels to film and TV shows to virtual publications like blogs and websites on the internet—a much faster and more reactive media than the standard publishing industry. The deliberate inclusion of these various genres is to demonstrate that the maps made up of contemporary Chinese diasporic narratives include both literary and cinematic visual representations. Even though this monograph focuses more on literary analysis, it does not intend to privilege the literary narrative; instead, it tries to be as inclusive as possible when looking at the idea of mapping in diasporic narratives. It looks at works in a variety of languages and formats: traditional novels, cinema, popular internet writings, Anglophone writings, Chinese-language literature, and works by male and female writers. Although the book cannot avoid an imbalanced proportion in these categories, it attempts to provide a comprehensive map of the contemporary diaspora with these multigenre, multilingual works. The different chapters deal with specific maps that capture interrelated yet distinctive flows, convergences, and divergences.

Chapter 1 opens by discussing some of the problematics already analyzed in this introduction: how to navigate the tensions between countries, families, and individuals. It focuses on the works of the renowned Chinese American Anglophone writer Ha Jin, arguing that his novel *A Map of Betrayal* (2014) challenges physical territories and geopolitical entities by mapping out the complicated, tortuous, and emotional trajectories of his immigrant characters. Ha Jin's characters locate home within themselves and their personal artistic creations. The historian and narrator, Lilian, the half-American daughter of a Chinese man, serves as a literary cartographer recounting her father's tragedy by reconstructing his map of betrayal—a complicated map pointing to him as both the subject and object of multiple betrayals. She displays a multilayered, intricate map of deterritorialization and reterritorialization that her father creates as a spy for the Chinese government living in the United States. From her father's story, Lilian and her nephew Ben learn not to define the nation as the site of loyalties and home and instead re-create a map that transcends national boundaries. The chapter further contends that Ha Jin's life and works display a multilayered, local–global map that allows its readers to transcend the limits placed upon them by geographical locales, physical boundaries, and political states. Instead of external geographies and nation-state locales found on maps, his works invite us to turn to an internal geography that he creates for himself, his characters create for themselves, and that we, by extension, must create for ourselves. In so doing, Ha Jin advocates literary cartography and geography not only as a way of coping with the tension between the nations and individuals but also as a way of cultivating an identity between different cultures.

Chapter 2 turns from national map to the familial map, further exploring the dynamic and tension between "nation" (*guo*) and "family" (*jia*) in Yan Geling's novel *The Criminal Lu Yanshi* (*Lufan Yanshi* 陸犯焉識, 2011). Whereas chapter 1 shows a positive future of transcending the national boundaries—allowing Lilian and Ben in the end to have a happy home—this chapter shows the possible turmoil that can result from a home without boundaries when individual and familial freedoms are taken away by the carceral rule of an authoritarian state, turning the home into a prison and perversely the prison into a home. A correlation and tension exist between the nation and family, inherent in the Chinese term *guojia*: the idea of "home" in Chinese culture is revealed in the interconnectedness of the two characters. However, during the Mao era, the notion of *jia* was threatened because the socialist authoritarian power and the unified Maoist ideology redefined the concept of family and marriage. Yan Geling's novel, set during this time, demonstrates this by focusing on Lu Yanshi's imprisonment experience and his tragic love story with his wife. Strangely, prison in some way provides him a sense of familiarity—not in the sense of comfort, but in the familiarity with the political system of China during the Mao era. Yan Geling uses Yanshi's imprisonment experience to signify a "home" experience that is problematic and traumatic, contradicting the usual implications of what an ideal home should mean: comfort and stability. Prison during the period of land reform is shown as a carceral dystopia, with its deployment of both hard and soft surveillance infrastructures. The tragic love story between Yanshi and Wanyu is a critique of this dystopia caused by the Mao regime. The chapter aims to examine the complicated and paradoxical sites of home destabilized between communist collectives and individuals, and between *guo* and *jia* in *The Criminal Lu Yanshi*. Yan draws a twisted route to home on her characters' map in resistance to the Maoist regime.

Chapter 3 moves inward from national and familial maps to personal, intimate ones by exploring another site of negotiation between homeland and new land—romantic and intimate love. In the narratives by new Sinophone writers, such as Shi Yu's *New York Lover* (*Niuyue qingren* 紐約情人, 2004), Chen Qian's *Listen to the Caged Bird Sing* (*Wang duan nan fei yan* 望斷南飛雁, 2010), and Rong Rong's *Notes of a Couple* (*Fuqi biji* 夫妻筆記, 2004), love represents a complex dynamic between home and diaspora. These stories chart an affective map for Sinophone readers to navigate homeland and diaspora, but the dichotomies of tradition versus modernity, East versus West, and home versus homeless are staged as an exotic spectacle for Chinese consumption. In these narratives, love is central to the protagonists' spatial imaginations of mobility and dwelling, as well as to the feeling of being both at home and away from home. These works challenge the categories of home and diaspora, but they do so by turning the diasporic experience into touristic, exotic adventures that can be consumed. Constructing Sinophone romance literature as tourist maps, these new immigrant writers create paths to self-identity through love and personal desire.

Chapter 4 turns to the cinematic and visual representations that highlight cinematic cartography in the Chinese diaspora. It looks at works that challenge the traditionally conceived view of the American dream and the Chinese dream, including *Beijinger in New York* (*Beijingren zai Niuyue* 北京人在紐約, 1994) and *The Way We Were* (*Gui qu lai* 歸去來, 2018). The chapter argues that the dreams portrayed construct palimpsestic maps, with each generation adding a new layer. While both critique the American dream, the latter show offers a new map to chart a way home: a map leading back to China itself. However, this is not simply a homecoming, as the journey itself has created a new sense of what is home for the returning characters. By creating a palimpsest with such layers, *Beijinger* rewrites the map of the American dream as being uncertain and unpredictable, while *The Way We Were* rewrites the map of the Chinese dream as more personal than political.

The coda examines the newest "site" at which diasporic subjects can generate a sense of home: virtual space. Internet-based multimedia writing, like blogging, online magazines, and journals (including Twitter journals), allows people to create identities even when being a part of a community in person is impossible, whether because of distance or during times of pandemic. By historicizing the Sinophone online literary community in North America and doing a case study of some online writers, including Hongwei Bao and Shao Jun, I argue that the internet is a new material form of transpacific mapmaking, both a response to and reaction against global capitalism—one that might provide the reader with a true sense of boundarylessness. These writings present global capitalism as an inherent part of the mapping practice that connects various transpacific spatial and temporal sites, but at the same time they portray the problems of global capitalism and advocate for universal humanitarian values and love. The coda reiterates some of the topics covered in this book, including identity, an atlas of homes, the global–local divide, elitism, diversification, and liminality. It also considers future endeavors by exploring multimedia cultural productions in the digital, global age of the Chinese diaspora.

And now, I present to you the maps of the contemporary Chinese diaspora.

1

Mapping Experiences of De/Reterritorialization

• •

Ha Jin's *A Map of Betrayal*

As I touched upon in the introduction, Ha Jin's novels show a strong interest in geography and boundaries. These can be national boundaries—with his immigrant characters' attachment to and detachment from their "old land" and "new land"—but those are only one part of Ha Jin's interest in conceptualizing space. Just as important, if not more, are boundaries between public spaces (e.g., Chinatown, restaurants, etc.) and private spaces (homes, neighbors' houses), as well as personal and psychological realms. These latter personal spaces, such as zones of poetic creation, prove most essential in Ha Jin's works. He masterfully uses the boundaries between these various locales— the geographic locations, dislocations, and relocations—to map out the emotional trajectories of his immigrant characters' journeys as they search to make a home for themselves.

Although this is a thread throughout much of his corpus, it is perhaps most revealing in Ha Jin's *A Map of Betrayal* (2014). The novel's protagonist, Gary Shang, tries and fails to inhabit two worlds. A physical map could have shown the names of distinct countries, yet this novel does not include any physical map. But any map based on physical or political geography alone cannot express the complexities of the protagonist's social and emotional relationships; Gary has not betrayed the countries on that map; rather, it is the map that has betrayed him.

24

In this novel, which is the focus of this chapter, space and emotional attachment are central to the characters' reflections on being migrants who still retain part of their homeland. Yet, ironically, their efforts to redefine home and space based on physical territories or political entities ultimately prove to be in vain. These characters' reconstruction of home and identity in relation to different geographical spaces and social relationships is instructive for our broader study of contemporary Chinese immigrants as a whole.

I argue in what follows that Ha Jin's life and works display a multilayered, local–global map that transcends geographical locales, physical boundaries, and political states. After a summary of his life and the reception of his oeuvre, I will briefly review theories of deterritorialization and reterritorialization and how they can help interpret Ha Jin's immigrant works. I then examine how transpacific mapping functions in Chinese diasporic narrative, using *A Map of Betrayal* as an example. I end the chapter by concluding that Ha Jin invites us to go beyond the external geographies found on physical maps, using his literary cartography as an example for how to create an internal map for ourselves where we can feel at home.

The Impossibility of Placing Ha Jin on a Map

Ha Jin's citizenship, chosen writing language, and subject matter have given rise to many questions around his identity and the classification of his works.[1] Are his works Chinese literature, American literature, Sinophone literature, or something else? In his extensive reading of Ha Jin's work, Lo Kwai-Cheung argues that Ha Jin's situation challenges the traditional view of national literature. In the current global age, Lo argues, Chinese literature and literary studies go beyond where the works are produced, or whether they are written in a common language. Thus, he proposes reading Ha Jin's works—created in the United States and written in English—as modern Chinese literature.[2] A brief biography of the author shows how these questions of where Ha Jin belongs ultimately matter less, as his works themselves attempt to transcend categorization.

Ha Jin was born in 1956 in Jinzhou, Liaoning Province, in China. He joined the People's Liberation Army at the age of fourteen, following the example of his father, a military officer. Stationed on China's northeast border as an ammunitions handler, he witnessed both the Cultural Revolution and the war between China and the Soviet Union. Not long after he left the army, the school he was attending closed down due to the Cultural Revolution. As a result, he worked as a railroad telegraph operator for three years. When the colleges reopened in 1977, Ha Jin studied English literature in Heilongjiang University in Harbin. He earned a master's degree in American literature at Shandong University in 1984, where he studied T. S. Eliot, Ezra Pound, and other "High Modernists." He met his wife, Bian Lisha, during his graduate years. A year later he traveled to Massachusetts to pursue a PhD at Brandeis University. He began writing his first volume of poetry in English while working part-time as a night watchman at a chemical factory. He planned to return to China after his PhD studies but changed his mind after the Tiananmen massacre in 1989, and he became an American citizen a few years later. After completing his PhD program, Ha Jin was appointed professor of creative writing at Emory University, before joining Boston University in 2002.

Although he abandoned plans to return after the Tiananmen incident, Ha Jin did later hope to return to China through literature, believing that "only through literature is a genuine return possible for the exiled writer."[3] He could achieve homecoming in the form of missives sent back home from a distant shore. And Ha Jin has made extensive efforts to reach the Chinese audience. If not for the censorship placed on his novels, Ha Jin would have more of his writing published in mainland China.[4] Being bilingual and bicultural, Ha Jin follows the Chinese translations of his own work closely. For the Chinese translation of *Waiting*, he provided considerable help and support by talking with his translator, Jin Liang, and reviewing the work. In particular, he encouraged the translator to use various strategies to portray the Chinese characters in the novel accurately, including employing a northeastern dialect and using cultural-specific metaphors and idioms.[5] Ha Jin also co-translated his debut collection of short stories, *Ocean of Words*, with his wife and translated his 2010 short story collection *A Good Fall*. All these efforts suggest that he values Chinese readership as much as his English-speaking one—that he desires his works to be free of the boundaries that he himself might not be able to overcome physically.

For Ha Jin, one way to stake out his identity is through literature, in particular, "minor literature" in Deleuze and Guattari's definition, that is, "literature a minority makes in a major language."[6] As previously discussed, when Ha Jin was writing about Chinese stories in his early works, he always hoped to reach his homeland through literature. Writing in English has allowed him to pass messages and be revolutionary in ways he could not in Chinese. As he writes in the preface of his first book of poems, *Between Silences: A Voice from China*, "If what has been said in this book is embarrassing, then truth itself is cold and brutal."[7] Some poems in this collection, as well as some of his earlier novels like *The Crazed* and *War Trash*, were not accepted in mainland China and were too hard to express in his native tongue: "only the English language—sterile, foreign—can penetrate into this cold core of truth, too brutal to touch with the warm heartbeat of a native language."[8] In that aspect, Ha Jin's stories fit into minor literature and are characterized by the connection of the individual and political."[9] For an immigrant like Ha Jin who came to the States in his thirties, English is a tool for Ha Jin's exotic yet powerful message.

Despite his efforts, Ha Jin's reception in China has been mixed. Rather than embrace his English writings, many Chinese scholars read his works as a form of "self-Orientalism"[10] and his choice of writing in English as a betrayal. They believe that his work conveys a negatively skewed image of China to a Western audience. This is especially true of his early writings, which focus on the historical setting of China during the 1960s to 1980s, portraying Chinese life under communist rule. In this early stage of his career, he viewed the purpose of writing as giving a voice to pain—the pain inflicted on the lives of oppressed Chinese who have suffered, endured, or perished.[11] He further explains in his essay "The Spokesman and the Tribe" that "I viewed myself as a Chinese writer who would write in English on behalf of the downtrodden Chinese."[12] But this approach has exposed Ha Jin to criticism from Chinese who believe that he is drawing on stereotypes.

Indeed, much of the criticism directed at Ha Jin stems from his stereotypes about China. Liu Yiqing argues that Ha Jin, in order to be successful, writes in a way that "curse[s] his own compatriots," as he "become[s] a tool used by the American media to vilify China."[13] Liu harshly criticizes Ha Jin's work for emphasizing China's backwardness. She even castigates the U.S. edition of *Waiting* for propagating traditional Chinese stereotypes by featuring a single braid of hair running the vertical length of the cover, representative of the outdated "queue" that was common during the Qing dynasty. In a similar vein, Sheng-mei Ma writes that Ha Jin sells the view of China as a primitive Third World nation to the First World country America: "Presented as ignorant and savage, rural China and totalitarianism offer glimpses into politically incorrect gender relationships and primitivism, so long repressed yet still craved by the advanced, democratic First World."[14]

However, what Liu and Ma read as a self-Orientalizing performance might more accurately be read as Ha Jin's strict commitment to realism. His early exposure to nineteenth-century Russian realists—including Nikolai Gogol, Ivan Turgenev, Anton Chekhov, Leo Tolstoy, and Fyodor Dostoyevsky—deeply influenced his style, which features a constrained realism. On the cover of the Chinese translation of Ha Jin's novel *Waiting*, the publisher advertises that the author "is one of the greatest realistic writers in the modern world." Setting his early stories in China in a time period that he experienced, from the Cultural Revolution (1966–1976) to the launching of Deng Xiaoping's "Reform and Opening Up" policy (1987), Ha Jin creates realistic Chinese stories, setting them in the army (e.g., *Ocean of Words*) or in townships or cities during the Cultural Revolution (e.g., *Under the Red Flag, Bridegroom*, and *Waiting*). He is successful in his realist aims in part because much of his early subject matter draws on events he witnessed himself. Having experienced the difficult years in China during the Cultural Revolution, Ha Jin is well informed about the culture and history of the 1960s to 1980s. These intense experiences of communist control and the Cultural Revolution provide valuable source material for his works. His work is therefore a far cry from an exaggerated, self-Orientalizing melodrama.

Nonetheless, the fact remains that despite Ha Jin's stated intentions to return home through literature, his somewhat negative reception and rejection by publishers in China makes Chinese literature an uncomfortable home for his works. For his critics, there is clearly an element of his work that sticks out when placed next to other writers from the People's Republic of China.

If not Chinese literature, one might instead suggest that Sinophone literature would be a better label. Indeed, Ha Jin has had better luck reaching audiences in Sinophone communities outside of the mainland; most of his works have been translated and published in Taiwan, and popularized among Chinese communities in Taiwan, Hong Kong, and abroad. Moreover, because they are mainly written in English and include a dimension of political engagement, and at times resistance, that can often be found in Sinophone literature's response to Chinese political and imperial hegemony, they might seem to fit more comfortably under the Sinophone category. After all, Ha Jin's article "Exiled to English" is included in *Sinophone Studies: A Critical Reader* (2013), edited by Shu-mei Shih and other scholars. Then again, because Sinophone literature emphasizes the centrality of the Chinese language, Ha Jin's English works do not quite match comfortably with that label, either.[15]

Without a nice and neat home in Chinese or Sinophone literature, perhaps as an American citizen writing in English Ha Jin is more precisely called a Chinese American writer. For instance, *The Asian American Encyclopedia* (1995) includes "all works by writers of Chinese descent who have decided to reside in America permanently."[16] Although this definition of Chinese American literature would include Ha Jin, he remains one of the few immigrant writers born in China who are regularly referred to as Chinese American.[17] It seems problematic to group him with second- or later-generation Chinese American writers like Amy Tan and Maxine Hong Kingston.[18] Compared to the "imagined homeland"[19] conjured by their second- or third-hand knowledge of China, Ha Jin experienced his homeland culture firsthand and has a real past to yearn for. To him, the homeland is just not imagined; it is also a mix of reality and imagination.

These discussions of Ha Jin's identity and the categorization of his works reveal the limitations of labels and categories that scholars impose on writers. Ha Jin is a good example to prove notions like Chinese, Chinese American, and Sinophone are not monolithic terms; rather, they are multiple, complex, and difficult to categorize. Ha Jin is transcending these boundaries to be at home in a place without such labels. What, then, do we make of Ha Jin's elusive shapeshifting?

This chapter turns away from previous critics who focused on politicizing or labeling his works. Rather than trying to place Ha Jin on a map, it is better to consider him as a map maker. To view Ha Jin as a literary cartographer allows us to reexamine his life and works from a geocritical lens. As we will see, his works challenge the very existence of a world with obvious geographical notions like "China" and "America." Consider the fact that maps in American classrooms show America in the middle, and maps in Chinese classrooms center on China. On which shelf does Ha Jin best belong? The answer is neither. Just as he is not simply an "American" or "Chinese American," neither does he fit on a "Sinophone" map, which might centralize the East and place the West on the periphery.[20] Instead, Ha Jin redraws the map, one that reveals the complexities and interdependencies of these two places, without a center of gravity or a focus on one over the other. It is a map without boundaries—or, if the boundaries remain, they are constantly shifting and being redrawn.

Ha Jin as a Literary Cartographer

Just like the immigrant characters Ha Jin constructs in his works, he himself maps out his literary trajectory through navigating different genres and themes in his writing career and immigrant journey. While his early works were set mainly in China, beginning with *A Free Life* (2007), Ha Jin decided to leave contemporary China in his writing and "negate the role of . . . spokesmanship."[21] Instead of continuing to attempt to speak for his country, Ha Jin sets that novel in America, relocating the subjects of his writing, just as he himself is relocated, though changing the setting of his novels takes much longer. Ha Jin is a transitional immigrant writer between the old and new. Through the lens of literary geography, we can see how he tries to break through the limits of immigrant writers to narrate his own space and home dwelling in the art of writing.

Undoubtedly, transnationalism and globalism are prominent themes in Ha Jin's works, yet localism plays an equally important role. Adopting the pen name "Ha Jin" shows his admiration and nostalgia for the city of Harbin, which shares its first character with his pseudonym and is where he attended Heilongjiang University for his bachelor's degree. Even though some critics like Ma believe his pen name is nothing more than a "Made in China" tag that helps his success,[22] I believe Ha Jin does carry more sentimental personal feelings for the place. He also uses Harbin as the main character's hometown in *A Free Life*. That character, Nan, has a complicated relationship with the city, as we shall see, but Harbin, where the Songhua River flows, remains a key locale on Ha Jin's imaginary map.

A prominent example of Ha Jin's mapmaking is through real or imaginary place names in his fiction. For instance, in his most famous novel, *Waiting*, the protagonist Lin Kong, an army doctor, leaves his family and wife from an arranged marriage, Shuyu, in a rural village for an army hospital in a made-up city, Muji. Lin is ashamed by his wife because of her bound feet and servility. Lin slowly develops affection for a nurse, Manna Wu, yet legal restrictions prevent him from showing affection or having an affair with her, even though she is frustrated with his passivity. They must wait for eighteen years until Lin secures a divorce without his arranged wife's consent. According to Shen Shuang, the novel "presents a spatial opposition between the army hospital in the city of Muji and the home village of Lin Kong."[23] Muji here symbolizes modernity and hope, in contrast to the older, traditional village. Yet at the same time, in the novel's spatial narrative of the city, the long suppressed romantic relationship between Lin Kong and his lover Manna suggests the city space as hopeful yet constrained. This middle part of the story is inserted between the first part, when Lin Kong takes a trip to the countryside to divorce Shuyu, and the last part, when he finally wins the divorce case after eighteen years. Therefore, Muji, the city occupying the middle part of *Waiting*, yet constrained by the countryside, is an illusionary place that gives Lin Kong temporary sanctuary and imaginary love, but could not be fully realized.

Real place names also appear in Ha Jin stories, including Dismount Fort, Golden County, and Dalian City.[24] But with these, too, our cartographer does not simply relate an exacting depiction of cities on an existing map. Rather than relaying these Chinese places to an English-speaking audience, Ha Jin re-creates them based on his memories and imagination. His early short story collections like *Under the Red Flag* (2010), *The Bridegroom* (2001), and *Ocean of Words* (2014) are mostly set in concrete locales in China at specific historical moments. Specifically, *Under the Red Flag* depicts stories in the bleak rural town of Dismount Fort, where people are blinded by repression during the Cultural Revolution. Depicting the cities in this way is part of his broader attempt to re-create a homeland based on his imagination and memories.

These examples show the importance of the "local" in Ha Jin's cartographical endeavor. While previous studies have focused on his contributions to global English and world literature and neglect the local elements, in reality it is the nexus of the local and the global that is at the real essence of his works—and the way that Ha Jin seeks to overcome the distinction in his imagination.[25]

I argue that Ha Jin's life and works display maps that transcend geographical locales, physical boundaries, and political states. Instead of external geographies found on maps, Ha Jin's works invite us to turn to an internal geography that one could create with literature and helps us use these maps to construct our identities. It is with that internal, map-making goal in mind that we turn to an analysis of the diasporic individuals in *A Map of Betrayal*. We may not have enough evidence to say that Ha Jin's works transcend geographic classification. Instead, we must examine theories of deterritorialization/reterritorialization that explain precisely why Ha Jin's every word points back to "country" being such a "very fickle and unreliable" construct.[26] As we will see, cartographic narratives establish Ha Jin's identities and help him navigate the tortuous journey in between the countries, while enabling the possibilities of deterritorializing the territory bounded by nation-state.

Concepts of De-/Reterritorialization

"When I grew up I was given the contract itself.
In it was the map of a whole country,

...

I took my contract to another land,

...

'Sir, this doesn't mean anything'"[27]

This poem, written by Ha Jin's protagonist Nan in his semi-autobiographical novel *A Free Life* (2007), implies the old map of his homeland—how to navigate its culture and society—does not apply to the new land. Without a legible, accurate map for the new land, immigrants like Nan are lost. Therefore, they need to draw their own new maps. I have described Ha Jin as a writer whose novels are full of geographical locales. I have further suggested how he as a mapmaker challenges and transcends physical geographies in place of new internal ones. But for a fuller understanding of my meaning, it is worth taking a step back to consider what boundaries are and how they operate. After all, we cannot understand why Ha Jin would have no recourse but to become his own cartographer without a deeper understanding of the myriad ways the maps at his disposal fail him. Indeed, understanding territory and territorialization is a building block for understanding the structures at play for Ha Jin's immigrant novels. But territorialization in and of itself does not account for the negotiations and renegotiations that immigrants make throughout the many phases of their diasporic journey; their movement can add dimensions of both deterritorialization but also reterritorialization.

The limits of a territory are defined by boundaries, with those lines drawn on maps defining states painted in different colors, lines within which states have sovereignty.[28] Boundaries demarcate geographical and political entities— as Anssi Paasi claims, "Boundaries, along with their communication, comprise the basic element in the construction of territories and the practice of territoriality."[29] Territoriality, the act of marking territory or boundaries, therefore, suggests sovereignty, surveillance, and jurisdiction.[30] Studies of political geography have focused on the study of states as containers demarcated by boundaries.[31] By drawing parallels between mathematics and politics in the seventeenth century, Stuart Elden argues that territory is partly about boundaries and partly about the political usage of the concept of space.[32] Territorialization, then, is setting up boundaries to give specific spaces political meanings. And the so-called political is not limited to politics, but broadly includes things that define a nation and its boundaries—such as culture, landscapes, and language.

Yet territorialization is not necessarily a static endpoint, especially for immigrants navigating diasporic journeys. In this discussion, we ought to consider also the theory of deterritorialization and reterritorialization as coined by Gilles Deleuze and Félix Guattari (1972).[33] According to them, deterritorialization is taking down the boundaries of a territory (land or place) that is already established—for instance, by destroying the political or cultural system, organization, or context. Reterritorialization refers to restructuring of a territory that has been deterritorialized. Their use of the terms had quite specific psychoanalytical meanings, yet they have been applied to describe the shifting of social and cultural practices, and of people, languages, and beliefs from their originating bodies, which is helpful in understanding Ha Jin's immigrant novels.

In relation to deterritorialization, Deleuze and Guattari's distinction between smooth and striated space further helps interpret Ha Jin's remapping. A "striated space" is a territory "drawn and riddled with lines of divide and demarcation that name, measure, appropriate and distribute space according to inherited political designs, history or economic conflict,"[34] whereas a "smooth space" is "one that is boundless and possibly oceanic, a space that is without border or distinction that would privilege one site or place over another."[35] A striated space is therefore appropriated, or (re)territorialized, while a smooth space is deterritorialized without being reterritorialized. The map described in Nan's poem in the beginning of this section is bound to a nation, and the place where it can be used or cannot be used is "striated space." On the contrary, the "country without borders"[36] that Nan and Ha Jin hope for and imagine is a smooth space, one that is boundless and borderless. Yet, any deterritorialized space is open to reterritorialization, and the places in Ha Jin's immigrant novels, both in *A Free Life* and *A Map of Betrayal*, serve as a medium where deterritorialization and reterritorialization take place.

Furthermore, Ha Jin has demonstrated through his own life and the characters in his fiction the Chinese diaspora's detachment from their homeland in a territorial sense, yet attachment to their cultural identity after they leave their homeland. The term "deterritorialization" is often employed in diaspora studies to refer to a process by which the loss of an old territory (in the homeland) leads to something else gained by that loss: "Deterritorialization implies staking identity outside ordinary claims to the land. . . . Many diasporic groups can be called deterritorialized because their collective claims to an identity do not depend on residence on a particular plot of land."[37] Indeed, most diasporic populations are taken out of the land they once were familiar with. Yet deterritorialization knocks down the boundaries while reterritorialization reconstructs those territorial and national boundaries.

In the case of Gary in *A Map of Betrayal*, he does not allow himself to be deterritorialized or try to see himself outside those national allegiances. Instead of reterritoralizing where that China–U.S. divide was gotten rid of, he very strongly did the opposite—to resist being deterritorialized, leaving a lot of striated space within the boundaries of him, which leads to the tragic ending.

For instance, part of Gary's identity is strictly tied to being Chinese and the territory of China: "Happiness lay elsewhere, and he could visualize it only in his homeland and in the reunion with his original family."[38] He is an example of those in the Chinese diasporic community who lay claim to their cultural identity and roots, perhaps even more than if they were back in their homeland.

Ha Jin's novel *A Map of Betrayal* is self-reflexive of his Chinese American identity, capturing the hardship he embodies in the subject and language he writes. As he told the *Paris Review* in 2009, "I live in the margin as a writer—between two languages, two cultures, two literatures, two countries. This is treacherous territory."[39] I will next discuss how the novel charts a multilayered map of betrayals and subjectivities.

Mapping Split Immigrant Subjectivities

Ha Jin's 2014 immigrant novel *A Map of Betrayal* recounts the story of Gary (born "Weimin" in Chinese) Shang, who initially appears to be the perfect archetype of a Chinese immigrant. He owns a comfortable home in Alexandria, Virginia, holds a reputable job, and marries an Irish woman, with whom he has an American daughter. In essence, Gary appears to be completely integrated into the fabric of American society. However, he hides a rather shocking secret: Gary is actually acting as a spy for the Chinese government, a mole buried deep within the CIA. It turns out Gary's life is marked by years of not only deceit but lost chances, incredible yearning, and devastating internal conflicts that both shape and transform not only his history but also the future of those he calls family.

While being the cause of such betrayals, Gary also becomes a victim of multiple betrayals himself. He becomes a Chinese spy purely by accident, and he finds himself in a "precarious situation, forced to act within a moral vacuum."[40] Moreover, despite promises made by the Chinese government, Gary fails to return home to receive honor and glory. When the FBI arrests and convicts Gary, the Chinese ambassador does not defend him, and instead denies any ties he has with China. The Chinese president at the time, Deng Xiaoping, goes on to advise that they "let that selfish man rot in an American prison together with his silly dream of being loyal to both countries."[41] It is clear then that China demands complete loyalty from its citizens. Deng seems to believe that embodying double loyalties and double identities serves to hinder rather than serve the Chinese national ideal. As a result, Gary is not defended but discarded, and eventually convicted and sentenced to 120 years in prison. He ends up committing suicide while in jail.

In an effort to uncover both heritage and history, Gary's story is told through the lens of his American daughter, Lilian, a professional historian. Her retelling of his stories is not only an attempted rediscovery of Gary's history as a spy but also a path to uncovering her family's complex and rich history. Structurally, the narrative alternates points of view. It includes narrations of Gary's life from 1949 to 1980, based primarily on his diaries, as well as Lilian's own journey to China to search for her half family, and also a narrative of her own life from 2001 to the present. In her journey, Lilian reunites with her father's Chinese family, and in doing so, she attempts to help them understand Gary's motivations, emotions, and affections toward them, almost as if it were her duty to justify his choices. The novel ends with the story of Gary's grandson, Ben, who runs a questionable computer business in Boston for the Chinese government before eventually running away with his pregnant girlfriend, indicating he has chosen his own life and happiness over sacrificing himself for his country.

The theme of espionage central to the plot of the story carries critical resonances in the backdrop of contemporary Sino–U.S. relations. Reading the novel at a time when Chinese academics have been fired and the Chinese consulate in Houston was closed due to the U.S. government's accusations of Chinese spying brings a chilling perspective to Gary's story.[42] For many Chinese people today, answering questions in the customs line can seem like an interrogation of national allegiance. While the vast majority of Chinese immigrants and visitors to the United States are not, in fact, engaged in espionage, the high-stakes world of international intelligence operations dramatizes similar conflicts in which average diasporic subjects find themselves stuck. Therefore, Ha Jin's novel is of great relevance to the understanding of the Sino–U.S. relationship during and after the Cold War; in fact, some scholars like Chung-jen Chen even argue that the novel functions as a proxy to reflect the Sino–American relationship during and after the Cold War, with the transcultural and transnational communication Gary and Lilian conducts being essential to main concerns of loyalty, citizenship, and patriotism in Asian American studies.[43]

Much work has been done to examine cultural and personal questions of identity that arise in this genre of Asian American espionage literature, specifically, regarding the notion of a "split identity."[44] Calling the impersonation in Chinese American novels "double agency,"[45] Tina Chen points out the split immigrant subjectivities that simultaneously pay homage to and challenge authority and authenticity. Chen proposes impersonation as a paradigm for understanding Asian Americans' multiple allegiances to various countries. This notion challenges the binaries of loyalty/disloyalty, real/fake, and Asian/American; rather, it considers Asian Americans as double agents.

Following on Chen's theories on the spy trope of Asian American subjects, we could say that Ha Jin's novel presents the split immigrant subjectivities as double agents to push against the seemingly clear-cut nature of aforementioned binaries. Gary develops two senses of self and identity in his diasporic journey. One of these identities represents his hidden self—empty, lonely, and constantly longing for his homeland. The other is his imagined and created self, a façade he casts upon the eyes of America and what he assumes to be the American ideal. Weimin and Gary, the same man with two names, embody both his Chinese and American identities. He hopes to establish himself as a loyal peacemaker to both countries, remarking that "the two countries are like parents to me,"[46] yet in this process, his sense of home and identity become ultimately shattered.

But this split identity framework, though useful, is limited. Instead, we should consider that Gary's split identities form one layer of the "map of betrayal" that the novel presents, but there are other layers to this map that are also essential to keep in mind, and I turn now to the concept of literary geography to parse out these other layers. The fuller picture of Gary's map encompasses external geopolitical relationships between the United States and China, the familial relationships of Gary's descendants, and—as with Nan and his personal poetry—Gary's internal geography. The tensions between these layers demonstrate the "treacherous territory"[47] between the two cultures, literatures, and languages Ha Jin and Gary both traverse.

Lilian as a Cartographer

While it is Gary's eponymous map of betrayal that interests us here, Ha Jin grants the role of cartographer not to Gary, but to his daughter, Lilian; she is given the ultimate authority to draw an atlas of her father's complicated relationships on longing, love, and betrayal. In this role, Lilian sketches a multilayered map of Gary in terms of his national, familial, and romantic relationships. On the map that Lilian constructs, she illustrates Gary's emotional connections with China, his motherland, and America, the new land he occupies with both his Chinese and American families. The novel portrays her piecing together—transpacific mapping—the places her father journeyed throughout his life, as well as the landscapes she witnessed while visiting family, and, finally, a reconnection to her father's family in China. The term "mapping" here denotes finding "a way of understanding the unknown, an ordering of the vastness and complexity of the space surrounding [us]."[48] For Ha Jin and his narrator Lilian, "mapping" is first and foremost finding a way to establish a tangible connection with Gary and his Chinese identity. Through the parallel narratives, Lilian attempts to piece together her father's life and career through his diaries, yet at the same time, she seeks understanding of what "home" truly meant for him. While the map portrayed in the novel may not be physical, we should by now be familiar with Ha Jin's literary cartography from this book's introduction. Indeed, Lilian's map is richer than a physical map of lines and territories in that it effectively embodies the intangible—the twisted and undulating sense of loyalties and betrayals that exist for Gary between China and the United States.

With personal and professional curiosity, Lilian is an active pursuer, cartographer, and narrator of her own father's story. A professional historian, Lilian writes "in her own fashion" with the third-person narrative, attempting to be as authentic as possible. Readers cannot be aware of how much she has revised or manipulated, but they do know that she is afforded an opportunity to map out Gary's story and reconstruct her own home in the process—to some extent, even her own identity. Casting her role as a historian enables her maps to be more useful to the public, and her map more likely to be used as reference for research and other purposes.

The map she draws first challenges the notion of patriotism and loyalties on national and personal levels. On the national level, she depicts Gary as a patriotic victim who gets betrayed in the end. In doing so, she questions if nation is a reliable place in which to invest our loyalty. Lilian's retelling of Gary's life explores the question of patriotism through Gary's double-agent career and life. Meanwhile, she reveals Gary's personal life entangling with three women, which will be further explored below. In sum, this map displays Gary's navigation of home through intricate relationships with dual countries and multiple women who inhabit them. Yet when she creates the map for her father, she realizes the map is what causes all the issues in the first place. Hence, she learns that in order to live a fruitful immigrant life, she needs to get rid of the boundaries of the map.

Ultimately, Lilian's map for her father is one of deterritorialization and reterritorialization. His homeland and his Chinese wife/family act as a source of his nostalgia. He still has an idea of what that territory is like when he left, but the reality conflicts with what he remembers. This territory slowly closes off from him, as he is reterritorialized in the United States as a spy, and he is no longer allowed to interact with his Chinese family or enter China. While Lilian remaps her father's experience from 1949 to 1980, she portrays on the one hand how Gary and his family are deterritorialized from their land, becoming victims of the policies and constraints that set them apart, and displays on the other hand how Gary's reterritorialization in America does not help to become more settled. As we will see, Gary's map of deterritorialization and reterritorialization interrogates the grounds upon which nation-states make promises of shelter and scrutinizes ways by which territories are defined.

A National Map of Betrayal

The map in this novel is not a single directional trajectory of immigrants coming from China to the United States; rather, it is a dual directional map rooted in both Gary's complex emotional connections and disconnections between family, country, and even his own values. Gary deceives himself not only with his patriotism and national loyalty but also with the belief that he is capable of creating multiple homes and identities that he can totally disentangle and delineate from each other.

This map first consists of Gary's relationships with the two nations (China and America), and then of his affectionate relationships with his Chinese family, American family, and his mistress. Ha Jin's novel shows us a map without the boundaries connected to patriotism and loyalties that are both personal and national.[49] Undoubtedly, Gary sees himself as a Chinese patriot and remains hopeful for the overall good of his home country, making tremendous efforts and taking many risks to serve it. However, he also wants America to be in peace. In his mind, he plays a significant role in the Sino–U.S. relationship during the Cold War, and he wishes to secure a peaceful relationship between the two countries, where the borders are not called into question by the specter of war. While working for the CIA, for example, Gary deliberately mistranslates important messages to better serve the interests of the Chinese government. On one occasion, in translating Chinese official documents into English, he chooses "determination" over "will" and "fight back" over "resist" in order to strengthen the tone of the messages conveyed, thus lessening the chance of conflicts between the two countries, he believes. While conducting espionage, Gary constantly warns China about dangerous situations and the possibility of being attacked by foreigners if they fail to strengthen their military. His only wish is that they heed his warnings.

All his loyal service to China is attributed to his imagined love and allegiance for his home country. Ha Jin writes, "For him, happiness lay elsewhere, and he could visualize it only in his homeland and in the reunion with his original family."[50] Although he cannot see his Chinese family, Gary believes that he is serving his homeland by remaining loyal and bringing it glory, therefore making a lifetime investment in his own personal affairs. His ongoing espionage work is out of his idealist belief that he could serve his country and return gloriously. He loves his country not for what it is, but for his own vision of what it could have been. Sara Ahmed points out that love can be a powerful emotion, even without reciprocity, because the unreturned love actually affirms that the emotion is meaningful.[51] Gary's homesickness develops into an obsessive longing, yet is also a catalyst for his nationalistic love.

Gary's homeland gets de- and reterritorialized constantly in his mind, causing him to try to delineate his loyalties externally and internally. Even though Gary is physically displaced from his homeland, he continuously makes territorial and emotional connections to China by thinking, even obsessing, that he can return to it physically one day. However, while in America he must appear on the outside to suppress his Chinese identity. His daughter Lilian reflects that "at times it was hard for me to penetrate the armor of detachment he had clothed himself in."[52] The detachment from China and subsequent attachment to the United States while being a spy creates this "armor," which as we will see does not defend him in the end.

Gary walks on one map while presenting another map to everyone else. He creates territorial connections and disconnections not only with his homeland but also with adopted land, as deterritorialization and reterritorialization of both take place simultaneously in Gary's life. From being a spy for China to working for the CIA, he slowly removes himself emotionally from Chinese territory and reorients toward America. In the beginning, Gary resists the seduction of America and is only pretending to fall in love with it, but he gradually grows to fit into the mask he makes for himself.[53] "He'd begun to be fond of this place, where he had a secure, decent job and a comfortable home with a little flower garden."[54] Lilian's nephew Ben talks about America as a place that is "very seductive and corruptive," that can "suck you in and make you forget who you are and where you're from."[55] Even though Gary never forgets his homeland, he slowly develops an attachment to America unexpectedly. In his speech after getting an award for his distinctive service to the CIA, he seems to genuinely embrace and appreciate this America—the America that took him in and gave him a family and a home.[56] Although the speech is meant to fit with his false identity, it catches him by surprise in that it echoes a feeling deep within his heart that he is not fully aware of yet.

The above analysis shows the constant negotiation between the two cultures, as well as that a continual de- and reterritorialization is inevitable in immigrants' lives. They become victims of the entangling relationships and growing tension between the two countries, which inevitably determines their fate. Along with this complicated map on a national level, their romantic and familial relationships consist of a map that echoes the entanglement in patriotism and loyalties. *A Map of Betrayal* complicates the romantic relationships of the male immigrant protagonist Gary, who has two families and three women in his life.

A Personal Map of Betrayal

Gary's complicated relationships with three women paint a map of his emotional connections and disconnections. Yufeng in China is the woman in Gary's subconscious, and the one he is perpetually longing for; he also finds comfort and confidentiality in Suzie; and finally, Nellie functions as Gary's "cover" of sorts, whom he has used as a means to an end to further portray himself as an almost archetypal American. His love for America and his American wife becomes a contingency for his false identity in the United States. As a Chinese spy working for the CIA, Gary tries to blend in, to avoid drawing attention to himself. As a result, his marriage to Nellie comes at the suggestion of his Chinese handler; the marriage will secure his American residency and better cover his true identity.

Gary striates the space within himself and how he sees the world, how he maps himself in that world. Within him is the country. The outside of him and inside of him are two different countries. On both the outside and inside, he is both American and Chinese, and he is trying to keep those divided instead of trying to transcend or integrate them. The women he is with symbolize different countries to him, and he keeps them separated. Within the boundaries of himself, he marks clear divisions of his emotional affiliations just like he marks his national affiliations.

Yufeng serves as the imaginary home to Gary. The long-term separation between Gary and his Chinese wife, Yufeng, transforms her into the same realm as his imagined homeland in Gary's mind. Throughout the novel, he demonstrates deep affection and longing for Yufeng, and although Gary never sees her after leaving China many years earlier, he is never able to stop thinking about her. In the end, Yufeng's absence strengthens their bond.[57] Gary's daughter believes that "she was rooted in his consciousness."[58] Even with his American wife, Nellie, Gary is "shadowed by the memories of his other wife."[59] Yufeng fits into an ideal image of a traditional Chinese woman. She remains "a good wife" and protects the family reputation,[60] thus embodying the characteristics and expectations of an idealized wife and maintaining a sense of "home" in Gary's own mind, despite only spending a month with her before leaving. Immediately after leaving China, he dreams of his wife Yufeng back home, "pregnant with meanings he couldn't decipher."[61] His mind turns some vague memories with Yufeng into codes he hopes to decipher someday.

Gary's longing for his Chinese wife deepens as she is distant from him. When Nellie gives birth to Lilian, Gary insists on using the first character from his Chinese wife's name, "Yu," as his daughter's middle name,[62] as if the baby might carry on his memories of Yufeng and his Chinese home in the name itself. He believes, by doing so, that his first wife would own part of this American baby. He even plants a pomegranate tree in the backyard of his American house as a way to connect to his Chinese family and homeland. Deep down, Gary hopes Yufeng might share his American life. Once, he even dreams of her speaking English to him.[63]

Like the way he hopes to sacrifice himself to bring glory to his country, Gary hopes to take care of his family financially from afar. Yet this is nothing but a wish. His Chinese family becomes part of his sacrifice. His handler Bingwen followed the Chinese government's order and does not tell Gary of his wife's pregnancy with his two children. Bingwen continues to emphasize that they would ensure the care of Gary's family, yet Gary is also told that he may never visit them. Financially, Yufeng is not taken care of as promised, since she could only share a small amount of his salary, and even that stops during the Great Famine. As it turns out, Gary's Chinese wife had to move away from the town in which they lived due to rumors of her being a widow shortly after the Chinese government stopped sending her money. The money they receive hardly helps them endure the famine; consequently, they suffer throughout their lives. Unable to connect with his Chinese family members, Gary carries an enormous amount of guilt in part because he believes he has treated them unfairly.

Gary's memories of Yufeng invoke fear and guilt, as "in the middle of the night he'd awake with a start, feeling his wife standing at the head of his bed and observing him. . . . Her breathing was ragged while her eyes radiated resentment."[64] His imagination of his wife's rage and resentment suggests Gary's growing and impending sense of overwhelming guilt. Once, he dreams that she hurts herself and is hospitalized,[65] causing him to feel downcast for several days. The thought of his family in China and his inability to take care of them pains him greatly. Gary seems to constantly ask of himself: *Is it right to leave my family behind in China? Is it fair to my Chinese wife? What could I do to make it up to them?* He feels guilty betraying his Chinese family. Ultimately, his nostalgia and remorse for them persists until the conclusion, which proves to be a direct result of sacrificing family in favor of serving his country, or patriotism over family loyalty. His tragedies indicate such sacrifice is not worthwhile.

While in the States, Gary does not stop longing and searching for his homeland emotionally. Yufeng's character symbolizes the lost homeland from which Gary feels such deep nostalgia, and also a home that he cannot return to. To fill this emptiness that has been caused by his disconnection with China and his Chinese family, Gary develops a secret relationship with his Chinese mistress, Suzie. In many ways, Suzie symbolizes the same emotional longing for a home that is trapped inside of him. Suzie articulates a feeling she has that Gary shares: "No matter where I go, I always feel I'm Chinese. . . . I mean something inside me cannot be changed, was already shaped and fixed in China."[66] Although Suzie is an American citizen, she identifies herself as Chinese and recognizes that this identity is internally fixed. Gary delights at these words, as if she were speaking with his own voice. Their shared trauma and open wounds caused by alienation from their homeland bring them close to each other.

Gary's affair with Suzie provides them with space to share their longing and nostalgia for homeland "for the sake of self-preservation."[67] They both "perform" as loyal and devoted Americans, yet inside they share a sense of loneliness and alienation. Both of them embody split identities within themselves and represent maps with boundaries. The emotional and physical connection between Gary and Suzie is a space of relief they create for themselves in order to survive in a difficult diasporic life. Among all the deception that defines almost every element of Gary's life, Suzie is someone who he can trust completely. Their trust in each other is symbolic. Suzie sustains his fantastic ideas of China and establishes for him a more tangible and visual image of "home" in his psyche, and Gary feel safe to Suzie, making her unveil her real self.

Both Yufeng and Suzie serve as the codes by which Ha Jin symbolizes homeland, using Chinese women that male protagonists long for emotionally and sexually as a cypher for China itself. Using female bodies as metaphor of a nation is not new or unique to Ha Jin—it is quite a common trope in modern Chinese literature,[68] as well as earlier overseas Chinese literature. Both male and female writers have figured their female characters this way. In particular, in Nieh Hualing's *Mulberry and Peach* (*Sangqing yu Taohong* 桑青與桃紅, 1976), the female protagonist Mulberry embodies all the traumatic, haunting experiences taking place in the homeland through her entangling relationships with different men in the novel. In Yu Lihua's *Again the Palm Trees* (*Youjian zonglü, youjian zonglü* 又見棕櫚, 又見棕櫚, 1967), the male protagonist, Mou Tianlei, expects his fiancée in Taiwan to embody the traditional Chinese qualities and imagines her as an idealistic homeland; yet the reality is the opposite. These female figures perform as landmarks on the map for the diasporic male characters, where they look for, search for, and develop attachments to and detachments from. However, the complicated and affectionate relationships in these novels cannot just be shown as coordinates in a geographical map. It is essential, rather, to decode these symbolic landmarks on a more affective map.

Compared to the female figures who embody homeland in Ha Jin's novels, his Irish wife in America is less imaginary and romanticized. Gary's relationship with Nellie is superficial and materialistic. Their changing residences marks their trajectory of climbing up the ladders of social and financial status. After they were married in 1956, the two moved into a larger apartment in north Alexandria, "on the third floor and had a living room; two bedrooms, the smaller of which he used as his study; and a narrow balcony—more than eleven hundred square feet total."[69] This is a marking point that Gary has settled in the United States, particularly with a white woman. The Shangs quickly moved upward on their financial ladder to afford a larger house, in a "quiet cul-de-sac at the end of Riverview Street in Alexandria. . . . Their home was a raised ranch with an attached carport; a huge rock sat beside the house, and holly hedges demarcated the property."[70] The house is "in a tranquil location, with brick exterior, living room with oak-paneled walls, and the finished lower floor."[71] On the surface, this description seems to be the epitome of the American ideal, or the American dream envisioned. However, under the seemingly glorious façade, the couple is not affectionate with one another, proving the image that they portray is merely an illusion. Nellie tolerates his life outside their home as long as he can take care of the family financially.[72] Nellie turns a blind eye to his affair with Suzie and later starts her own affair with her boss.

Gary's relationship with Nellie portrays the materialism that links to the perceived American dream. Gary and Nellie's marriage is one built more on convenience for each party: for Nellie, it is a way to get out of her parents' house and settle down, and for Gary, it is a cover for his American life. This novel points to a disappointing immigrant life caused by materialism and distrust in the United States. Gary's material success and seemingly happy marriage are a façade, and underneath it is the obliteration of their idealistic American life. Therefore, both the glorious titles Gary wins and the nice house Gary owns and all other material success are at the price of the personal ideals. The wide gulf between Gary's material success and mental suppression makes them both feel emotionally displaced in the United States. Gary's failed relationship with Nellie interrogates the grounds upon which the American dream promises.

Lessons Learned from Gary's Map of Betrayal

The preceding discussion displays a map of betrayal surrounding Gary's entangled relationships with two countries and three women. It appears that Gary betrays all of them. As a Chinese agent he betrays China by developing an attachment to America. He also betrays America by performing as a devoted and loyal American while spying for China. In love, he betrays his Chinese wife by leaving her alone and not being able to take care of her. He betrays his Chinese mistress by using her to console himself yet not making any commitment. He betrays his Irish wife in America as she is a part of his story created out of an American ideal. Most important, he betrays himself with the belief that he could create distinct boundaries between multiple homes, identities, loves, and patriotisms.

Gary is a victim of the irreconcilable relationship between the individual and the state. Like many of Ha Jin's novels, *A Map of Betrayal* illustrates the tensions between individual and political circumstance. Critics also comment on how Gary is victimized by forces larger than himself, remarking, "Ha Jin painstakingly chisels a morally bankrupt traitor—Gary Shang, into a sympathetic human being/victim/victimizer burdened with forces that are bigger than himself."[73] King-Kok Cheung's study "Fate or State" focuses on the espionage life, double agencies shared by Gary, Ha Jin, and Larry Chin (the real-life spy upon which Gary may have been based). She carefully outlines the conflicted loyalties many double agents and immigrants (including Ha Jin) face. She claims that "through Gary, Jin has mapped a nuanced and poignant psychological journey of someone whose destiny is determined by fate or, more precisely, state."[74] Critics rightly highlight how individuals can be subsumed and victimized by states. Gary is betrayed and victimized by the two countries he serves, and his sense of home is divided when he attempts to inhabit multiple identities, pledging his loyalty to both countries.

Both of his families are sacrificed for his attempts to make peace with two countries. Eventually, he transforms into a "stranded traveler," in Lilian's words, someone who is unable to settle down anywhere mentally.[75] His attempt to situate home between China and America is, in essence, his homelessness.

His sense of belonging is severely disrupted by the double identities he attempts to occupy—a tragic ending that suggests the failure of a dream for dual loyalties. His ambition to inhabit dual identities and dual allegiances leads to crushing anxieties, resulting instead in a Chinese husband feeling guilt about neglecting his Chinese family, and a husband to Nellie who takes advantage of her as a cover, and also as a spy living in constant fear of the discovery of his deception. In essence, Gary embodies the duties of a responsible husband, a loving man, a reliable translator, and an accomplished spy. He tries to be all of these, but in doing so is none of them. The dramatization of Gary's tragedies suggests that national loyalty and patriotism is unworthy of pursuing. Gary ultimately becomes a victim of the complexities of his allegiances and identities.

Gary's life trajectory proves that his dual patriotism fails to serve as a remedy for his loss, or a resolution for his conflicted identities. In the end, he chooses to end his life: he "smothered himself with a trash bag tied around his neck with two connected shoestrings."[76] Tragically yet ironically, this is the only decision he makes for himself after first accepting a career in deception: to die quietly. The end result of his attempt to inhabit dual identities is the ultimate withdrawal from life. Betrayed by both countries, Gary becomes the victim of the boundaries of the nations, and eventually he chooses to end his life and leaves his story for his later generation to remap and reconstruct.

Lilian is now entrusted with this task. She makes a map of her father's experiences of de/reterritorialization, which proves the limits of geographical and nation-state boundaries. Her unveiling of her father's tragic stories maps another possible trajectory for future generations of immigrants. Here, the distinction between limits and liminal would help point out a possible direction. Robert Tally has drawn out the difference between limits (in Latin *limes*, plural *limites*) and the liminal (site of the *limen*, a threshold). While the former suggests an end, boundary, and closure, the latter indicates an in-between space of potentiality, an opening and unfolding. He claims that "the liminal is figured in the form of the Deleuzian nomad, living in the intermezzo, ever deterritorializing without reterritorialization."[77] Therefore, to overcome the limits, one could transform *limes* into a *limen* and create a liminal space. This is something Gary fails to do himself but that Lilian accomplishes when mapping out her father's history.

Through revealing her father's story, Lilian comes to realize nation is not necessarily a place to invest one's loyalty, and she defends migration as a way to find one's belonging. When talking with Ben during her visit to China, she states:

> I believe that a country is not a temple but a mansion built by the citizens so they can have shelter and protection in it. Such a construction can be repaired, renovated, altered, and even overhauled if necessary. If the house isn't suitable

for you, you should be entitled to look for shelter elsewhere. Such freedom of migration will make the government responsible for keeping the house safe and more habitable for its citizens.[78]

After Gary's espionage was discovered, citizens from both countries perceive his acts as betrayal of his country and family, and his migration as "bourgeois disease."[79] However, in Lilian's eyes, patriotism and allegiance should be adhered to on the principle that the country has not betrayed individuals or violated the basic principles of humanity. With this belief, Lilian convinces Ben to abandon his espionage.

Ultimately, Ben leaves Boston with his lover, Sonya. Unlike Gary, Ben fears loving and embracing two countries, thus being emotionally torn between them. Instead of making an attempt to claim loyalty and attachment to either country or both countries, he chooses to live a life "as an independent man, also as a man without a country."[80] He feels satisfied and "at home" on the condition that Sonya is with him. The joys and sorrows of their life are the only aspects that signify "home" to him. Instead of futile attempts to anchor himself in multiple homes, he chooses to disassociate himself from a national identity. Instead, he finds his emotional belonging in his own individual freedom and personal love.

Just like Ben's example, Lilian shows the hope of Chinese youth pursuing their own happiness without reliance on national allegiance. When she teaches in China, she realizes the nation's essential values, such as the idea of "national sovereignty" being upheld and promoted.[81] Citizens are expected to serve the motherland. Despite the fact that Lilian's students are taught to follow routines and protocols, they admire and pursue the freedom and individualism in Western society, like the famous tennis player Li Na whom they admire, and who embodies "rebellious, independent spirits" and says, "Don't talk about bringing honor to our country. I'm competing for myself."[82] From this, some young people in China prioritize individuality and self-esteem over loyalty to a nation.

In *A Map of Betrayal*, Ha Jin suggests that one's home may not be solely located on a map or in a nation, for otherwise the sense of home would collapse when one was inevitably betrayed. In this sense, Gary is a victim of the hostile Sino–U.S. relationship during the Cold War. Gary theorizes, "If only China and the United States had not been hostile nations so that he could travel back and forth easily. If only he could become a citizen of both countries, a man of the world."[83] Gary envisions himself as a global citizen facilitating the relationship between China and United States, yet he falls victim to the entangled relationship between the two. Lilian serves as a literary cartographer displaying her father's tragedy by reconstructing his map of betrayal—a complicated map pointing to him as both the subject and object of the multiple betrayals. From her father's story, Lilian and Ben learn not to define nation as the destination of loyalties and home. The map Lilian draws for herself, Ben, and her students, therefore, goes beyond the limits nation-states and national ideals set upon their citizens.

By mapping out her father's relationships with his families and the two lands, as a literary cartographer Lilian leads an alternative way to find home beyond geographical boundaries. Like the protagonist Nan in *A Free Life* writes in his poem "Homework" (discussed in the introduction), Lilian's telling and mapping of her father's story is her way as an immigrant's daughter to find her place and reconnect with her father. This creative act of mapping and storytelling to seek one's sense of belonging creates an internal geography that transcends the territorial one that caused her father so much suffering.

Much like Gary in the novel, neither Ha Jin's homeland, China, nor adopted land, America, provides him with a sense of home. Rather, literature serves as a retreat from realities where one could possibly establish a sense of belonging. Literature can powerfully yield to a sense of belonging, beyond the realm of reality. In Virginia Woolf's early essay "Literary Geography" (1905), she discusses the relationship between real and imaginary spaces or places. She writes, "A writer's country is a territory within his own brain; and we run the risk of disillusionment if we try to turn such phantom cities into tangible brick and mortar."[84] Woolf discourages readers from visiting the real places that appear in William Thackeray or Charles Dickens's novels, as those visits would diminish the affective power of imaginary places. Likewise, by highlighting the affective power of the imaginary homeland and creating it through his own writings, Ha Jin challenges the ability of political entities called countries to provide a sense of shelter, a feeling of belonging, a stable place called home. But instead, he urges us to map out our imaginary homeland and calls for a withdrawal from national allegiance. The real heaven and paradise live within, only existing in the immigrants' imagination; their sense of home is generated from their own creation.

By examining Ha Jin's literary cartography, this chapter has looked at the way he maps out the complicated, tortuous, and emotional trajectories of his immigrant characters. Like Ha Jin, Lilian becomes a literary cartographer of her own, carving out a new map based upon internal geography beyond physical boundaries. Only through this way could these immigrant subjects find a sense of belonging.

2

Cartographing Carceral Dystopia in the Mao Era

· · · · · · · · · · · · · · · · · · · ·

Yan Geling's *The Criminal Lu Yanshi*

Zhang Xiaogang's surrealist painting *Bloodline: Big Family* (1993) offers insights into how families were affected by Maoist ideology.[1] Three figures form the subject of the painting: a father and mother with a son between them. They appear to be posing, as if for a family photograph, though all three look in slightly different directions. The painting is almost monochromic with its use of dark shades—with the three figures wearing black and gray, sitting for their portrait in front of a gray background. The parents wear typical Mao-style clothing; the mother tilts her head toward her husband and child, and the child's face is unusually red. The faces of the family are halfway in the shadows, with only a patch of fractured light illuminating their expressions, though on each face, the light appears to be coming from a different source. The figures' eyes are empty and still, making it difficult for viewers to connect with or identify with the family. They do not smile, neither with their mouths nor their eyes. Although they stand close to each other, the family does not look intimate or happy, as if each had some secrets in their hearts. The father looks straight ahead, the mother slightly to the right, and the child straight ahead, though one of his eyes is crossed, suggesting isolation and distance from each other, even amid physical proximity. A thin, red string, almost invisible, loops through the mother's jacket button, around the child's wrist, and over the father's ear.

Because of the connotations of red in this context, the viewer is invited to associate the red string with the Communist Party. Yet the string here is thin, almost imperceptible; if this string is meant, like communist ideology, to bind this family together, it does so only weakly. In that way, the title "*Bloodline*," a term often associated with ancestral strength and connection, becomes ironic, as this red string "bloodline" is fabricated and external, whereas the internal, familiar "bloodline" is invisible, but not creating any sense of apparent intimacy among the subjects. The question is, would the Communist Party and Maoist regime bring the ones who share a bloodline closer together or push them further away?

This is one of the key questions I explore in this chapter. If the unity of the family is threatened under a certain political regime, how would one survive? The red bloodline tying together the family could extend beyond the frame of the picture to connect those who straddle their country and their family, the collective and the individual. While the red bloodline vaguely and loosely connects these individuals to the collective and situates them in the Maoist political situation, the connection is thin and weak, yet visible and obvious. The evidence of the thread is from the red color distinct from the plain and dark colors of the figures. Therefore the connection between the family members is inseparable from their connection with the communist government, indicated by the color red. The whole dark picture with isolated individuals visualizes another set of hidden boundaries *within* the nation-state—ones that could cause individuals to feel as "diasporic" within their national boundaries for political reasons. The previous chapter has shown how not allowing the strict boundaries between one nation and another to dictate one's identity can provide a new home for an immigrant, one not bound by the territories of any nation, past or present. This chapter examines how mapping one's home, especially for Chinese individuals, can be distorted, where breaking down the barriers between family and country can have damaging effects.

As mentioned in the introduction, the nation and the family are inherently connected, as implied by the Chinese compound term *guojia*, with *guo* (國) meaning nation and *jia* (家) referring to family. However, during the Mao era, the notion of *jia* was threatened because the socialist authoritarian power and the unified Maoist authoritarian ideology undermined the notions of family and marriage, allowing Mao Zedong himself to become the patriarchal "head" of a Chinese family. After the communist government gained central power following the internal civil war with the governing Nationalist Party (known as the Kuomintang) in 1945, it sought new ways to govern the land. During the 1950s to 1970s, Chairman Mao developed a guiding philosophy for the new country. This, however, led to an extreme cult of personality surrounding Mao in later years. As often portrayed through various forms of propaganda, he was cast as the ultimate patriarchal figure and icon.[2]

In Maoist discourse, individuals were sacrificed for collective benefits, becoming victims of the communist revolution as their personal loves and ideals were mostly destroyed. Love became subordinated to or worked in service of revolution: "The relationship of the revolutionary husband and wife should be first and foremost that of comrades. . . . The feeling between husband and wife is first of all that of revolution."[3] Some revolutionaries responded to the communist nation-building project by suppressing their desires and love, yet many of them became victims of this ideology. As Jianmei Liu points out, "Political ideologies called for the postponement of love and the subordination of sexual relationships to the revolutionary agenda."[4] Maoist ideology categorized love and marriage as bourgeois ideas and redefined home to be represented by the collective proletarian masses. During the Cultural Revolution (1966–1976), "private feelings, sex, and personal love, which were regarded by the Communist Party as harmful and destructive elements, were expelled from literary production."[5] The expulsion of those emotions from cultural productions like books and plays shows the extent to which personal love and feelings were suppressed under Mao. This often produced a huge void in terms of family and emotions during the Mao era. After the Cultural Revolution, however, personal love, interpersonal connection, and sexuality reemerged in literary representations. Avant-garde writers publishing in the 1980s, like Su Tong, Mo Yan, and Ge Fei, employed love and sex in their novels to deconstruct the national myths of the Mao era.

With this context in mind, I discuss a contemporary female Chinese immigrant writer and dancer, Yan Geling, who continues to address how to negotiate the individual's need to map their own home when faced with a regime that has tried to turn the home into a part of the state. Her novel examined in this chapter, *The Criminal Lu Yanshi* (*Lufan Yanshi* 陸犯焉識, 2014), dramatizes the dynamic of nation/politics and family/marriage. By largely focusing on the protagonist Lu Yanshi's imprisonment experience and his tragic love story with his wife, the novel criticizes a Mao regime that suppressed individuality and replaced it with political discourse. I will now examine how individuals respond to this institutionalized Maoist ideology as portrayed in *The Criminal Lu Yanshi*, and how a sense of "home" is generated in Yan Geling's novels set during the Mao era.

In *The Criminal Lu Yanshi*, prison in some way offers the protagonist Lu Yanshi a sense of home—not in the sense of comfort, but in familiarity with the political system of China during the Mao era. Writer Yan Geling uses Lu Yanshi's imprisonment experience to signify a "home" experience that is problematic and traumatic, contradicting the comfort and stability that represent the usual implications of home. The prison during the Land Reform is shown as a carceral dystopia caused by the Mao regime, with the installation of both hard and soft surveillance infrastructures, which the tragic love story between Yanshi and Wanyu critiques.

This chapter examines the complicated and paradoxical sites of home straddled between communist collectives and individuals, between *guo* and *jia* in *The Criminal Lu Yanshi*. Ha Jin's China and America in chapter 1 can be described at times as a "utopia," an imagined, idealized place, and other times as a "dystopia," a depressing, frightening space that causes disillusionment. Yan Geling portrays dystopic spaces that are controlled by national discourse and authorities, showing the extreme way that the state has interfered with individuals' notions of the boundaries of their private familial lives and being part of a nation, distorting one's ability to map a home. Whereas Ha Jin shows how collapsed boundaries of the nation-states can lead to individuals' freedom to choose their own identity, Yan points out that when the state oversteps its bounds and interferes with the individual's familial relationships, it can create a diasporic need to map with terrible consequences, even within China's own borders.

Yan Geling as a Chinese Diasporic Writer and Literary Cartographer

In contrast to the previous chapter, in which I discuss one of the most famous Anglophone Chinese American writers of the present day, this chapter looks at one of the most renowned Sinophone Chinese American writers, Yan Geling.[6] Yet their roles as cartographer overlap. Like Ha Jin, Yan Geling had firsthand experience in China and with the People's Liberation Army, which serves as an inspiration for her many works. Born in 1958 in Shanghai, she was a dancer before embarking on a literary career and performed in the People's Liberation Army during the Cultural Revolution. In the 1970s, she served as a journalist for the military on the border between China and Vietnam. In late 1989, Yan went to the United States and was awarded a scholarship by Columbia College in Chicago, studying creative writing and earning a master of fine arts degree. Although she wrote in English while earning this degree, Yan mostly publishes in Chinese, writing about Chinese stories.

Although many of Yan Geling's works are set in China, her immigrant experience is essential to understanding these novels in particular, and her writings in general. Yan has defined immigration as the "weakest, vulnerable existence of life," which is "most sensitive to the cruel environment" and "tragic destiny."[7] Yet it is this condition that "forces one to react to the cruelty of one's environment in a most truthful fashion."[8] Therefore, Yan's immigrant experience is essential to her rich portrayal of cultural vulnerability and the cross-cultural conflicts suffered by early Chinese immigrants to the United States, as in her most famous novel, *Fusang* (扶桑, 1995). Yan insists that it is unfair to categorize immigrant literature as marginal.[9] To her, the ease of traveling between China and America gives her many opportunities to narrate Chinese stories

50 • Transpacific Cartographies

from a liminal perspective that is different from Chinese nationals in mainland China and gives her privilege to be able to speak out what she may not be able to within China.

Previous scholarship on Yan Geling largely focuses on the gender perspectives and historical discourse in her works.[10] To some scholars, Yan's novels set in the Cultural Revolution serve the social function of rejecting efforts to erase the tragic events of China's modern history from its greater history. Shenshen Cai posits that Yan's two novels *A Woman's Epic* (*Yige nüren de shishi* 一個女人的史詩, 2006) and *The Criminal Lu Yanshi* "probe into the political and cultural catalysts that contribute to the authoritarian rule of Mao and the subsequent social and human catastrophes of this traumatic period."[11] Similarly, Namyong Park asserts that *The Criminal Lu Yanshi* in particular resists the forgetting of China's tragic modern history.[12] While these scholars rightly highlight these efforts at recovering history, their focus on the historical and political representations in the novels overlooks the complex personal relationships and emotions that are at the heart of Yan's works—relationships that are central to understanding how her book critiques the forced remapping of the family under the Mao regime.

While gender and historical perspectives are both important elements of Yan's writing, I believe it is beneficial to read her works from a spatial perspective, as doing so allows us to discover more complex layers of her literary construction as a multilingual, transpacific diasporic writer. Feng Pin-chia is one of the few scholars who incorporates spatial dimension into her analysis of Yan Geling's works, albeit in a very limited way and with only a brief mention. She argues that immigrant works by Yan Geling "involved a systematic exploration of Chinese American women of different temporal locations and geopolitical positions."[13] Feng reads *Ren huan* (人寰, *The World of Man*, 1998) as Yan's attempt to create a transitional space for the narrator to simultaneously remember China and construct her diasporic subjectivity. Vera Schwarcz's borrowed concept of "transitional space"[14] allows that "Chinese abroad seek to create some continuity between past and present, between old selves imprinted by the mother tongue and new ones invented with painful freedom."[15] Built on Feng's initial attempt to bring in the spatial perspective in researching Yan Geling's work, this chapter further examines the spatial literary construction in Yan's novel, in particular what map of her characters she is charting to display a China in the Cold War as a Chinese diasporic writer.

While *The Criminal Lu Yanshi* might not have the explicit mapping metaphorical framework of Ha Jin's *A Map of Betrayal*, I want to highlight the spatial and geopolitical aspects of Yan's writing so as to establish her role as a literary cartographer. Indeed, one might say that Yan Geling is obsessed with space in her works. For one, many of her stories literally start with place or space. Like in "Riddles in Las Vegas" (*La si wei jia si de miyü* 拉斯維加斯的謎語), with its first sentence, "Las Vegas, we call 'la si wei jia si,'" followed by a map of the city from the perspectives of a Chinese immigrant tourist, and zooming in to the disastrous life of a Chinese professor reduced to a gambler. Another example of this is "Bird of a Lime Color" (*Qing Ningmeng se de niao* 青檸檬色的鳥), which unveils the empty, lonely space in which a Chinese immigrant lives at its opening: "The house on the second floor hosts empty loneliness for a year."[16] These are just a couple examples out of many when Yan Geling opens her stories with descriptions of place and space.

As was noted earlier, Yan Geling was a trained dancer who served in the Cultural and Dance Troupe of the People's Liberation Army beginning when she was twelve.[17] Her dancing experience makes her aware of space and spatial imaginations in a way that parallels the acts of a mapmaker. There are numerous studies on the intertwined relationship between body and space, as "it is through the body moving with space that we construct meaning of the world around us and create relations to that world."[18] Therefore, dancing and choreographing the movements for bodies in space is comparable to placing the characters on a map. Just like dancers' movements create meanings of the world and relations between the bodies and the world, characters' experiences on the map create relational connections with the real or imagined places on that map. I would argue that spatial construction—the mapping of space—is essential in Yan's literary works, and reading her works through geospatial theories reveals a deeper meaning to how her characters perceive their existence in China.

In talking about space, I mean both the abstract, metaphorical, and symbolic spaces like those created by gender and racial hierarchies, and specific places like homes, houses, prisons, and so on. The boundaries between metaphorical and realistic spaces become blurred, as theorists in critical cartography would argue that maps make places realistic as they represent them. Geographer John Pickles emphasizes the need for us to "focus on the ways in which mapping and the cartographic gaze have coded subjects and produced identities."[19] Pickles asks us to pay attention to how mapping is a production of place, space, and identities. Following this definition of cartography and space, I consider Yan Geling as a literary cartographer who actively creates multiple spaces, places, and identities through her novels.

Yan Geling's novels not only cross different gendered and geographical spaces inside her novels, but her works and cultural identity also challenge categories of literature. For instance, Wen Jin discusses Yan Geling's most famous immigrant novel, *Fusang*, a novel first published in Chinese in 1995 and translated into English in 2001. Comparing and examining the novel and its translation, Jin asserts that the multilingual circulation of the novel destabilizes the nation-based focus of literary culture. The novel has been "translated into English and read in the country where most of its plot is set, [and] the novel also resists literary categories based on language, such as 'Sinophone' and

'Anglophone' literature."[20] Just like her own cultural and linguistic crossing, Yan Geling crosses the linguistic and cultural boundaries in her literary creation.

I believe that Yan Geling, being a female cartographer of the Chinese diaspora, paints a picture where her characters map out a distorted sense of home during the Mao regime. While the boundaries between the state and family are destroyed, their sense of home is threatened, leading them to a diasporic state with a distorted sense of home. Through focusing on how her characters map out multiple spaces and places in her novel *The Criminal Lu Yanshi*, Yan demonstrates how Chinese bodies are collectively "misplaced" and "displaced" in the mainstream society not only outside China but within China. Whether it is in her immigrant stories or Chinese stories, Yan captures a "diasporic space" in which one hardly finds a sense of belonging and faces existential angst. Yan has her characters go beyond boundaries by questioning the limits on space, family, and nation through spatial analysis and Foucault's carceral geography, in particular, in her novel *The Criminal Lu Yanshi*. The novel shows that when personal connections are based on political ideals as a viable container for a nation's hope and future, mapping one's identity becomes distorted, with the era destroying many people's sense of home.

Carceral Geography in *The Criminal Lu Yanshi*

The Criminal Lu Yanshi describes a tragic story between an intellectual, Lu Yanshi, and his wife, Feng Wanyu. Yanshi was born into a privileged family in Shanghai and is arranged to marry Wanyu after his father's death. He goes to the United States for further studies, where he indulges in "Western freedom," including free expression of his political beliefs and numerous love affairs. Upon his return to China, he becomes a professor and leads a complicated life between his dedicated wife and the demands of his shrewd stepmom. In the 1950s, he is judged as a counterrevolutionary and is sent to a northwest prison. In the deserted land, Lu Yanshi is torn by fights and struggles with the counterrevolutionaries, which takes away his pride as an intellectual. During his twenty years in the labor camp, he has been waiting to reunite with his wife and their daughter. His intellectual aspirations have been vanquished, yet his affection toward Wanyu grows as he waits out his sentence. After he is released from the labor camp he is reunited with Wanyu, who has lost her memory of him and can no longer recognize her own husband. Finally, they remarry not long before she passes away.

David Der-wei Wang suggests that the novel *The Criminal Lu Yanshi* is in many ways a "scar story."[21] In arguing that Yan Geling's two Cultural Revolution–era novels—*A Woman's Epic* and *The Criminal Lu Yanshi*—undo the process of cultural forgetting, Shenshen Cai compares her works to the scar literature (or the "literature of the wounded," *shanghen wenxue* 傷痕文學) of the late 1970s and early 1980s that recaptured the suffering of officials and intellectuals during the Cultural Revolution primarily through narrations of personal experience. Indeed, the theme of *The Criminal Lu Yanshi* echoes what happens in the archetypical example of this genre, Lu Xinhua's story "The Scar" (1978).[22] In both stories, the relationships (husband and wife in *Lu*; daughter and mother in "Scar") are torn apart by the political regime, and neither narrative ends in reunion. Both Lu Yanshi's endless waiting in the labor camp and Wanyu's eternal waiting for her husband's homecoming have similarities with the ending of "Scar," in which the daughter's return is too late to meet her mother one last time. These works reveal an awareness of the feelings that had been suppressed during the Cultural Revolution. Yet, other elements of scar literature—its expressions of hope for the future of the Communist Party or narrating simply the historical details of the traumas during the Cultural Revolution—diffuse the political agenda of these stories and any critique of the Mao regime.[23] Thus, comparing Yan's works with earlier scar literature is useful but limiting. Because of the time period when this kind of literature was published, scar literature could not present direct criticism of Mao or other social problems without risking censorship by the government. Under such restrictions, the personal feelings and individual stories in the genre were fashioned to serve the purpose of the collective. For instance, the Gang of Four are scapegoated as the cause of the suffering, therefore reinforcing the ideals of communist leadership and the party rules. Unlike those earlier works, however, her novels conclude neither with hope for the Communist Party nor with characters "finding salvation and happiness in the West,"[24] as often happens in the Anglophone Cultural Revolution memoirs that began to appear at the end of the twentieth century. Rather, Yan's novels use personal and intricate relationships to retrieve the cultural memory of the Cultural Revolution and the critique of Mao.

Although previous readings of Yan's novel do not extend to its spatiality, reading it as "scar story" implies a spatial aspect. Scar stories create an Odyssean kind of request where there is a separation of the family followed by the reunion, just like the protagonists in *The Criminal Lu Yanshi*. This relationship inherently creates the loss of home and the need for homecoming, which necessitates mapping. Because the story is largely based within and without prison, I am interested in how identities are created and shaped within carceral space. Strangely, but significantly, prison in some ways provides Lu Yanshi with a sense of easiness and calmness, not in the sense of comfort but through his familiarity with the political system of China during the Mao era. Yan Geling uses his imprisonment experience to signify a "home" experience that is problematic and traumatic, contradicting the usual implications of home—comfort and stability—which leads to questions of whether the nation can provide a home for individuals. The prison that confines Lu Yanshi during the Labor

Camp Movement demonstrates the Mao regime to be a carceral dystopia, with the installation of both hard and soft surveillance infrastructures. The tragic love story between Yanshi and Wanyu is rather a critique of the carceral dystopia caused by the Mao regime that extends beyond the prison and into the home.

Scholarship on carceral geography is rich, diverse, and multiscale, focusing on wider structural, political, and institutional contexts, as well as on everyday experiences, practices, and agency; it is sensitive to change and difference across space and time, and between cultures and jurisdictions. Of particular note is the breadth of empirical focus of carceral geography; on spaces of "mainstream" incarceration of "criminals" for custodial sentences imposed by the prevailing legal system; the overlaps and synergies between these spaces, their functional and postfunctional lives, and also their porosity, in recognizing that techniques and technologies of confinement seep out of "carceral" spaces into the everyday, domestic, street, and institutional spaces with which both former inmates and their loved ones (such as prison visitors) come into contact. It also increasingly recognizes "the carceral" as spatial, emplaced, mobile, embodied, and affective.

The carceral inherent link with prison is reinforced by Michel Foucault's influential work *Discipline and Punish: The Birth of the Prison* (1977). Foucault describes a "carceral system" that reaches far beyond the prison, based on its disciplinary control that encompasses the most "coercive technologies of behaviour."[25] This idea of the carceral as affecting how people map their space beyond the physical prison is an essential part of Yan Geling's novel, which portrays the carceral system as not only existing within the labor camp during Laogai (reform through labor) in the 1950s, but also outside it. Yan powerfully displays how the sense of confinement seeps out of the traditional carceral spaces into the everyday life during the Mao era. Indeed, by depicting the extreme hardship Lu Yanshi experiences in the labor camp and how his family is impacted outside the camp, she shows how the prison discipline penetrates the whole of society during the 1950s and 1960s.

The novel spends many pages on the labor camp movement and the prisoners' lives, showing the terrible experiences that the prisoners go through. The titular character's name, Lu Fan Yanshi, contains two Chinese characters (陆犯) that imply "land offense," a symbol of his status in the political movement. The protagonist Lu Yanshi is one of the many labor camp (*laogai* 劳改) prisoners who were sent to the countryside for reeducation in Qinghai—one of the major labor camps during the Anti-Rightist Campaign (1957–1959) and afterward. According to an official document, more than four thousand prisoners in Qinghai died during the Great Famine (1959–1961). Three years after the Great Leap Forward (1957–1960), more than ninety-five thousand prisoners were sent to the labor camp in Qinghai, and in 1965 the whole Shanghai *laogai* troupe moved to Qinghai.[26] Setting Lu Yanshi's experience in this huge *laogai* camp is intentional given its importance, indicating that his experience is not just an individual one, but a collective one shared by many.

Before the prisoners are moved into their actual prison, a virtual prison made by powder thrown onto the grass already exists: "One line is 'internal wall' one is 'external wall' and the one at the most outside is 'big wall.'"[27] The fact that the carceral "walls" exist not only inside the prison but also outside signifies the imprisonment of these innocent people. Such virtual, soft lines as carceral walls draw the ground as a prison, and only a select lucky few have been able to escape. These invisible walls are indicative of the communist regime, which sets up a restrictive confinement. Outside the prison where the labor camp prisoners work in the open grass, the narrator, Lu Yanshi's grandchild, notices an interesting fact that "every pickaxe coming down, deserted land uses head of the pickaxe and his arm bone to hit his internal organs instead of the other way around. Therefore it is not humans reclaiming the land but land reclaiming humans."[28] Such inhuman punishment shows the extreme impossible work imposed on the prisoners and how the brutality pervades into their everyday work in the labor camp.

As mentioned previously, the novel does not merely present how the labor camp prison redefines space for the prisoners but, more importantly, expands to the whole society during the Mao regime. Lu Yanshi's journey of studying abroad in the United States is brief, yet his personality and life abroad are completely different from when he is in China. Returning to China after six years overseas, he laments that "the ship on the Pacific is the beginning of his imprisonment."[29] The word "imprisonment" shows the lack of freedom for Chinese even outside a physical prison: "Like all the other kids in China, and all the boys from intellectual Chinese families, he has never had enough freedom."[30]

This lack of freedom has a profound impact on how Lu Yanshi maps the space around him. With the boundaries between what constitutes home and what constitutes the state totally broken down, he maps the space of his incarceration not as other prisoners might, but as something that feels familiar, that feels like home. "My grandpa feels calmer than other prisons in the labor camp prison, because he is used to living without sufficient freedom."[31] In fact, Lu Yanshi feels calmer when in the labor camp, drawing an analogy to the restricted society beyond the prison. His identification with "prison" therefore is a critique of the authoritarian Mao regime.

This sense of a disturbed sense of home can be found in the novel's introduction, which uses a metaphor that compares prisoners of the state with grassland creatures who are corralled by men with guns. These state prisoners, many of whom are convicted for nebulous or unknown crimes, are forced to migrate, to be moved around like cattle, and live in the rural countryside. The labor camp movement and the Cultural Revolution pushed a lot of people like Lu Yanshi to exile, to becoming diasporic within their own country. This move largely limits the use of his intellectual talents while forcing him to be emotionally away from his family, thereby completely taking away his freedom in career and love.

Instead of the sense of freedom that one might feel with the boundaries of home being erased on one's personal map, Lu Yanshi feels trapped, as the state has taken over every aspect of his personal life. He advocates freedom and political ideals that run against the core values of Chinese communism at the time, acting on the beliefs he held consistently during his five years abroad. Shrewd, quick, funny, and competitive, he constantly attends political speeches and frequently makes his own. He particularly speaks about topics that would be taboo in China: the Soviet Union, conflicts between Japan and America, secret treaties, and more. He pursues social freedoms as well, actively participating in clubs and organizations, flirting, and having affairs.[32] It seems that America is his space for freedom, where he has full control of his own life and love, where he can feel at home without interference from his family or the government.

When Lu Yanshi returns from America, however, his freedom and pride become embarrassing to his family.[33] He does not feel like he belongs in his old home. He feels more *at home* in liberal environments, like his campus or American associations and American-style restaurants and cafes. His American friends seem to bring abroad the American cultures and ideals, creating a space for themselves where they call home. Although his personality and experience make him dedicated to a pursuit of freedom in both politics and love, this dedication and idealism create problems for him in his later life.

We can also see Lu Yanshi's pursuit of freedom in his love life. He is never ashamed of his affairs, which take place throughout the early years of his marriage. He first has an affair with an Italian girl while abroad, and later keeps a mistress when he returns to China. He sees his affairs as a courageous pursuit for freedom instead of stepping outside of boundaries as legal husband. These affairs are blatantly rejecting the fake closeness that was enforced by the Mao regime. Whereas the protagonist's body and emotions are restricted in China, while abroad he feels released, and these affairs are the articulation of his true desires without enforcement. Therefore these affairs are like his mapping beyond the restrictive boundaries.

Lu Yanshi's mistress Nianhen embodies his ideal of freedom, as the mistress in Ha Jin's novel did for Gary (see chapter 1). Compared to his wife Wanyu, Nianhen is more of a modern woman, determined and independent, with a business of her own. At the same time, Nianhen is portrayed as kind, generous, and understanding. When Lu Yanshi is in prison, she helps send his letters to his family; when he loses his job after getting out of prison, she financially supports him. But underneath her gentleness, she possesses a spirit of "combat."[34] Yanshi has a passionate, close relationship with Nianhen; his love for her has much less to do with Nianhen herself, and more to do with the fact that he is free to choose to love her. At the end of the novel, he leaves his family, taking only his clothes and Wanyu's ashes, as if he were helping to make his wife's eternal return to a real "home," as the Chinese term *luoye guigen* (落葉歸根, returning to one's homeland when one dies) suggests. The family—an imposed unit that has been taken over by the state—no longer offers him a sense of home, and he wants to go look for an open possibility for the future.

The women in Lu Yanshi's life are not the only way that he seeks freedom from a state that has taken over his personal life, whether in a physical prison or outside of it. Lu Yanshi and his fellow prisoners long for freedom, yet under the communist regime their freedom is restricted. Therefore, they look for secret ways to have freedom—expressions that might go undetected or concealed. As mentioned earlier, dancer and writer Yan Geling has set the labor camp as a limited stage for the prisoners. People in prison have limited space to choreograph their lives and perform their identities. Suffering the limitations, the prisoners find extreme ways to articulate their lives. Even suicide, which might be thought of as a desperate expression of freedom, is deemed acceptable, considered as being "resistance, protest and expression of antagonism."[35] When one prisoner is sentenced to death, he writes these final words: "Long live the motherland."[36] Even at the moment of his death, one carried out by the state, he must conceal his sarcasm in the guise of patriotism. For instance, the prisoners pretend to be sleepwalkers at one point, getting up in the middle of the night and wandering around the compound. When asked to go back to their own beds, they interpret "return" differently in order to wander around longer.[37] The dream-wandering charade suggests their hidden desire to be set free, meanwhile suggesting that their freedom is strongly suppressed and could only be achieved while dreaming. Yanshi realizes his mind is awake to the shouts of the wardens, whereas his body wanders to other places that it wants to be. He and the other prisoners straddle the country in reality and the country that they long for—one that grants freedom and benefits to its citizens.

Hierarchical Observation and Normalizing Judgment

According to Foucault, "prison discipline pervades all of modern society."[38] The modern approach to discipline is to produce "docile bodies"[39]—bodies that not only do what we want but do it precisely in the way that we want. Foucault further discusses the modern means of producing these docile bodies, including *hierarchical observation*, meaning intense observation that becomes coercive and intrusive; and *normalizing judgment*, denoting that individuals are judged by where their actions place them on a ranked scale that compares to everyone else. *The Criminal Lu Yanshi* demonstrates both means with vivid examples to illustrate how the home has now become a prison just as the prison offers a sense of home-like familiarity for Lu Yanshi.

Over ten years, Lu Yanshi writes Wanyu numerous letters; for each letter, he creates two versions: one is an open version that he knows will be screened by the XXXX letter box and the eyes behind it; the other is his private version, read by no one but himself.[40] The "XXXX" symbols do not represent the English letter X, but rather refer to crosses. Normally, the letter box has numbers on it, but the author represents it with these four crosses, implicating a pair of eyes from an anonymous official that strictly follows the government's orders. In this way, he struggles through a double existence—one that is public and shaped to please the government, and another that he keeps to himself. In this scenario, the true emotions he has for Wanyu and his family can only remain buried in his heart, or be expressed in a hidden letter that no one else could read. For instance, in the private version of one letter, Yanshi writes to Wanyu about the day he was arrested, saying that his thoughts often return to how he said farewell, remembering how Wanyu followed him into his study before going downstairs and watching him being taken away by the police. When he looks back, he writes, he sees her holding his slippers in her hand, making him believe he would eventually come home.[41] Comparatively, the open version of that letter is businesslike, asking Wanyu to deliver some daily necessities to the prison.

Lu Yanshi's private letters are only for the prison, his home, while the ones that actually communicate with his wife are exposed to the public, showing the loss of boundaries between home and state. He knows the letters are read by the eyes behind the letter box through which they communicate: "The eyes behind XXXX letter box made him feel as if he and Wanyu were being seen naked."[42] The effect, though, is far beyond mere exposure—beyond private emotions becoming a public spectacle. Rather, the letters are exposed to pairs of eyes described as dirty—those that have "watched violent killing and atrocity, and have become accustomed to blood and dung."[43] This is a form of hierarchical observation, which not only negates and disrupts Wanyu and Yanshi's intimacy but also projects an intrusive observation from the political regime that has forced them to be nothing but "docile."

Another way of producing docile bodies in Foucault's definition is "normalizing judgment," which means making people conform to or reduce to a standard or norm; yet this so-called norm may actually not be very normal or good at all. In the novel, the protagonist's family has their judgment "normalized," not to reflect their family love, but to conform to the communist ideology. When Lu Yanshi is labeled as a counterrevolutionary, his family has to choose between him and the government. The novel shows that his family, consciously or unconsciously, follows the Maoist ideology and rejects Lu.[44] Without much knowledge of Lu Yanshi's life in the labor camp, his family tries to define him based on how the government instructs them to. Rather than try to understand the love between his parents, Lu Yanshi's son Ziye prioritizes the benefit of the family and the collective. Ziye is a product of Maoist ideology. Traumatized from losing his first girlfriend because of his father's background, and worrying that the family will suffer further because of his father's crimes, he encourages his mother to sign divorce papers.[45] On hearing the news that Lu Yanshi has been released from prison, Ziye feels only worried and nervous. He first disbelieves the letter, thinking that his father has possibly run away instead of being released. He then believes Lu Yanshi's return will only bring the family trouble and does not show any sympathy toward his father but instead denies any relationship with him. He also tries to convince his sister to write a letter to keep Lu Yanshi away from their household. When picking up his father at the train station, Ziye asks his daughter to greet Lu Yanshi as a generic "grandpa" instead of calling him "father" directly, which would reveal their more direct blood relation. To him, their family has been the real victim, its members invisibly imprisoned because they lost the trust of the government and the masses.[46] Instead of trying to figure out if his father is actually guilty, Ziye blindly believes in the government's judgment. The ties that should bind the family together—love, trust, honor, and respect—have been dissolved by the actions of the government, which encourages family members to distrust and suspect each other, redirecting that familial love to the state instead. The home is no longer a unit of the family, but one that has the government (or Mao himself) as a patriarchal figure dictating what views will exist in the home. There is no independence, no barrier, just "docile bodies" and minds under the power of the communist regime.

Such disciplinary power that incorporates hierarchical observation and normalizing judgment shows that the home has become nothing but a small unit in the communist collective, and that the family has to conform to the communist ideology to survive. Yanshi and Wanyu's only daughter, Dantong, the offspring of their passionate love making just before Yanshi went to prison, becomes the main actress in an educational film that aims to achieve what Chairman Mao promotes—an attempt to "cure all the blood-flukes" (meaning to eliminate all the bad elements from society).[47] By being a main actress in propaganda films, Dantong is unconsciously absorbed into the communist course. Lu Yanshi's wife, Feng Wanyu, though trying to hold on to her feelings for Yanshi, cannot avoid the Communist Party's impact on her daily life. Gradually after her husband's long absence, she begins a new life that concedes to communism. She moves to live in an area where several communists reside; the neighborhood committee visits her and gives her *The Quotations of Chairman Mao* to study. Encouraged by her neighbors, she joins the older women's club and the party itself. She drifts into the Maoist ideology without much thinking or deliberately choosing to.

Although Maoist ideology and politics play such dominant roles in their lives, the characters in the novel show a marked ignorance of them. Lu Yanshi's family and friends either romanticize communism without understanding it, or they prioritize politics over their family and friendship. His nephew, Pierre, who grew up abroad, is very idealistic about China. He runs away from home and fights for the communist revolutionary course with Yanshi's old schoolmate David. David and Yanshi dislike each other because of their different beliefs in communism.[48] The fact that Pierre becomes a revolutionary after such a short time is ironic, since it seems the public are all ignorant of what revolution even is. No one in the novel can define it. The ambiguity of the concept leads Yanshi's daughter to naively say, "If all the counter-revolutionaries gather together and establish a nation, it would be a mess."[49] She assumes that being counterrevolutionary is bad, but she does not know why. She changes her mind when two of her favorite teachers become counterrevolutionaries. Whether Lu Yanshi and these teachers are actually counterrevolutionary or not is never explained; if they are, the reasons are never clear.[50] These "counterrevolutionaries" are all sent down to the countryside without even knowing what crime they have committed. Revolutionary is presented as an ambiguous concept, and the state is dissolved in all these characters' activities.

Ironically, although Lu Yanshi is judged as "counterrevolutionary," he seems to be as innocent as one could be during the time of the Cultural Revolution. Wang points out that the protagonist's name, "Yanshi," in traditional Chinese means "How to know this?"[51] The "crime" he commits remains unknown in the novel, which spends many pages describing how Yanshi is accused of his crime, yet never identifies clearly what crime he actually committed. The narrator explains that it is a way for Yanshi's family to clarify his crime because "at that time the crimes were all abstract."[52] It is as if the story looked away from his crime (how he is victimized, the tortures he endured in the labor camp, etc.) yet the very nature of the crime is omitted. This represents the irrationality of labor camp[53]—that everyone is obliged to obey the Maoist ideology and the counterrevolutionaries are sent to prison; yet it is never clear how they become criminals in the first place. When Lu Yanshi gets a fifteen-year sentence, this attracts attention from other prisoners, as if he won the lottery, because it is lighter than most other punishments. His sentence is later extended twice, then escalated to a death sentence, and then lowered to life in prison. Just like people's belief in communism, the reasons for Yanshi's imprisonment and sentences are arbitrary, which was common during Mao's time. The fickle nature of the sentences suggests the instability and randomness of the political judgment of the time. Lu Yanshi's family never figures out what kind of crime he has committed, and yet some of them blindly believe the government's assertion of his guilt.

The Distorted Love between Lu Yanshi and Feng Wanyu—Personal Spaces of Confinement

In this irrational environment, the love between the married couple Lu Yanshi and Feng Wanyu develops as a means of enabling prison identities to move beyond the confines of the prison. Despite their arranged marriage, Yanshi develops his love for Wanyu over time. Wanyu becomes the "home" he wants to return to. When he runs away from prison and faces the possibility of death, he makes sure to face the direction of Wanyu,[54] as if the direction he is running would bring him back home. Despite the vague image of Wanyu in his heart, Yanshi makes every effort to reconstruct her image in his mind and to maintain a connection with her through his letters, which makes him survive through the despair of the labor camp. The biggest hope he has in the prison—to get out and return home to reunite with his family—keeps him alive. Although Wanyu and Yanshi do not have a strong attachment with each other, Lu Yanshi identifies her as an imagined homeland for him when he is in prison.

However, Wanyu's symbolizing of Yanshi's imagined homeland is not necessarily good. She represents an ideal, traditional Chinese woman who is loyal to her husband and family. Not at all outspoken like Yanshi, Wanyu seems quiet, gentle, and obedient in appearance. Her name, "Wanyu," not only suggests "curvy, as if," as Wang suggests, but like its Mandarin pronunciation, symbolizes "like a jade." Jade, which was a rare and strong material in ancient China, helps to suggest Wanyu's purity and strength. Even when she lives under the same roof with Yanshi and his young stepmother, Wanyu yields to their wishes. She only disobeys Yanshi once in the novel—when he begs her to divorce him in order to spare the children from sharing his disgrace. Wanyu refuses to do so, always hoping that they could be reunited someday. She embodies the qualities of a woman of the Maoist state instead of what the liberal Lu Yanshi originally wants. But the Maoist politics and prison have changed him so much that he identifies her as an ideal wife figure and home that he wishes to return to.

Lu Yanshi embodies "home" to Wanyu because he is the only one on whom she could project the wildness and freedom inside her. In other words, he sees much in her that is hidden from anybody else. For example, the novel constantly implies that her beauty is hidden. "Her beauty has to be discovered, and Yanshi has never discovered it. . . . He's never carefully looked at her," and "she hasn't let him carefully look at her face."[55] Her husband is not attracted to her at first, but he cannot help noticing her beauty and stubbornness over time. Yet he discovers her beauty not when they are together, but when he is remembering her while in prison. This further proves that Wanyu serves as his imaginary home. She has to hide her desires because of the social and cultural role she has to fill as a traditional, reserved Chinese woman. But inside her is a wild, unknown, unexplored pure body waiting to be discovered. After the couple remarries in 1986, Wanyu seems to emancipate herself fully. She gets rid of her conservative self and becomes another person. She rejects clothes and just stays naked all the time. This extreme emancipation of her body suggests her strong wish to escape the strict social protocols and rules under the Mao regime that the clothing represents. Her son, in wanting to put clothes back on her, also wants to put social restrictions back on her, but Yanshi keeps him and others away from Wanyu. When all her clothes are taken away from her body, her "pure, white body is emancipated"[56] when she dies of pneumonia. While Yanshi is in prison, Wanyu exists in a prison of her own. She follows the protocol as a traditional, loyal wife for Yanshi yet suffers from the waiting and restrictions. Wanyu's reunification with Yanshi releases her from those restrictive controls. She sets herself free from the suppressed desires once Yanshi comes back, liberating herself from the expectations of a traditional Chinese woman who is reserved and conservative. Different from the reuniting in previous scar literature, the happy reunion in this novel no longer exists. In fact, their longing for each other shows more how they are both trapped by the Maoist ideology instead of their actual longing.

We see that although Lu Yanshi is externally outspoken and rebellious, internally he has deep love for Wanyu and his family. Wanyu, while being quiet, gentle, and obedient on the surface, secretly longs for freedom. At the same time, Wanyu holds onto an idealistic love based on her conceptions rather than reality. Throughout their lives, Yanshi has been absent: from when Yanshi pursues education, love, and freedom abroad; to the time when Yanshi's stepmother monopolizes his time, dividing him from Wanyu; to the years Yanshi spends in prison. Yet these absences do not decrease her love for him; in fact, the opposite occurs. This suggests, however, that the Yanshi that Wanyu falls in love with is not the actual man, but the image she clings to— an image that she has desired and fantasized about since she was seventeen, before she even knew him. Her desire rather represents her persistent and unconditional pursuit of an idealized, fantasized love, though by different means from Yanshi.

Their love story in the end turns into perpetual waiting, loss, and absence. This long waiting, both Lu Yanshi's waiting and longing for his wife in the labor camp, and Wanyu's waiting for her husband's homecoming, represents the "scar" of the Cultural Revolution—turning all forms of personal happiness (intellectual and romantic powers, physical and mental abilities, personal relationships) into tragedies. In *The Criminal Lu Yanshi*, after their reunion Wanyu loses her memory and cannot recognize him; Wanyu must continue to wait for the Yanshi in her memory. Yanshi tries hard to help Wanyu retrieve her memory, but at times he needs to act as someone else accompanying her to wait for Lu Yanshi, though ironically, he is the very person she is waiting for. The Cultural Revolution's impact on individuals proves devastating in the novel. Yet compared to traditional scar literature, Yan Geling's novel retains a final, celebratory tone because in some ways, the waiting does not damage but instead strengthens the novel's central relationship. Yanshi's absence keeps Wanyu waiting, thereby giving her hope and something to long for. Wanyu has always been waiting for her love to come back, the reunion with her husband and the idealistic love. For Yanshi, he hopes Wanyu can recognize him and their love could be realized. Waiting in the novel functions to give characters hope. Meanwhile, the fact that the imaginary love between the two enables Yanshi's prison identities to move beyond the confines of the prison indicates that individual experiences can facilitate people to move beyond confinement during the Mao era.

Conclusion

The absence of home presented in Yanshi and Wanyu's love, marriage, and relationship dramatizes the emotional void during the Mao era, and reinforces the restricted emotional spheres of life under the Maoist regime. Politics and nation are irreconcilable with family and marriage, and people like Yanshi and Wanyu find it difficult, if not impossible, to generate a sense of home in these conditions. Through portraying the extreme hardship Lu Yanshi experiences in the prison and his impossible love with his wife in *The Criminal Lu Yanshi*, contemporary female Chinese immigrant writer and dancer Yan Geling demonstrates how Chinese bodies are collectively "misplaced" and "displaced" and are trapped within the carceral spaces inside and outside labor camp prison within China under the Mao regime. The displacement and diasporic experience not only exists in Yan Geling's immigrant novels but also in novels set inside China like this one.

In *The Criminal Lu Yanshi*, prison in some way provides the protagonist Lu Yanshi a sense of "home"—not in the sense of comfort but in the familiarity with the political system of China during the Mao era, a limited space where they can choreograph their own lives. This special kind of land reform prison, which includes both actual and virtual prison, is a carceral dystopia caused by the Mao regime. Whereas I discussed in chapter 1 how one could possibly create a borderless map beyond the nation-states, in this chapter I show a possible disastrous home on a map with the collapsed boundaries between the nations and families.

The boundaries between home and the state have been dissolved, but not in a way that leads to freedom for the novel's characters, as it does for Lilian and Ben in Ha Jin's *A Map of Betrayal*. Mapping in *The Criminal Lu Yanshi* is all out of whack, especially Yanshi's, because of the authoritarian system that has totally taken control of their home space, so much so that he feels at home in prison. In a way, this distorted feeling of home contrasts with chapter 1, where a home without boundaries was positive. A distorted sense of home mirrors what diasporic characters feel, so this chapter shows how such mapping could occur within a country as much as from without. Given the author's immigrant status, it could be read metaphorically as a diasporic experience.

Addressing political topics and ultimately offering a political critique—while seemingly writing apolitical novels that focus on love and waiting as the movie adaptation *Coming Home* shows—make Yan Geling's works even more interesting. Interestingly but expectedly, the movie adaptation *Coming Home* (*Gui lai* 歸來, 2014), directed by Zhang Yimou, deliberately deletes the whole part of Lu Yanshi's imprisonment and focuses on the love and waiting between the couple after Yanshi returns from the labor camp. Another adaptation, *One Second* (*Yi miao zhong* 一秒鐘, 2020), takes a small plot from the novel about Lu Yanshi trying hard to get out of the labor camp to see a film his daughter acts in, and develops it into a movie about a prisoner from the labor camp escaping to see movie and meet someone. Both movies simply identify that the main protagonists are from the labor camp movement but do not show any scene of prison life, which is understandable due to censorship in China.

Until 2022, Yan Geling was well acclaimed in and outside of mainland China. Unlike Ha Jin, who has been banned from traveling to China and whose many works are not allowed in China, Yan has been very active in the literary circles and activities in China. Yet since February 2022, after her comments on how the government treated a woman chained in Xuzhou, which went viral online, Yan Geling's name has been "wiped out" in China, with few searchable results on Chinese websites except that her books are still available on Chinese book sites. This swift, partial censorship of Yan Geling in China has again proved the instability of Chinese American identity and the unreliability of state-bounded sense of belonging. Luckily, Yan's ability to voice and publish is not easily wiped out in a short time, especially in a digital age like today. And her already established reputation would not suddenly disappear, yet her current situation would force her to reposition herself in the literary market.

3

Affective Mapping of Touristic Diasporic Experience

• •

Contemporary Sinophone Chinese American writers Shi Yu (施雨), Chen Qian (陳謙), and Rong Rong (融融) are not exactly household names. I often hear "I've never heard of them," "I've not read them," or "Where are they selling their books?" from other scholars when I mention these writers. I picked up some of their works mixed with other contemporary Chinese fiction in bookstores in China, and some from my Chinese immigrant friends in the United States. Whether their works belong to the canon of literature or to popular fiction remains undetermined, yet these works are still worth reading as cultural productions and literary phenomena that create their own unique set of maps.

The writers examined in this chapter, Shi Yu, Chen Qian, and Rong Rong, are all female Chinese American writers who emigrated from mainland China to the United States in the 1980s.[1] Their works are published in mainland China and target a mainland Chinese readership, as well as Sinophone readers at large.[2] Just as Franz Kafka wrote from Bohemia in the German language in order to converse with a larger German- and Eurocentric literature,[3] these Sinophone immigrant authors write from America in Chinese to speak to a larger Sinophone and Sinocentric readership. The Chinese readers and Sinophone readers abroad "consume" this literature mostly as commercial, popular fiction.[4] Indeed, the commercialization of literature has been a broad trend in mainland China since the 1980s reform and opening period, when

65

these authors traveled to the United States.[5] Though living outside the mainland, these Sinophone Chinese American writers have also followed this commercialization trend in their literary productions.[6]

Some might argue that this kind of popular fiction is not worth scholarly attention.[7] First, there are the formulaic plots—a husband and wife's values are transformed after coming to the United States, for example. Then there is the straightforward narrative style—either a chronological narrative or a parallel narrative of the past and the present. Clearly, many of these works are not of the same level of literary craftmanship as the more celebrated writers we have examined. Nevertheless, beyond aesthetics—and in fact even because of them—they have a multilayered value. The commercialization of portraying contemporary Chinese immigrants' lives, continual negotiation of cultural differences, nostalgia for their homeland, and fascination with the new land make these novels worth exploring. In this regard, although they have not received as much scholarly attention as some of the other works I examine in this book, the commercialization of the diasporic narrative offers us another strategy for addressing the need for home examined in previous chapters.

While these novels portray immigrant experiences that are similar to those in other works in this book—interracial relationships, fascination with and debunking of the American dream, the negotiation of cultural differences, nostalgia for the homeland, and so on—their primary themes revolve around romantic love. This focus on romantic love marks a shift toward more personal and individual accounts in Chinese diasporic literature that we have seen also in the novels by Ha Jin and Yu Geling. Even though the earlier Chinese diasporic writers touch on romantic love and individual experiences, those mostly serve as metaphors for the characters' nostalgia and longing for their homeland, and the changes that globalization and the American dream have brought to them. Generally, the sense of home that those previous diasporic Chinese works project is more informed by national identification—even love itself was a metaphor for one's relationship with the homeland, as was noted in previous chapters. As we will see in analyzing the works of this chapter, however, recent Chinese diasporic writings are more personalized and romanticized: contemporary, cosmopolitan, and free-spirited characters define their sense of home and identities through their relationships and attachments as an end in itself.

In the context of popular fiction, the result of this affective turn is a new challenge to the idea of home. Instead of creating a map for readers for dealing with existential issues of finding your place in the world, these books commercialize the need for home, creating more of a tourist map for the reader. The touristic narratives often come packaged with promises of individual self-discovery and sexual and affective awakening.[8] As will be explored in this chapter, many of their diasporic writings present exciting, realistic immigrant stories that interest Chinese readers in their homeland and abroad. But unlike stories by forced exiles, the diasporic experience they convey in these novels becomes a voluntary act on behalf of the reader, almost like tourism, manufacturing the affects of homesickness and lovesickness to render their experience back home and among Sinophone communities. This demonstrates how Chinese diasporic writers have commercialized the loss of collective investment in home as a particular geospatial location in a globalized society. Instead of describing diaspora as a traumatic event, these writers turn it into a medium for offering their readers tourist-like experiences that destabilize notions of home for those who have not left their homeland physically.

The tourist-like, voluntary diasporic experiences prevalent in these narratives likely stem from the milieu in which the authors grew up and the ever-changing China they left behind. Having lived in China during the transition from socialist-planned to market-driven economy to a period in which individual desires and a search for existential meaning are prevalent, these writers' sense of home is much less connected to the nation but depends on individual affects. Moreover, the relatively open time allowed readers glimpses into Western culture while still in China, making such stories exotic and interesting.

In commercializing diasporic stories into tales of romantic travel, however, a new vision for the home also begins to emerge. The series of dramatic historical and social changes in China during their time abroad no doubt has affected these writers, causing them to focus their work away from the national concerns of earlier generations. Put another way, how are these authors to write about their nation if they cannot identify that nation as home? Unable to recognize China, let alone identify strongly with it, these authors map their home not in the land of their birth, but in the very same romantic and personal relationships that make their fiction popular in the first place.

Composed of giving and abandonment, love mirrors the departures, arrivals, and resettlements in a diasporic journey. Romantic love in these novels is a mechanism through which the diasporic characters constitute their identities and conjure up the sense of "home" in their diasporic experience. I call this "affective home" (i.e., the emotional/affective sense of home one ascribes to a specific topological and social setting). Following the notion of "affective geographies,"[9] my concept of "affective home" emphasizes how we are "affected" emotionally by particular places, spaces, and relationships, and in turn, this affects how we experience and interpret home and diaspora.

This chapter examines the trivialities in the diaspora's emotional journeys and affective relationships in novels such as Shi Yu's *Niuyue qingren* (紐約情人, *New York Lover*, 2004), Chen Qian's *Wang duan nanfei yan* (望斷南飛雁, *Listen to the Caged Bird Sing*, 2010), and Rong Rong's *Fuqi biji* (夫妻筆記, *Notes of a Couple*, 2005). We will explore the struggles of identity formulation for contemporary Chinese immigrant subjects and how they deconstruct and reconstruct their sense of "home" through relationships. Although these

Sinophone writers draw "tourist" maps of their immigrant stories, turning their personal narratives into romance travel fiction, they offer another path for transcending the territorial boundaries that restrict one's identity—a path to self-identity through love and personal desire.

Literary Cartography and the Tourist's Affect

In tracing a metaphor of critical importance for understanding Chinese diasporic literature, as demonstrated in the previous chapters, I argue in what follows that these authors can also be seen as literary cartographers. Doing so allows me to conceptualize how the writers imagine, negotiate, and articulate the sites of home in relation to romantic and familial relationships. What I call literary cartography is not drawing maps in a literal sense, but rather the way that authors figuratively map social, spatial, and affective spheres in their literary works.[10] These Sinophone writers' articulations of their emotional topography and the trajectory of affective home are their cartographic attempts to chart their complex diasporic relationships. I examine how their works draw the lines between notions such as diaspora, nostalgia, home, and romantic love through the lens of what Weijie Song terms an "affective map."[11] Using the works of another Chinese writer, Lao She, as a case study, Song shows how the author performs an affective mapping of Beijing's teahouses, streets, and courthouses by detailing an atlas of emotions and projecting modern Beijing as a locus of pain and pleasure. "Affective mapping" highlights the emotional atlas associated with the places, including nostalgia, anger, hatred, and happiness. This cartographic endeavor leads these diasporic writers to focus on an affective home that challenges the earlier definitions of diaspora and nostalgia. If we interpret these writers as cartographers, then to draw the affective maps of their immigrant characters is to redraw the routes or maps of diaspora and redefine notions of diaspora and nostalgia along the axis of personal relationships rather than national ones.

In diaspora and nostalgia studies, a common tendency among scholars over the past several decades has been to reduce diaspora to geographical and spatial movement and nostalgia to homesickness. Some earlier diaspora theorists define home in opposition to diaspora, while later scholars define it as a construct on a diasporic journey.[12] This latter view has certain advantages as it rightly highlights the fluidity and complexity of the notion of home. But even while these later studies emphasize that home is not merely a single place from which one is unidirectionally uprooted, much of this scholarship has focused on the collective experience of diasporic populations.[13] This collective approach has its merits—it can tell us about the general pattern of modern migration, the collective experience of a diaspora, and the historical maps of the Chinese diaspora. However, it falls short in describing individual stories' particular nuances, and glosses over the personal, private affective experiences that shape their journeys. Those individual affective stories are precisely the focus of this chapter, as they represent an important medium through which readers of Chinese diasporic literature experience more deeply the emotional journeys that Chinese immigrants undergo when living in the United States.

To navigate those affective journeys, we will need a map. The works I examine here are cartographic attempts to give a living account of the diasporic affective space. They provide a new way to read the link between romantic love and diasporic journey. The map these works draw is not merely a geospatial one, even though some specific places in the novels are essential to the diasporic characters' experiences. It does not necessarily provide specific spaces, places, or directions to guide us through the stories. In fact, there is no actual map at all. The works discussed reduce descriptions of physical settings to a minimum. They instead detail the interior psychic and romantic space. Therefore, they construct an affective map consisting of remembering, reconstructing, and representing the geography of love and how it can create a sense of home. In *Atlas of Emotion: Journeys in Art, Architecture, and Film*, Giuliana Bruno walks us through the connections between "sight," "site," "motion," and "emotion." Her book argues that specific locales would remind one of specific emotions based on their experience of a place. It suggests that we could draw a map of places that connect to various emotions for each of us. Similarly, we might view this chapter's literature as maps that lead us to observe characters' intricate emotional relationships and their back-and-forth movement between different cultures. These maps—composed of narratives, characters, chapters, and titles central to their immigrant identities and relationships—display nostalgic attachments, displacements, and other feelings. By studying these affective maps, we can learn about complex webs of space, bodies, and identities in contemporary Chinese diasporic journeys.

In these works, love is more than a vapid trope to entice readers. Instead, it is an important site through which diasporic subjects mediate personal desires and cultural expectations. Most prominently and bluntly, love is at the intersection where East meets West, becoming the axis along which what counts as home is drawn. Often in these narratives, characters struggle to balance perceived social constraints in Chinese traditions with their cultural exposure to the West. This struggle can involve the intimate relationships between couples and within their families, which operate as sites to represent and complicate affectionate and emotional relationships. The characters' negotiation of their love relationships and cultural traditions impact their imaginations of mobility/dwelling, home/away, and home/diaspora beyond physical geospatial relationships.

Formulaic in nature, these romantic narratives tackle many tropes. Some debunk the traditional American dream. Others show how female Chinese immigrants can remake their identities in the West. But for all of these narratives, they primarily convey this complex negotiating of home through love on an exotic map of diaspora as a spectacle for Chinese consumption. Svetlana Boym's definition of nostalgia could be used just as well as a slogan for the global tourist industry: "The imperative of a contemporary nostalgic: to be homesick and to be sick of being at home—occasionally at the same time."[14] In a global society where many people have lost any sense of collective investment in home as a particular geospatial location, tourism profits precisely by manufacturing the affects of homesickness and lovesickness. The fruit of these authors' cartographic labor is in the end essentially a tourist map. Their works consist of locales, directions, and landmarks that could be appealing to Chinese readers both in China and abroad.

While they are touristic maps, these narratives also contain the underbelly of what tourism often seeks to hide.[15] Anthony Carrigan, in analyzing stories of postcolonial tourism, foregrounds intersubjective differences, thereby helping the subaltern make a voice in the tourism history.[16] Indeed, by telling stories from the minorities and about the minorities, like the Chinese immigrants or women in the United States, the Sinophone writers in this chapter contribute to the kind of "narratives" that Anne-Marie d'Hauteserre claims are essential in moving past colonial narratives of travel, as they would help "resist their erasure from the tourist imagination, and especially from networks of capital accumulation."[17]

These touristic, affective maps in these works contribute to the picture of America to the Sinophone audience's imagination, either by reaffirming the exoticism and excitement as they have heard, or by presenting the realities and trivialities contrary to what they imagine, or a combination of both. Either way, they, as bicultural cultural ambassadors and tour guides, present diverse touristic maps that help navigate the cultural landscapes and relationships in America. Of course, the "locales" and "landmarks" on these maps are metaphorical. I am not speaking of landmarks as in the Empire State Building or Golden Gate Bridge. Their works create, after all, *affective*—not geographic—maps. The points of interest on these affective maps are things like relationships, American lovers, and Chinese husbands. By navigating through these relationships as locales, these writers orient readers in such a way that they can explore the diasporic journey as tourists from the comfort of their own homes.

Three Diasporic Women Writers:
Shi Yu, Chen Qian, and Rong Rong

Before analyzing each of their works, we need to understand the diasporic narratives that these three female Chinese American writers have lived through. Shi Yu, Chen Qian, and Rong Rong are all highly educated intellects who are active in the Sinophone literary circles in America. Both Shi Yu and Chen Qian had full-time jobs while becoming writers. Shi Yu was a doctor before she "abandon[ed] her medical career for literature."[18] Though Shi Yu believes in the Lu Xun–esque value of saving people through literature instead of medicine,[19] she still uses her medical background quite directly in her writing. In her 2004 novel *Niuyue Qingren* (紐約情人, *New York Lover*), Shi Yu says in the afterword, "Because I was a doctor, every person and detail I write in this story is familiar."[20] Some of her other representative works include novels *Daofeng xia de Mangdian* (刀鋒下的盲點, *Blind Spot under the Blade*, 2006) and *Xiacheng jizhenshi* (下城急診室, *Inside the City Emergency Room*, 2011), many of which draw on her experience in the hospital.[21] After Shi Yu left the medical field, she became active in the Sinophone literary scene and took on some leadership roles. She serves as the head and the editor-in-chief of the *Wenxin* (文心, *Literary Mind*) literary circle and was invited to serve as the dean of Beijing Writers' College. She is a columnist for *Qiao bao* (僑報, *The China Press*), *Ming bao* (明報, *Ming Newspaper*), and *Xingdao ribao* (星島日報, *Sing Tao Daily*).

Similarly, Chen Qian's career did not begin in literature. She grew up in Nanning, China, and came to the United States in 1989 to study electrical engineering and is now a senior engineer. She has worked in the Silicon Valley chip design industry and continues to live in northern California.[22] At the same time, she loves writing and is one of the pioneers of Chinese network writers,[23] which I will discuss in depth in this book's coda. Chen Qian has become popular on a North American well-known cultural website called Guofeng (國風, National Styles) with her *haishang xin'qing* (海上心情, mood of the sea) column. Her novels include *Ai zai wu'ai de guigu* (愛在無愛的硅谷, *Love in Loveless Silicon Valley*, 2002),[24] *Fushui* (覆水, *Gone as Falling Water*, 2004), *Wang duan nan fei yan* (望斷南飛雁, *Listen to the Caged Bird Sing*, 2010), and *Wuqiong jing* (無窮鏡, *Infinity Mirror*, 2016), some of which have won many awards.[25] Despite the fact that neither Shi Yu nor Chen Qian come from a literary background, they were able to work their way to becoming professional writers. In other words, writing is a luxury for them as part of their cosmopolitan lifestyle—a lifestyle that in turn also becomes an inspiration and background for their works.

Comparatively, the third author in this study, Rong Rong, has more training in literary writing. She graduated with a major in journalism and worked as a journalist and editor in Shanghai. She came to the United States in 1987 and is currently the editor in chief of the U.S. publication *Qing Zhou Publisher*. Her first work, *Zao'an, Yexiong Xiansheng* (早安, 野熊先生, *Morning, Mr. Wild Bear*, 1997), is included in the *Chinese Overseas Students Series*. It describes a romantic story of biracial newlyweds as they camp in a deep valley. Rong Rong then spent almost two years writing a novella called *Yuan xing* (遠行, *Journey*, 1999), centering on a couple who experienced the Cultural Revolution but still love each other from across the ocean; however, tragedy befalls them when they try to start a new life. In 2002 Rong Rong published *Su Su de Meiguo lian'qing* (素素的美國戀情, *Su Su's American Romance*). Many of her works focus on "emotion" or "sentimentality,"[26] especially *Notes of a Couple* (*Fuqi biji*, 夫妻筆記, 2005).

It might not be a coincidence that these three writers came to the States in 1989 around when the Tiananmen incident took place.[27] The demonstrations leading up to this incident mark a period when young people were growing dissatisfied with the ruling Communist regime and desired to pursue a more open and democratic living condition that they had been accustomed to growing up with in the advent of the Cultural Revolution, along with the awakening of personal advancement and individual pursuits. The early reform era in the late 1970s to 1980s implemented a series of reforms that were intended to drive Chinese economy away from Mao's central planning and high socialism. Despite being uncertain about the correct way of achieving that goal, people used art and literature to liberate themselves from the Mao regime and also to reinscribe subjectivity. These writers, who came of age during the early reform era in the late 1970s and embraced the opening-up policy, sought subjectivity and individualism through their migration, as well as their literary works that focus on the personal over the collective, and the romantic over the patriotic. Their focus on popular (and commercialized) romance does have its detractors in the academy, as the scholar Zhang Zhen criticizes their work as "unreflective self-absorption."[28] Yet the way they chart an individual's sense of home around relationships makes the maps they draw no less interesting in their more personal and affectionate orientation.

To understand how these Sinophone writers' works present touristic maps, it is important to review Chinese readers' reception of the three female writers' "nostalgia" and fantasy. And among Sinophone literary readers inside and outside China, these writers emphasize their connection to their roots in China,[29] making it easier for Chinese readers to relate to; yet the exciting, exotic, and seemingly realistic America they present raises Chinese readers' curiosity. Having experienced the two cultures, these Sinophone writers in the United States can serve as tour guides leading Chinese around American tourist sites, telling the Chinese audience about the interesting historical and cultural sites of various places, and narrating engaging immigrant stories to which a Chinese audience can relate or stories that could surprise the audience in various ways. In studying the Chinese readers' reception of their stories, I look at two specific readerships in China: literary scholars and popular readers. I found that most of these reviews do not judge the literary merits or quality of writing in the novels but rather focus on how the novels present the romance stories in an American setting.

Shi Yu's *New York Lover*, even though it is widely available for purchase on all the Chinese websites, does not have many comments on popular websites like Douban (豆瓣). However, it has received a decent rank overall, with 15.4 percent of readers ranking it five stars, 38.5 percent ranking it four stars, and 46.2 percent ranking it three stars, out of a total of thirteen people. Literary scholars in China praise it for its realistic and detailed portrayal of America, as well as how the novel paints the picture of a beautiful New York and an engaging portrait of the emergency room. For instance, Yanyan Wang argues that the novels of Shi Yu present a three-dimensional, detailed picture of American culture, further elaborating in three points that Shi's novels cover details of American history, literature, music, and art, giving readers an in-depth introduction to the history and culture of America; the legal and medical system from multiple perspectives; and different ethnicities within the States.[30] Another scholar, Han-ping Chen, sets Shi Yu apart from previous Sinophone writers who focus on scar literature, the Sino–U.S. cultural conflicts, or nostalgia, arguing that her writings, even though touching on cultural conflicts and rootlessness of the Chinese diaspora, focus on the mainstream society of America in the areas of culture, medicine, and news.[31] These comments, on the one hand, show Chinese readers' curiosity for the West; on the other hand, they show an interest in a West introduced by a nonwhite, non-American Other, someone just like them yet not exactly like them. Shi Yu, who has been a doctor for over a decade in the United States, describes in her work a story of an Asian woman who is both a heroine for many patients and a victim in relationships and immigration. Many new emigrants from China who aim to pursue an advanced degree in the United States and stay there to work can relate to this protagonist.

Chen Qian appears to have the most significant audience in China among the three authors. She has won multiple literary prizes in mainland China.[32] Many of her novels are collected and reviewed on Douban in China—her most popular novel, *Wang duan nan fei yan*, has been reviewed by over one hundred people, and her second most popular novel, *Teleisha de liumangfan*, has been reviewed by almost fifty, making them among the most-reviewed works of contemporary Sinophone literature in the United States. Among the public reviews, some comment that her literary quality is average, yet some like the simplicity of her language. Most reviews focus on the romance in her novels and express their own opinion on the independence of women. Only one criticizes them for their "rigid portrayal of America." However, the majority of reviewers seem to pay attention to the more general themes regarding relationships and gender roles. Chinese literary scholars on Chen Qian's works are much more diverse in their critiques. Xu Xiaoya, in comparing Chen Qian's novels with early overseas Chinese student literature, such as *Youjian zonglü, youjian zonglü* (又見棕櫚, 又見棕櫚, *Again the Palm Trees*, 1967), argues that new immigrant works like Chen Qian's are no longer concerned with the topics of diaspora and rootlessness, but center more on general themes like values and global perspectives.[33] Some others share similar interests with the common readers, and have turned the focus to studying women's pursuits in her works.[34] Yet some read her *Wang duan nan fei yan* from a diasporic perspective, discussing the conflicts between nostalgia and the American dream in the protagonist's search for self and personal fulfillment.[35] Even though several discussions of her works focus on gender perspectives, the characters' American experiences indeed separate her works from other Chinese stories that share similar theme. Therefore, the space of America adds a layer of excitement and exoticism to the protagonist's story that Chinese women's stories in China would not have.

The other writer examined in this chapter, Rong Rong, is comparatively less read and discussed among the Chinese public, as there is very little mention on Chinese reading websites, perhaps due to the explicit sexual depictions in her novels. The cover of her novel *Fuqi biji* (夫妻筆記) seems to use sex and love as the selling point, and includes the statement "Rong Rong is the first in the North American Sinophone literary scene to use sex and love as a trope to pry open the in-depth 'transplantation of life.'"[36] Numerous reviews of Rong Rong and her books are found on websites and blogs frequented by Chinese Americans. She is active in the literary scene in North America and has been instrumental in coediting some collections, including one of the most comprehensive collections of new immigrants' short stories, as well as the scholarly criticisms of those works, *Yidai feihong* (一代飛鴻, *A Generation of Flying Swans*, 2008). Currently, she is working on a collection of stories from Sinophone writers about the pandemic. The very few websites that introduce Rong Rong to the Chinese audience in China promote her work *Kaizhe fangche zou Beimei* (開著房車走北美, *Touring North America in an RV*, 2011), which won the popularity prize among the top one hundred books for tourists. An article in a magazine called *Chuguo* (出國, *Going Abroad*), written by a Chinese journalist in America, introduces the American experience that Rong Rong tries to capture in her travelogue. At times, it is unexpected, like, "After her marriage, Rong Rong who is used to busy Shanghai metropolitan life moved to the forest, having trees, flowers, fruits, hares and deer as companions . . . is this America? Why is it so rural?" At times, it can be shocking, such as when she hears her American husband say "good morning" to Mr. Bear; she cannot imagine befriending wild animals after experiencing "class struggles" during the Cultural Revolution in China.[37] All these are interesting and exotic experiences to Chinese readers who have not been to the United States. The fact that readers in China are particularly fascinated with Rong Rong's works on her realistic tourist experience and her unexpected family life in America is telling of the touristic, exotic experiences found in her works.

To explore the affective maps these writers draw, the following section will discuss three novels that focus on the themes of romance, family, and love.[38] They are all romantic love stories that present complicated relationships immigrant characters have with their lovers and their projection onto their diasporic journeys. Written from the perspective of Chinese immigrants who have lived in China before encountering unexpected American experiences, these novels have more familiarity and resonance for Sinophone audiences than perhaps an American writing about America would. Therefore, their selling point is to lead Sinophone readers in China and abroad around America through tourist sites, nature, food, and culture, presenting exotic, interesting, unexpected American experiences in a way that maps a sense of home that is primarily personal.

The first novel I will discuss is Shi Yu's *New York Lover* (2000). This novel narrates the romances of a beautiful female doctor, He Xiaohan. The book opens with great promises, beautiful scenes of New York City, and passionate romance. The introduction shows the paradox of the city; it is filled with opportunities, albeit transient ones. It also introduces the protagonist Xiaohan as a romantic young female doctor who is eager for love. In China, she had a serious relationship with an intelligent and dexterous surgeon, Dr. Gao, which is revealed in flashbacks. Yet her insecurity with him and his previous marriage dooms their relationship. Escaping the disappointment of her relationship in China and the hope for finding romantic partners in the United States, Xiaohan pursues a doctoral degree in medicine. She hopes to start a new life in New York, but her first attempt at a relationship fails when a man she begins to love turns out to be gay. She eventually develops a romantic relationship with Dr. Shi, who resembles Dr. Gao in both his personality and skills. However, not long after the romance begins, she disappears in the tumultuous aftermath of the 9/11 disaster. The ashes and darkness of the novel's end strongly contrast with the beauty of its beginning. In the concluding scene her gay friend Kevin plays Kenny G's "Returning Home" beside Xiaohan's graduation photo. In this novel, He Xiaohan serves as a tour guide, leading the readers through tourist sites, as well as her romantic experiences in New York, mapping an affective sense of home projected in the city and her lovers.

The second novel is Chen Qian's *Listen to the Caged Bird Sing* (2010). It narrates a story of a couple's diasporic experience in the United States. The story starts with the protagonist Peining's flashback to when he spends a winter night by himself thinking of his wife, Nanyan. Peining is a biologist who has pursued a life in academia. When he gets an admission letter from Columbia University, he also meets Nanyan, who immediately fills the emptiness that his previous girlfriend, Lei Wang, left in him. Lei Wang is an ambitious scientist herself and is driven to achieve great success in her career. She breaks up with Peining when he refuses to follow her to a prestigious university to further advance her studies. Meanwhile, Nanyan gladly agrees to go to the United States with Peining, although Peining assumes she would be happy to take on a housewife role. However, years of her housewife life dissatisfy her, and she finally decides to venture into her American dream in San Francisco—to go to art school. Through depicting Nanyan's emotional changes that take place in her American household, the novel maps the journey of a Chinese woman from the role of a traditional household woman to one who actively pursues her own dreams beyond household.

The third novel to be discussed is Rong Rong's *Notes of a Couple* (2005). This novel describes a Chinese couple's struggles and conflicts before applying for green cards in the United States. The husband, Renping, comes to the United States for his studies, and his wife, Peifen, works to support the family. The Chinese couple's American life is at first disappointing, draining, and dull. They are students and are financially strained, stressed, and unable to get a green card.[39] One day, however, Peifen gets an opportunity to become a nanny, which would allow her to apply for a green card. She takes the job and moves into the household of her American employer. After that, she becomes a model, which pushes her to realize and pursue her own desires. In the American household, Peifen develops a strong sexual desire for the employer Gracia's ex-husband, Bailey; at the same time, Renping cannot resist his beautiful American colleague Nicole. The couple's encounter with Americans unveils their sexual desires and finally leads to their separation. This novel charts a map of both protagonists' romantic, exotic encounters in the American household.

Displacement as Self-Invented Nostalgic Love: *New York Lover*

For our first example of touristic, affective mapping, we turn to Shi Yu's *New York Lover*. This novel challenges the notion of home by turning Shi Yu's own diasporic experience into a touristic experience and voluntary movement away from the "pressure of an alien reality,"[40] which comes packaged with promises of an exciting, affective experience. Shi Yu's experience—her entangling romantic relationships with the Chinese men in her homeland and abroad—is appealing. Her immigrant experience is less about the discrimination, suffering, and identity problems of the sort that earlier immigrant novels focused on, but is more like a tourist experience for readers to consume, being more individual-based and defined by social fabrics surrounding them.[41]

This novel adopts the third-person point of view, asking readers to trace the main character He Xiaohan's trajectory as her inner thoughts, desires, and fears are revealed to us. The other characters, though described by the third-person narrator, are observed from Xiaohan's viewpoint. This allows Xiaohan to be a tour guide, showing the readers around the American geographical and cultural landscapes. Her personal experience shows another layer of the Chinese immigrant story with which readers could empathize.

Readers follow the map to trace Xiaohan's touristic experience in the United States through the places she has been and people she comes across. The introduction opens with vivid portrayals of the West Village in New York City, so vivid and detailed that it is as if readers were watching a movie following the camera. "West Village stretches from the Prince Street to the South and Fourteenth Street to the North.... The architecture, community and cultural atmosphere of this area displays postmodern flavor and vitality.... There are prime areas close to NYU and Washington Square on Main Street, filled with educators and professionals; there are lower class men who are alcoholic or drug addicts in the poor alleys on the West side, struggling to live; there are continuous flows of common people on the Sixth Avenue."[42] After one and a half pages of detailed descriptions of the streets, architecture, and people, the novel zooms into a scene in a classroom in New York University, where a pharmacology professor is giving a lecture to medical students. But only briefly, as the narrative quickly zooms back out to the campus of NYU. In introducing Washington Square, it quotes Henry James's novel *Washington Square* (1980). The focus zooms in on the protagonist He Xiaohan, who meets an American, Jack, in the park. Their encounter there reminds Xiaohan of French American novelist Raymond Federman's novel *Smiles on Washington Square* (1985). The reference to these American literary works shows Shi Yu's familiarity with American culture and literature. Like these American works, this novel could also serve as a new narrative that interprets the American places from a new Chinese immigrant's perspective.

Yet, rather than provide an alternative narrative to interpret American places, Shi Yu's depiction of New York City gives readers a vivid picture of the tourist sites. At times, the novel even namedrops the famous tourist attractions, including the Statue of Liberty, the headquarters of the United Nations, Times Square, the Metropolitan Museum of Art, Central Park, Fifth Avenue, the Rockefeller Center, Broadway, and Chinatown.[43] All these famous tourist sites would attract readers to follow along, as if they are led around the city without having to leave their home. Particularly, the novel provides an elaborate description of the West Village, explaining that it "used to be a British territory.... The Federal-style townhouses and roads filled with big trees render a rare flavor of a little town in the middle of a metropolis."[44] Such details teach the readers the history of the places, just like what tourist guides do when they are talking about various sites. To make the trip more interesting, the novel continues to bring in literary references, such as when Kevin takes Xiaohan to a building built in the eighteenth century; he says, "This is the house that O. Henry writes about in *The Last Leaf* (1907)."[45] Such a reference brings in familiar American literature that tourists or readers may have heard of. However, for those who have not heard of these Western classics, they get a nice introduction to Western landscapes and culture.

Xiaohan is fascinated with Western art and cultures. Through her, then, readers get to tour around famous tourist sites and are introduced to some famous Western literature, paintings, and songs, including Vladimir Vasilyev's paintings, ballets like *Swan Lake* and *Sleeping Beauty*,[46] Kenny G's song "Going Home,"[47] and Bob Dylan.[48] With her, we the readers visit the Cultural Center,[49] World Trade Center,[50] Brooklyn Bridge,[51] and many other sites. Xiaohan's love for Western art is such that her admiration for her first love is partially due to it. When she works on her first surgery with Dr. Gao in China, she is reminded of a Western painting called *The Surgeon*. The narrator then goes into a brief description of the surgeon in the painting, comparing his "beautiful and lean fingers of the surgeon [that] have surprising charm" to "Dr. Gao's hands[, which] are no worse than the oil painting's, giving people endless imagination."[52] Later in the book, the narrator mentions Gao's charming fingers multiple times. Xiaohan's obsession with him stems from the reminder of the painting she likes, as if he were a form of ideal beauty that resembles the Greek statues. Even when Xiaohan is in the United States, she often thinks of Gao. By drawing such a comparison between Gao and Western art, Xiaohan shows how she has broken down the national boundaries in her love, blending her fantasy of the West and nostalgia for her homeland so that they become one and the same.

Xiaohan's relationship with Dr. Gao is thus an analogy of how she has turned her relationship with America and China into a personal, affective one. While Xiaohan clearly has a fantasy of the West, she also displays nostalgia for her homeland. "Xiaohan has a special affiliation with Chinatown, all the Chinese shop and road signs, Chinese dialects, Chinese groceries . . . walking in the narrow old alleys, as if one could travel through space and time, dishes from the wok emits a special Eastern flavor, and it feels especially cozy and familiar to Chinese who live abroad."[53] Xiaohan's paradox—fascination with the West and nostalgia for China—comes to resemble what the Chinese readers themselves feel. While the tourist sites and landscapes provide readers with a tourist map that allows them to walk with the protagonist Xiaohan, we are also led into an affective map that tours into Xiaohan's emotions and feelings because of the third-person point of view.

Xiaohan's longing for her homeland while she is in the United States is thus transformed into her longing for love in the story. One can draw a parallel between homesickness and lovesickness in this story.[54] She feels lonely in New York: "America, particularly New York, is still peoples' country and city, they are distant, not home, and not as close as hometown. Coming far away from a foreign land, what pains us is homesickness and loneliness. Homesickness comes anytime and loneliness always follows."[55] Rather than seeing America as an immigrant's paradise, as she might have imagined, she finds herself "cast away" from the surrounding cultural environment and becomes a truly isolated individual, desperate for love. The narrator comments, "After all she needs love and care, she needs to feel the meaningfulness of life."[56] Lovesickness and loneliness are the vectors through which she communicates her feeling of diasporic displacement. Indeed, what stands at the core of Xiaohan's longing is the loss of her emotional home—the man she left behind in China, Dr. Gao.

The narrative alternates between Xiaohan's past and present, with one chapter describing her present life in the United States and the next one focusing on her past in China. Xiaohan's past romance with Dr. Gao is put side by side with her memories of him in the present. Her past and present experiences, and mapping across time and space, are a "double exposure" in Boym's term, "of home and abroad, of past and present, of dream and everyday life."[57] Her emotional attachment to and vivid memories of Dr. Gao are shown in her experience in the United States, where Xiaohan constantly thinks about him: "Gao Fanwei, this name that sounds familiar but strange, a shadow that is both distanced and close, comes up in Xiaohan's heart all the time. How is he doing now? Suddenly, an irresistible reverie arises; Xiaohan wants to cry."[58] Xiaohan's emotions are mixed with yearning and loss, desire and fear. Her nostalgia for him, in Boym's words, is a "romance with (her) own fantasy."[59]

Her complicated experience with Dr. Gao sets her on the route of a diasporic journey. His ability to save her and his patients gives Xiaohan a sense of security; however, the doctor's privileged background and his previous marriage make her insecure as a lover. Her dissatisfaction grows when his ex-wife comes back into his life after her new husband passes away. "Tell me the truth, are you already attached to her?"[60] Xiaohan asks, displaying jealousy and insecurity. Eventually, Xiaohan leaves China for the United States on an impulse to avoid this awkward situation, without notifying Dr. Gao. "Xiaohan gets on the plane flying to JFK Airport. . . . Just like that, she uproots herself and goes to a foreign land solitarily."[61] She chooses a path typical of diasporic subjects; by running away from insecurity, she attempts to regain control in her relationships and her life by traveling to the United States, looking for a new home where she can find love.

Rather than just a physical movement, diaspora examined in this novel is an emotional and existential state. It is nothing less than a survival tactic for Xiaohan, one that allows her to cope with her insecurities in her relationships by leaving her homeland in search of one where she can find love gain, even if it is, somewhat paradoxically, the love for Dr. Gao. Partly because she feels abandoned by Gao, she abandons China altogether. Only through distance can she restore a balance in her relationship with him. She hopes, by walking away, to prove that he needs her as much as she needs him. He looks for her after she leaves, and would have married her if she had not left. Indeed, it is as Boym says: "Nostalgic love can only survive in a long-distance relationship."[62] Xiaohan's way of retaining their love is to transform the present into the past through physical distance, to give up the potential future to the nostalgic past, thereby retaining the longing in both her and Dr. Gao's minds.

Their separation becomes a driving force for Xiaohan to look for her emotional home in her foreign experience. Yet, what essentially constitutes her diasporic identity is the escape and distance she creates herself. Like the diasporic identity that Marianne David and Javier Muñoz-Basols describe: "of the homeless self in search of both a home and a land, a *home-land*,"[63] Xiaohan clings to Gao's memory as a defense against the "pressure of an alien reality" in New York.[64] Gradually, Xiaohan finds her new home in a new love—Dr. Shi Jie, who resembles Dr. Gao in many ways, as they both have the same professional and romantic circumstances. They even both hesitate to approach Xiaohan because they are both afraid that their previous marriages would affect her. Perhaps these resemblances draw Xiaohan close to Dr. Shi Jie. Yet the sweet moment of their relationship—as it becomes sexual and intimate—soon becomes a vain hope and a desperate waiting. "Not long after, misfortune falls upon them and Shi Jie feels desperately painful."[65] The day after 9/11, Shi Jie begins to feel anxious when Xiaohan disappears. Like with Dr. Gao, Xiaohan vanishes from Dr. Shi Jie's life shortly after they become intimate.

The disaster takes her and the world by surprise, robbing her of any free choice. By the end of the novel, we are not given a clear explanation of her disappearance. She may have died in the disaster, like the news that Shi Jie watches indicates: "From the lens, we can see a wounded Asian-looking woman lying on the floor, with blood on her face; lying beside her are bricks that fell down from the building and wreckage from the planes."[66] Judging from Shi Jie's reaction to the news, it may be her, as he "stares at the TV screen for a long time, until his eyes feels stabbing pain and filled with tears."[67] If she died with the other victims on 9/11, her death would reaffirm the fragility of life she observed in the hospital. Yet with little evidence we the readers are still not given a clear hint that she dies or not. Regardless, one thing is clear: Shi Jie suffers from losing her: "He habitually glances at the direction of the Twin Towers, and cannot see that pair of beautiful shadows he used to see, in between the buildings in the dark; that absence and emptiness makes him particularly anxious, heartache and heartbroken."[68] Her disappearance causes serious heartbreak to her lover and evokes his nostalgia for their time together.

Xiaohan may alternatively have run away from the chaos, mirroring her initial flight from Gao. If we follow this interpretation, by leaving her lovers Xiaohan would be turning herself from someone waiting and searching for love into someone who others wait for and search for. This inversion shifts the role of diaspora—both in the sense of her move to the United States and her flight from Dr. Shi Jie after 9/11—to a strategic decision. Her voluntary diaspora is a means of retaining the lovers' longing and nostalgia by strengthening their feelings. While away from Dr. Gao, Xiaohan thinks of him often: "Gao Fanwei, this familiar yet unfamiliar name, this far and close shadow, jumps ups and downs in Xiaohan's heart, how is he now?"[69] Xiaohan indulges in this nostalgia, as it gives her a sense of control and excitement. Therefore, she constantly runs away because of her fear of love and the loss of control of her life. She creates a home for herself that is not dependent on others, individual or collective, where nostalgia can bring her happiness at a safe distance. She becomes a tourist of both her past and present, never attaching herself too closely for fear of abandonment.

Xiaohan exists in a gray area between what Boym terms restorative and reflective nostalgia. Because our broader focus in this chapter links the complex experience of nostalgia to diasporic subjects' larger sense of self, Boym's nuanced understanding of nostalgia will help us grasp how Xiaohan wrestles with her mental image of Dr. Gao, and, by extension, China. Boym defines nostalgia both as "a sentiment of loss and displacement" and "a romance with one's own fantasy."[70] She distinguishes two types of nostalgia: restorative, which "stresses *nóstos* (home) and attempts a transhistorical reconstruction of the lost home"[71]; and "reflective," which "thrives in *álgos*, the longing itself, and delays the homecoming—wistfully, ironically, desperately."[72] The former highlights the past, the origin, the truth, and the homeland, whereas the latter "dwells on the ambivalences of human longing and belonging."[73] Restorative nostalgia drives her to reconstruct the image of home—in this case, her lover in China, Dr. Gao. The "reflective nostalgia" stays in Xiaohan's sense longing and belonging and delays her homecoming. Kevin plays the song "Returning Home" at the end of the story, seemingly wishing her to return home after her disappearance, hoping her isolation from society would help her find a sense of belonging. Yet coming with the end of her diasporic journey is the impossibility of homecoming. While she replaces one diasporic journey with another, Xiaohan is further and further away from her homeland.

Xiaohan's story exemplifies Boym's conception of nostalgia, seeing it as "a strategy for survival, a way of making sense of the impossibility of homecoming."[74] Xiaohan's self-invented distance from her lovers and homeland creates a nostalgic love that is based on both memories of the past and fantasy of the future. The backward- and forward-looking aspect of nostalgic love plays an essential role in diasporic identities. The contradiction of the restorative and reflective nostalgias exemplifies an existential angst within herself. Diasporic nostalgia becomes a survival tactic for Xiaohan to deal with her pain. In this novel, Boym's argument that "the imperative of a contemporary nostalgic: to be homesick and to be sick of being at home—occasionally at the same time"[75] is translated into "to be lovesick and to be sick of being in love." Love becomes the axis around which Xiaohan finds her sense of home along her journey, whether through nostalgic love (Dr. Gao) or a new love (Dr. Shi).

Besides the affects of homesickness and lovesickness, another theme that Sinophone writers portray in their writings is the dichotomous relationship between security/home and adventure/diaspora. *New York Lover* shows that

Xiaohan has a paradoxical desire for security/home and adventure/diaspora, constructing a paradox. It is the reconciliation of this paradox that sustains the desire to be always in love. In the following section, I will elaborate on this dialectic through Chen Qian's *Listen to the Caged Bird Sing*.

Security/Adventure versus Home/Diaspora: *Listen to the Caged Bird Sing*

Like Xiaohan in Shi Yu's novel, the protagonist Nanyan in Chen Qian's novella *Listen to the Caged Bird Sing* is constantly leaving people behind. She leaves her family in China to follow her artistic interests. She hopes to find life in the United States to be adventurous and exciting. Yet once she arrives, she ends up being a housewife to her husband, Peining. He makes it clear that in his opinion, her hopes and dreams are secondary to his. As Xiaohan disappears after some time in the States, so too does Nanyan partake in a second diaspora. She leaves her husband and kids behind to pursue artistic endeavors. However, neither situation is a forced diaspora or exile. Instead, Nanyan twice makes the voluntary act of seeking some exciting adventure—moving to the United States or embarking on her artistic journey, rending her experience a touristic one. It is through these diasporic experiences that Nanyan generates a sense of belonging. Home in the traditional sense generates no sense of belonging for her; in fact, it is precisely the traditional notion of home her husband values that makes her feel so uneasy. Paradoxically, it is physical detachment—leaving home— that creates a home for Nanyan.[76] Diaspora becomes a prerequisite for her to establish a sense of belonging.

This novel fits a general pattern among such works that suggests different motivations for and attitudes toward migration that split along gendered lines. The men in these novels come to the United States for professional reasons, while the women come for more personal ones. Or, at least, this is purported to be the case. As Nanyan reveals to Peining many years after their marriage, "The most important reason she married him is that Peining represents a very attractive possibility in her future—America."[77] For Nanyan, the opportunity to pursue art in America far exceeds the value of settling down and having a family once they get to America. Simultaneously, although Peining assures himself that his professional work will guarantee a happy and secure family, he ignores his wife's frustration, and in the end his family breaks apart. Through portraying the tension between security and adventure within the household, the story challenges the idealistic notion of a stable home as a nuclear family living under one roof. Instead, the novel emphasizes the divide between the home and the pursuit of one's dream, more specifically, the pursuit of a woman's dream. Nanyan's home cannot be the one that Peining imagines; she finds it instead in pursuing her own personal ambitions.

Just like Peining, who comes to the United States to pursue his degrees and establish a career, Nanyan is as eager to pursue her own dream. From early on, Nanyan demonstrates a strong desire to make sure that she is properly prepared to live in the United States. She works hard to improve her English and takes the initiative to correspond with Peining in English. In Guangzhou, she tells Peining, "I really envy those girls who pursue studies in the United States!"[78] She wishes she could be someone who can achieve their dreams in a foreign land: "Hidden in Nanyan's heart there is a seed, which would crazily grow once it encounters suitable soil."[79] When the reality of her American life goes against her expectations, and her American dream is taken away by her housewife chores, she says to her husband in English, "Too bad, that is not my American dream."[80]

Eventually, however, Nanyan leaves her family for San Francisco to pursue her dream of learning art and design. Just like the English title *Listen to the Caged Bird Sing* suggests,[81] Nanyan chooses to step outside of the socially restrictive boundaries and listen to her own heart. She decides to find her own value not in the family and traditional ideals, but in her own dream. Near the end of the novel, Peining is told that Nanyan is going to the Art Center College of Design, one of the best design schools in the United States. Unlike Lu Xun in his influential story "What Happens after Nora Leaves Home" (1923), which shows a pessimistic view of Nora leaving her home, predicting that she would either be a prostitute or return with humiliation, Chen Qian's Nanyan is able to pursue her own dream and freedom. In some ways, the novella sells the typical American dream in which an immigrant can achieve their independence and dream, but in particular, it is a story of a new female immigrant, who straddles an identity between her housewife role and her artist's dream, her home(land) and diaspora.

Meanwhile, the Chinese title makes no reference to a "caged bird," instead quoting a line from a poem written by Chairman Mao: "Tian gao yun dan, wang duan nan fei yan" 天高雲淡, 望斷南飛雁 (Sky is high and clouds are light, looking at swans flying to the south).[82] Written in 1957, Mao's propagandist poem was created in memory of his Long March success in 1935, dedicated to the army and showing ambition for capturing the Kuomintang. Such a direct citation of Mao's poetic line as her book's title can be interpreted as Chen Qian herself being unconsciously caged by the Maoist language and metaphors. And more so, she may try to show that in order to get out of the "cage" of the Maoist regime, women like herself and Nanyan have to flee to the United States. With this title, the book shows the paradox of loving her motherland in her memory, which in Nanyan's case is the home she shares with Peining in America, and anxiously trying to escape the cage forged by Chinese tradition and her marriage.

While embracing physical detachment, the novella shows Nanyan's effort to connect to homeland and her family. Nanyan moves to San Francisco, where the large Cantonese community and proximity to the Pacific resonates with her hometown in China. From the Pacific Ocean, Nanyan "can see Beihai's Silver Beach under the shiny starts over the South China Sea,"[83] suggesting her nostalgia for her hometown.[84] Meanwhile, she maintains her ties with her kids. When she leaves, her husband takes a picture of her and her two kids on the beach, a happy moment indeed. Nanyan's departure, which Peining rejects, calling it "abandonment,"[85] brings memories of her back to Peining. Not until she is gone does he cherish what makes him feel comfortable at home: "the open pencil box, cards, books, Barbie dolls . . ."[86]

Therefore, it is not *just* physical detachment that generates Nanyang's sense of home. Emotional detachment is a key element, as well. Interestingly, it is precisely this tension of physical detachment and emotional detachment that defines diaspora. As William Safran writes, diasporic subjects are those who "have been dispersed from a specific original 'center' to two or more 'peripheral,' or foreign, regions," who, nevertheless, "continue to relate, personally or vicariously, to that homeland in one way or another."[87] In this story, drawn by the tension between traditional and liberal ideology, home and diaspora become part and parcel of each other: diaspora becomes a prerequisite for establishing "home" (i.e., a sense of belonging). Nanyang is leaving her home (and homeland) to find it on a personal level through her ambition to be an artist. She models for readers a diasporic experience that is more of an exotic, exciting adventure than a forced exile—a touristic trip rather than exodus.

In sum, this novella focuses on Nanyan's negotiation of her role as a domestic housewife and her artistic dream. While being a virtuous woman, wife, and mother, Nanyan has buried her ambitions in her mind, but she eventually decides to pursue it. The novella presents these relationships as not static but dynamic; just like the black-and-white symbol of yin–yang, they are fluid and mutable. The writer is charting a map to show how Chinese diasporic subjects find security in adventure and home in diaspora, a home not limited by the boundaries set up by societal ideals.

The next novel that I will discuss in this chapter expands on this discussion of yin–yang into the geospatial sphere and asks how the dynamic of *nei–wai* reflects or challenges it. In *Listen to the Caged Bird Sing*, love becomes a site through which diasporic subjects negotiate personal desires and cultural expectations, social, gender role constraints. The next novel, Rong Rong's *Notes of a Couple*, reiterates these conflicts more explicitly in love and sex.

Self-Discovery and Sexual Awakening: Transformation in an American Household in *Notes of a Couple*

The space of the American residence in *Notes of a Couple* is the main arena for conflicts that play out between personal desires and traditional ideals—conflicts that we have seen dramatized in the previously discussed works in this chapter. In this novel, the American residence is advertised as a transformative space for the protagonist Peifen, who had little knowledge of her own value: "In [my husband's] mind, I am the rubbish he picked up, he let me eat swan meat."[88] Emphasizing Peifen as trash reduces her to something other people throw away, not only in her husband's mind but in her own. This is clear from how she has changed the Chinese phrase "toad eating swan meat," which usually implies an ugly man desiring a beautiful woman, instead of the other way around. In reversing the common logic of the Chinese phrases, it reflects just how much her husband's depreciation of her value has filtered into her self-depreciation—that is, at least before they move into the American household where she works. In a new environment, Peifen eventually turns into a confident person who feels "[she] can do whatever others can."[89]

By portraying the American home this way, the author presents a deliberately voyeuristic image of the American home to her Chinese readers. Rong Rong's American household setting is primarily a form of cartographic tourism, one that sells the transformational powers of the American ideal to its Chinese audience, one that shows that what one calls home does not need the boundaries placed upon it by society, particularly traditional Chinese society. As the events of the novel unfold, the residence of Gracia and her ex-husband, Bailey—where Peifen works as a nanny for the family—serves as a space for liberation and expression of Peifen's own personal and sexual desires outside of her limiting role in her own household as a married woman supporting her family.

The American home acts as a liberatory space outside her own home, which is comparatively restrictive, and complicates the relationship between *nei* (interior space) and *wai* (exterior space). This novel posits that *nei* and *wai* are not opposing, but can become fluid and even interchangeable.[90] Unlike Nanyan or Xiaohan, who abandon the domestic space entirely by the end of their stories, for Peifen, it is not the "outside world" but the domestic realm of another culture and another land wherein she may step beyond her role as daughter, wife, and mother and instead become an independent, self-sustaining woman slowly discovering her own worth.[91] Her transformation challenges the meaning and boundaries of *nei*. In America, the familial realm of the home does not define "proper women" but instead is the place where Peifen transforms from a traditional Chinese wife to a liberal, self-sufficient woman under the influence of a Western man and his love.

It is not just the physical home, however, that becomes a transformative space for Peifen. The novel also plays with the symbolic ideals and spheres Eastern and Western men embody. The husband represents a restrictive sphere where her personal desires have been suppressed. Fearing her husband's rejection and intolerance, she hides from him the fact that she has taken on a modeling profession and her affair with Bailey. By the end of the novel, when she goes to a dance party with her husband, her husband finds her like an evil spirit filled with desire and passion. For Renping, Peifen taking on a modeling profession is like "a devil escaping from a bottle; a devil that once come out can no longer be put back."[92] Her confident, courageous, and eager self takes over in the end and enables her to get out of the restrictive sphere her husband embodies.

Comparatively, Bailey, her photographer and Gracia's ex-husband, represents an open space for Peifen to explore her personal and sexual desires—like she describes, "his body is like [her] vast sea, where I am an airship crossing through."[93] Ironically, there is barely any description of Bailey's appearance and character in the novel. It seems that Peifen is less attracted to him as a person and more because of what he represents. Gracia and Bailey's openly sexual scene exposes Peifen to a new way of love—passionate and revealing, different from the conservative, traditional love she is used to. With Bailey, she could freely express her desires, and through him, she reinvents herself and gradually realizes her own value.

Part of her transformation comes from her desire to be like the Western woman in the household and her sexual awakening through her voyeurism of the Western couple's sexual intercourse.[94] We as readers could read through Peifen's eyes the shocking, exotic, and erotic adventures this Western household brings her. She becomes a tour guide of a world that is foreign to her Chinese readers, not just geospatially but also sexually. The fantasized Bailey later becomes her sexual partner in reality, and the fantasizing Peifen is reinvented into someone bold and confident, who openly expresses her desire. The novel associates the different experiences with cultures, as if most Americans had sexual intercourse like this. The novel establishes a bifurcated space between Chinese culture and Western culture as symbolizing the traditional, restrictive sphere and liberal, open sphere, respectively.

While Bailey serves as the Western, liberal sphere that rouses in Peifen a wild sort of yearning and a passionate physical desire, Renping has found a similar sort of person at his work—Nicole. Like Bailey to Peifen, Nicole provides Peifen's husband Renping with a sense of security and comfort. "I finally found my home, my graveyard,"[95] he says, indicating where he wishes to return. Yet alongside this image of home, there appears an image of conquest. With Nicole, Renping imagines himself as a bandit in Western movies, with Nicole being his horse and his gun being a sexual organ.[96] The masculinity he gains from his affair with Nicole equips him with confidence and strength to continue his own difficult journey in the West. His admission demonstrates the equation of stereotypical American outlaws with sexual domination, which implies overtaking the stereotypical feminized, weak Asian American male figures.

The novel sets Western bodies as sites where the Chinese protagonists attain their sexual power and discovery. Exaggerating the Chinese–American cultural difference and associating the sexual adventures with the Western bodies would most likely satisfy her Chinese readership. However, it is important to note how the author uses both Bailey's and Nicole's bodies to serve as foreign locales that the Chinese diasporic characters experience as exotic spaces, almost like touristic attractions, leading us to watch how such new experiences can transform the characters' identities. This observation returns us to the theme at the start of this chapter—that these novels are chiefly commercial, touristic endeavors.

Readers follow Peifen and Renping as if they were adventuring into some exotic land where they settled into this American residence. More than the dichotomous relationship between the domestic and foreign, this house projects a complex, intersecting relationship of the two. It serves as a container of complicated affects between the immigrant couple, between the Americans and the Chinese immigrants, between Eastern and Western cultures, and between tradition and liberalism. By going beyond the traditional *nei–wai* dynamics, Rong Rong charts the emotional changes in the Chinese immigrant characters and depicts an adventurous but insecure, exciting but disappointing journey of self-discovery in this American residence and on American soil.

All in all, Peifen and Renping's story challenges and complicates the *nei–wai* boundaries of a traditional Chinese wife–husband relationship. Interestingly, in this novel, Peifen's transformation from a traditional wife figure to an independent woman happens within an American residence—*nei,* in a sense. The symbolic meanings go beyond the physical boundaries the terms *nei* and *wai* carry. *Nei* could also be interpreted as traditional values and Chinese cultures, with *wai* being liberal ideology. Thus, while Peifen transforms from *nei* to *wai*, her husband is torn between the two, still leaning to *nei*. Struggling with the tension between the two, both of them set on a self-liberating journey in different forms: the wife pursues her sexual and personal desires, and the husband ultimately leaves without any woman. The ending seems desolate, yet the couple realizes that their home in the diaspora is a personal one within themselves. Once they leave their homeland, the reconstruction of home is facilitated by them moving further and further away—a voluntary type of diaspora.

Conclusion

The Chinese immigrants' emotional attachments in their relationships indicate the emotional longings for their homeland and new land. In these novels, love, desire, and other emotions depict the tensions between security, traditional ideals, and social constraints on the one hand, and adventure, liberal values, and personal desires on the other. America and American lovers are the vehicles by which Chinese immigrants realize and achieve their personal desires. At times, American lovers represent illusory American dreams to Chinese immigrants, such as Xiaohan's gay friend Kevin, as well as Renping's and Peifen's American lovers. On the contrary, Chinese lovers evoke a nostalgic love for their homeland. In these stories, lovesickness signifies homesickness: In *New York Lover*, Xiaohan leaves her lover Gao in China, yet fantasizes about him all the time in the United States; the husband Peining in *Listen to the Caged Bird Sing* agonizes over his wife's abandonment of the family and draws closer attention to the trivialities of home once she is gone; and the Chinese couple in *Notes of a Couple* frets about each other's changes and loss of their traditional family ideals after moving to America and developing their new identities.

Their navigation of these affects reflects the real-world feelings that many diasporic subjects experience. Upon leaving their homeland, diasporic subjects often feel homesick; at the same time, they feel sick of being at their old home because of their changing perspectives of cultural values. In this conflict between being away from an old home and being at a new home, one straddles security and adventure, social constraints and adventurous desires. The relationship between home and diaspora has changed. Diaspora could be a voluntary act immigrants choose to be physically or emotionally away from their homeland, lover, or family; yet it also becomes a precondition for their new concept of home. In global societies, one can no longer necessarily secure a sense of belonging (home) in a physical space or geographical locale, but must constantly locate and relocate "home" as opposed to homeland. Diaspora becomes a medium to constantly relocate between home/security and journey/adventure.

These works challenge the categories of home and diaspora, transforming the diasporic experience to touristic, exotic adventures. They turn the "pressure of an alien reality" into exciting, romance-filled stories packed with melodramatic notes of romance and nostalgia. Therefore, Boym's idea of "the imperative of a contemporary nostalgic," that is, "to be homesick and to be sick of being at home—occasionally at the same time," may well be used as a slogan to advertise the Occidental experience for Chinese immigrants to readers back in China and among Sinophone communities.

These works paint interesting and provoking touristic, affective maps of diasporic adventures of romance, sex, and love. Their love-seeking journeys symbolize the protagonists' search for their identities and home in the new land. The trope of love represents a complex dynamic axis around which the characters chart their new homes while in diaspora.

These novels appear to chart a map for Sinophone readers to navigate homeland and diaspora. But the dichotomies of tradition versus modernity, East versus West, and home versus diaspora are more staged as an exotic spectacle for Chinese consumption. The dilemma and complexity of the diasporic identities they present in these stories mirror the ambiguity in the identity of their works, asking us to answer interesting questions about whether they belong to Chinese diasporic literature or part of a contemporary Sinophone genre of travel romance. While these questions remain debatable, it is obvious that these Chinese immigrant Sinophone writers are invested in charting a multilayered affective map that portrays the Chinese diaspora's journey of home and identity.

4

The Palimpsestic Map of the American and Chinese Dreams

● ●

Contested Sites in Overseas Chinese Immigrant Stories

> *"If you love him / send him to New York,*
> *'Cause that's where Heaven is.*
> *If you hate him.*
> *Send him to New York,*
> *'Cause that's where Hell is."*
> *—Beijinger in New York*

These lyrics, repeated several times in Cao Guilin's novel *Beijinger in New York* (*Beijingren zai Niuyue* 北京人在紐約, 1991; hereafter *Beijinger*), implicate the city as a space of paradox—a simultaneous juxtaposition between heaven and hell. The protagonist in the novel, Wang Qiming, lives through and demonstrates this paradox. In New York, he turns from a poor, helpless immigrant to a rich, successful businessman. However, he eventually loses all his fortune and his daughter. In his sorrow over his losses, he says, "New York. You're Heaven in Hell, you're also Hell in Heaven. And you might say I'm a little demon who's just about done for."[1] As he squanders his last bit of money at the casino, he realizes that this global city is just like a place where people gamble—a source of excitement, hope, insecurity, and anxiety. Using this metaphor, Cao compares the pursuit of the American Dream to gambling. Both can be addicting, and the belief that you can win increases that addiction. The casino captures what America as a national and public space means to immigrants—it could be colorful and exciting, yet it could be dark underneath. As Lydia Liu claims, the TV serial adaptation of this novel (1994), using the same title, sets up a perfect locale of reconciliation between the desire for American goods and cultural products and anti-American sentiments in contemporary China.[2]

As Liu points out, within less than a year of *Beijinger* airing, it "became a product of post-cold war diasporic Chinese cultures,"[3] spawning a surge of TV serials and films centering on immigrants, diasporas, and foreigners, such as *Chinese in Tokyo* (*Shanghairen zai dongjing* 上海人在東京, 1996), which is often considered as the sister show to *Beijinger*. This genre has won continuous popularity for the past two decades, spawning subsequent film spin-offs in the 2010s, including *Finding Mr. Right* (*Beijing yushang Xiyatu* 北京遇上西雅圖, 2013) and *Book of Love* (or *Finding Mr. Right 2*; Beijing yushang xiyatu bu'er qingshu 北京遇上西雅圖之不二情書, 2016).

In more recent TV shows about overseas Chinese students, however, there is an added element to how people in diaspora map their worlds. In *Gui qu lai* (歸去來, *The Way We Were*, 2018, hereafter *TWWW*), students pursue academic and ideological advancements in the United States, but instead of staying they find their way back to China. *TWWW* compares the national spaces of America and China, or more precisely, the American dream and the new Chinese dream. The show further examines how China as a national space now provides a new goal to those who once embraced and pursued the American dream.

This chapter examines the changes in how Chinese immigrants have begun to map their sense of home during a time of global precarity. By analyzing two TV series produced by Chinese directors in China, *Beijinger* and *TWWW*, we can trace the change in what constitutes the goal for diasporic Chinese—the endpoint of their journeys. The two shows, produced roughly two decades apart, give us a stark contrast of trajectories between the American dream in one and the Chinese dream in the other, particularly the Chinese imagination of these concepts. *Beijinger* presents an intricate transpacific map of the American dream, breaking down the heaven-and-hell dichotomy and presenting a potential third space, or no space, where immigrants can exist; in contrast, *TWWW* suggests a new map for immigrants: the return to a home(land) that now has just as much of an appeal as the one they left it for.

I see these television shows as palimpsestic maps revealing the many layers—good and bad—that make up the original American dream of a home, a family, and financial success. Their new maps show the lived experience of first-generation Chinese immigrants navigating the historical challenges and new struggles embedded in pursuing either the American or Chinese dream. The chapter argues that *Beijinger* reveals the uncertainties of the American dream by uncovering the layers of the map that are hidden, layers created by older immigrants and their experience in the United States. Instead of stripping this palimpsest to chart a space for immigrants, *TWWW* adds a new layer—the map of the Chinese dream and the possibility of returning to China—offering a new endpoint to the diasporic journey: back where it started. This new layer does not erase the ones below, however, especially the layers promoting the individual and the personal. In fact, it is only by navigating the different layers of the palimpsestic map that the characters can chart a new home in their homeland that is more personal than political. In a certain way, then, this final map becomes more literal, showing the way back home, but it also keeps the traces of the journeys we have seen throughout this book of diasporic subjects charting a home that transcends political borders, even if that home happens to be back in their homeland.

Demystifying the American Dream and Replacing It with the Chinese Dream

This chapter joins current scholarly endeavors[4] that move past assessing whether a novel attempts to uphold or debunk the American dream to analyzing new-immigrant discourse attempts to refine it. How is the American dream perceived by Chinese immigrants today? How have immigrant novels responded to the changing American dream? What does America as a national and public space mean to immigrants? Although the chapter cannot possibly answer all these questions, it attempts to explore some of these in the following pages.

The "rags to riches" idea exemplified by the American dream is attractive to many who have migrated to this new land, especially during the mass migration in nineteenth-century America. The American dream is not just about material success, however. As Truslow Adams's book *The Epic of America* (1931) states, it is "not a dream of motor cars and high wages merely, but a dream of social order in which each man and each woman shall be able to attain the fullest stature of which they are innately capable, and be recognized by others for what they are, regardless of the fortuitous circumstances of birth or position."[5] For Adams, writing during the Great Depression, this aspect of the American dream as an aspiration for a better social order perhaps stems from it being a necessary motivation for people in the 1930s. In addition to material and social success, there is a part of the American dream that looks to personal fulfillment and self-actualization. In his book *American Dream: A Short History of an Idea That Shaped a Nation* (2003), Jim Cullen points out that the American dream is not singular, but plural.[6] The core of these multiple dreams are the ideas of religious and political freedom, upward mobility, self-reliance, and individualism.

What interests us here is not the American dream per se, but its significance in Chinese immigrants' views about America. The idea of prosperity in particular has been a large part of the American dream throughout the history of Chinese immigration to the United States. A Cantonese folksong from the early twentieth century mentions Gold Mountain, which remains the Chinese name for San Francisco: "O, sojourner from Gold Mountain: If you have not one thousand in gold, you must have at least eight hundred. / O, uncle from the South Seas: Just look at your money bag. It's empty, it's empty. / O, young man from Hong Kong: You earn money in Hong Kong, and you spend it all in Hong Kong too."[7] This folksong compares Chinese immigrants to the United States with immigrants going to other places, implying that those who go to America become richer than other immigrants. California, where immigrants discovered gold, becomes "Gold Mountain," where immigrants are expected to make more than those who venture to the South Seas or Hong Kong. From early on in Chinese immigrant history, achieving prosperity and America have been closely entwined.

While the "Gold Mountain" American dream occupied the minds of early labor immigrants, the *liuxuesheng* (留學生, overseas Chinese students) immigrants have aimed to pursue advanced science and technology to help their country back home. The figure of *liuxuesheng* was born in the mid- to late nineteenth century, when learning about foreign cultures was seen as a necessity in the face of foreign invasions and the Chinese defeat in the Sino-Japanese War of 1894 to 1895. The so-called national humiliation gave birth to a generation of young men who sought opportunities to study overseas in Japan, Europe, and America.[8] They hoped to bring modernity to their motherland in the midst of political turbulence. With the implementation of Deng Xiaoping's Reform and Opening Up Policy in 1978 and the establishment of U.S.–Chinese diplomatic relationships in 1979, China's attitude toward the United States became more positive, and their relationship significantly improved. Since the 1980s, Chinese popular culture has portrayed the United States as a land of promises and material abundance, resulting in a huge wave of going abroad (*chuguo re*, "going abroad fever"). Since then, a multitude of students from China have departed for the United States to pursue advanced degrees, making China the world's largest source of international students in 2017.[9]

Regardless of whether they belong to the working class or are economically privileged immigrants, or if they are coming to the United States for further studies or business, most of the Chinese immigrants share the perceived notion of the American dream: financial and social upward mobility, freedom, and individualism. We have seen some of the same ideals at work in Chinese diasporic literature examined in this book so far, but not without reinterpreting and challenging this concept. As was noted in chapter 3, for instance, fellow Chinese back home would find some excitement and intrigue in the immigrant tales these stories present, being able to partake in the diasporic experience from a safe distance. As Margaret Hillenbrand summarizes, "These texts trade in triumph and disaster and American dream and American nightmare because readers consume them as instruction manuals and cautionary tales about life in the US."[10] Hillenbrand then uses *Beijinger* as an example of both triumph and disaster in an immigrant tale. Her comment indicates the importance of binary or duality in many earlier Chinese diasporic stories, as well as how readers perceive these texts. As the main protagonist in *Miss Bieji* (*Bieji Xiaojie*, 别基小姐, 2016) points out, "Chinese readers are misled for many years by reading two types of books about America—one describes America as heaven, the other deems America as hell. The former one includes stories like Chinese going to Harvard, opening businesses, succeeding in business, becoming millionaires; the latter portrays Chinese being discriminated."[11] Critics have emphasized that Chinese immigrant literature written in the 1990s and 2000s often describes America as either a utopic or dystopic space. For instance, Zhou Li's *Manhadun de Zhongguo nüren* (曼哈頓的中國女人, *Manhattan's China Lady*, 1992) and *Hafo nühai Liu Yiting* (哈佛女孩刘亦婷, *Harvard Girl*, 2000) paint a rosy picture of an exemplary immigrant businesswoman and star student succeeding in the United States, while some others like Yan Geling's *Fusang* (扶桑, *The Lost Daughter of Happiness*, 1995) and Ha Jin's *A Good Fall* (2009) present America as a land where immigrants face discrimination and suffer depression and displacement.

The portrayal of the American dream varies greatly on screen. There are certain films that present a pessimistic, tough story of the dream, like *Ai zai Biexiang de Jijie* (愛在別鄉的季節, *Farewell China*, directed by Clara Law, 1990). The movie traces Zhou, who smuggles himself to New York to find his wife since he stops hearing from her. They are both first filled with hope that her immigration into the United States would bring their child a brighter future, yet in the end she completely forgets who she is and kills her own husband. Such a tragedy almost reads like a propagandistic film to discourage Chinese from pursuing the American dream. Other films present more ambivalence toward the image of America. As Michael Berry claims, early American-themed films of the reform era used the "strategy of absence"[12] to "satisfy public curiosity about the United States" while avoiding direct mention of it to "offset the allure of the West"—a strategy in film that lingered for quite a while. Examples include *Liushou nüshi* (留守女士, *Those Left Behind*, directed by Hu Xueyang, 1991), *Da sa ba* (大撒把, *After Separation*, directed by Xia Gang, 1992), and *Bu jian bu san* (不見不散, *Be There or Be Square*, directed by Feng Xiaogang, 1998).

In this chapter, I look beyond the simplistic heaven–hell dichotomy in earlier discussions of *Beijinger*, focusing instead on how the palimpsestic map offers a gray space between the two extremes that immigrants must navigate. The fictional America in these Chinese immigrant narratives is neither utopia—a heavenly place that embodies the American dream—nor dystopia, a hellish place where immigrants suffer. Rather, there is a possibility of either, neither, or both—or even something else altogether. The works show that in each idyllic, rosy picture of the immigrants' American life, much darker layers always exist. Through reconstructing home and identity on their diasporic journey, Chinese immigrants attempt to balance and struggle between utopia and dystopia, the American dream and the American nightmare. Reading the shows through the lens of palimpsest helps bring in the connections between earlier and contemporary immigrant literature, showcasing the lineage of immigrant literature while drawing out the distinctive features of these shows.

In the case of *TWWW*, however, the show adds a new but important layer to the palimpsest for how the characters map home: the Chinese dream. The notion of the Chinese dream (*zhongguo meng*) was first coined by President Xi Jinping in his 2012 visit to the exhibition "The Road to Revival" at the National Historical Museum. There, he said, "in my opinion, realising the rejuvenation of the Chinese nation is the greatest Chinese dream." In 2013 he touched on the idea again.[13] The notion of a "Chinese dream" is still not fully understood, but it is often compared with the American dream, which is based on prosperity and wealth. Some scholars bring up the importance for China to have its own dream. For example, Thomas Friedman upholds that "China Needs Its Own Dream"—a dream that "marries people's expectations of prosperity with a more sustainable China." He explains that "because the next government's dream for China's emerging middle class—300 million people expected to grow to 800 million by 2025—is just like the American Dream (a big car, a big house, McDonald's Big Mac for all) then we need another planet."[14] The content of the Chinese dream is still up for debate, but we saw some policy shifts and changes that President Xi promoted in his regime, including improving morality, fighting corruption, promoting democracy, pushing economic development, and defining China's global role.[15]

Is the "Chinese dream" just a collective dream to rejuvenate the party? Or does it fulfill people's individual or personal dreams? According to some interpretative documents,[16] the Chinese dream emphasizes a collective mission of rejuvenating the nation and providing a society with an environment for technological and economic advancement. It is also a discourse to compete with America. In fact, many scholars have posited that "China and the United States are involved in a Cold War–style contest of the American Dream vs. the China Dream."[17] The Chinese dream is built on the advancement of the nation and society, providing better environment for personal achievements, whereas the American dream is built on individual financial success. If this dream is a national imagined space set up by official government discourse, how individuals live within this national imaginary space is a crucial question, as we will see in the maps that the characters from *TWWW* chart.

Charting the Palimpsestic Maps

The notion of palimpsest, a document on which the original writing has been replaced with a new layer of writing and so erased from the surface, emphasizes the process of deconstruction, overlaying, and overwriting. These new immigrant works write over the maps of previous generations to demonstrate the continuous Asian diasporic experience of the hardship, as well as the constant shift in how characters develop their identities. Multiple layers of the palimpsestic maps interact with each other and are written over each other, layer under layer. According to André Corboz's "The Land as Palimpsest" (1983): "To represent the land means to understand it. But such representation is not a tracing but always a creation. A map is drawn first to know and then to act. It has in common with the land the fact of being a process, a product, a project."[18]

Because a palimpsestic map reflects the traces and remains of the past, previous scholars have pinpointed the significant role of palimpsests in ethnic and postcolonial literatures: "The palimpsest is a way of writing back and challenging the authority of established texts and associated power hierarchies by showing how they re-emerge with new meanings."[19] The experience of indenture[20] and the American dream myth expose the journey of lived experiences through time, which can be written over with each new immigrant story but cannot be fully erased. If we read these TV series from the lens of postcolonialism, they too contribute to the remapping of the American dream—and in the case of *TWWW*, the Chinese dream. The multilayered, interactive movement of the palimpsests challenge and complicate the simple definition of these aspirations that focus on material success and upward mobility, and meanwhile show in *TWWW* how the Chinese dream and American dream intersect in the immigrant discourse. The changes of the trajectory also change characters, relationships, and personalities. If we see immigrants as the characters on a map, they change their locations along the way. Yet the journey also shifts the characters, too, so it is more of an iterative, ongoing process.

This chapter examines how the two visual productions chart the Chinese immigrant lives in the United States differently at two historical points in time. Through the creation of a palimpsestic map, these two works chart a similar trajectory of Chinese immigrants turning from privileges to vulnerabilities. To Chinese immigrants who come to the United States to pursue upward mobility or education, their version of the American dream has evolved from wealth and material success to the ideals of freedom, individualism, and self-reliance. Meanwhile, new immigrants who came to the States from mainland China after the 1990s are often viewed as being privileged in terms of economic and political backgrounds and the social status of their family. Under this new context, their privileges are taken away, and their vulnerability surfaces. Their hardships are caused by cultural conflicts, racial boundaries, solitude, and their difficulties with constructing a new home and identity. Through portraying the privileges and vulnerabilities of the contemporary Chinese immigrants, these two overlapping palimpsestic maps demonstrate America, New York, and Stenden University as a heterotopia: both real and imagined, utopia and dystopia. The palimpsestic maps destabilize the preconceived center of the maps that defines the American dream and the Chinese dream. In these TV series, the immigrant characters struggle to define their new home and identity between Chinese and American cultures. Nevertheless, they redefine their own values and systems after observing and critiquing the social problems of the two countries. They show that the American and Chinese dreams should not be defined in terms of material wealth and national boundaries but rather on an emotional and personal level. While *Beijinger* presents how to find a sense of home within the ups and downs of being a diasporic subject in the United States, *TWWW*'s palimpsestic map adds a new layer, one where the return home—even if a home that is transformed by one's travels—becomes a real possibility.

Beijinger in New York (1994): The Palimpsest of the American Dream for Chinese Immigrants

Written by Cao Guilin in 1991, *Beijinger in New York* was adapted into a twenty-one-episode TV drama by Feng Xiaogang and Zheng Xiaolong in 1994. The story narrates a famous cello player in China, Wang Qiming, and his wife, Guo Yan, who follow their American dream fantasy by moving to the United States. Once arriving there, Wang realizes life in America is not as rosy as they both thought. Wang first works at a Chinese restaurant and later establishes his own clothing factory, where his wife also works. After some years, they have become wealthy, and their daughter travels from China to reunite with them. Yet the good days do not last long—ultimately, they lose all their money, their home, and their daughter. The story ends with Wang witnessing a new batch of immigrants coming from China, and a sense of sympathy and confusion wells up in him.

Immigrants like Wang follow the example of the earlier newcomers who left for the United States to be railroad workers or laundrymen. They worked hard during the day at low-paying jobs, always hoping for the upward mobility of the sort that Wang achieves by successfully building up his career, making a lot of money, and gaining admiration from all those around him. Immigrants like Wang were privileged in China in terms of social status, yet they leave their privileges behind and come to the United States; through hard work and economic success, they hope to regain their social status. As *Beijinger* shows, however, they can also lose it very quickly.

In *Beijinger*, America, specifically New York City, at first serves as the site of the American dream for the couple. It later becomes simultaneously a site of dystopic realities. New York City, which is also symbolized as the factory and casino, stands in between heaven and hell, or embodies both. The TV series dramatizes the "heaven" images like Times Square, Fifth Avenue's fashion district, Wang's mansion, Wang's competitor's lake house, and Manhattan over the bridge, contrasting them with the "hell" images/spaces—a basement apartment, Wang's daughter's window, a drummer on the street, dishwashing in a restaurant, and knitting day and night in the factory. While the heaven–hell dichotomy is embedded in the show, and many have read it that way, viewing it through the lens of palimpsest allows us to move away from this simple comparison. In this way, we can dissect the process whereby the last map made by Chinese common assumptions is overwritten while examining the makeup of the subjective, lived experience in diasporic fiction. The last map is not destroyed, however, and the show captures what is left along the new information. By creating a multilayered palimpsestic map, the TV series dramatizes the romance, affairs, and intergenerational conflicts, keeping the trace of the American dream and experience of indenture (labor workers' hardship), yet reveals a new map that targeted the Chinese audience in the 1990s, offering a more realistic way to grapple with the diasporic experience in America than seeing it in black and white.

The opening of *Beijinger* vividly conveys a craze for America and the American dream in the 1980s and 1990s. The TV series starts with a brief scene of two successful businesspeople in New York. One is an Irish immigrant, David, who *Zhongguo tong* ("knows all about China") and drives home with the song "Dirty World" (1988) in the background. Another is a Chinese immigrant who owns a Chinese restaurant, Ah Chun, who arrived in the States earlier than Wang. One early scene that perfectly captures their hopes depicts Wang and Guo's excitement on their first ride to Manhattan from the airport. Wang calls out "New York, Manhattan" while pointing to the skyline. The aerial shot of the skyline overlooks the skyscrapers in the evening, while the song "Stars and Stripes Forever" starts playing.[21] The repetition of this song sets the tone of American patriotism on the one hand and the dreamy image on the other. The camera then zooms to the car, where Wang looks as though he is conducting the orchestra playing the song. Meanwhile, Guo busily looks around with curiosity, peering out the window while her husband is enraptured by the song—at times smiling at him, and at other times, pointing to something that captures her attention. The medium close-up of the couple in the back of their aunt's car shows their extreme excitement upon entering this new world. It is as if they are composing new music, with Wang's hand conducting. Passing through Times Square, Wang says with a sonorous tone: "New York, I, Wang Qiming, have come!" The camera turns to a scene of the hustle and bustle in Times Square, where people are standing alongside the streets. Wang waves in the car, as if he were a celebrity. Even though only instrumental music is playing, the song conveys the message of pursuit for liberty and freedom like the lyrics render:

FIGURE 4.1 Guo Yan sitting across the river from Manhattan. Source: *Beijinger in New York/A Native of Beijing in New York* (北京人在紐約), directed by Zheng Xiaolong (鄭曉龍) and Feng Xiaogang (馮小剛), aired on January 1, 1994, episode 12, 37:32, accessed February 22, 2023, DVD.

"Sing out for freedom and the right / Sing out for Union and its might." The photography, cinematography, background music, color, and lighting together paint a dramatic picture of a rosy American dream that excites immigrants. If anything, this is one of the "heavenly" images displayed in the TV series.

Manhattan and Times Square, as well as other "heavenly" spaces, embody the kinds of places that immigrants long for and inhabit when they get wealthy. Yet these same spaces are not unilaterally demonstrated as being fully ideal. Instead, they often have two sides to them—good and bad, bright and dark. The visual representations in the TV series elicit the interchangeability of the opposite sides—the heavenly, rosy images are only a layer of the palimpsestic map, being prone to being overwritten by less bright ones at any moment.

One scene in episode 12 demonstrates the different layers of this map. We first get a long shot of a bridge across to Manhattan, and then the camera lens moves to an overview of the landscape of the island before leading the viewer to this side of the bank, with Guo Yan sitting on a bench, her back turned to the viewer (see Figure 4.1). This shift from a long shot of Manhattan to a zoomed-in image of Guo Yan creates a greater sense of distance between her and the beautiful landscape of Manhattan, suggesting her great distance from her ideal American life. This scene is interrupted when Yan is caught off guard and has her bags taken by the thieves. We see a closeup shot of Guo Yan with a disappointed look, followed by overexposed images of Manhattan across the sea, as if the cruel nature of New York now overwhelms her. This place, like the out-of-focus image, seems distant to her. Her alienation and nonbelonging all swell up. In this image, then, one side is the beautiful, dreamy landscape of Manhattan; the other side is the disappointed Guo Yan, filled with regrets and a sense of loss.

Meanwhile, the TV series also portrays the more explicitly "hellish" spaces for immigrants—the dark spaces in which immigrants occupy, live, and work in the United States. One of the best examples of these spaces is the basement apartment their aunt puts them in when they first arrive. The dark image in the basement sharply contrasts with the bright skyscrapers with their radiant, flashy lights. We follow Wang, who slowly explores the basement, from the graffiti-filled wall to the small door at the back, then to another graffiti-filled wall, a hallway only big enough for one person, leading to a kitchen. When Wang calls for Guo Yan to come in and look, she sits in the dark hallway outside and cries, complaining that no one cares about them. The dark, cramped visual space of this basement marks the beginning of Wang and Guo Yan's immigrant life as poor and humble. When Wang goes to work in a Chinese restaurant, Guo Yan finds herself stuck in the basement. The sense of imprisonment and the restrictive space they have contrast strongly with the freedom and prosperity they longed for in the beginning—the expectation of an open map where they can create their home is quickly limited by the tight spaces of their first apartment in the United States.

Other images in the show that project hellish darkness include Yan and Wang's daughter Ningning's window and the blinds from which she looks out angrily at her dad's lover, the drummer on the street who appears frequently, the sewing machine, and the knitting factory where a lot of immigrants work day and night. In these spaces, Chinese immigrants such as Wang and Guo Yan suffer from depression, alienation, discrimination, and displacement. The portrayal of the difficulties of immigrant lives and the restrictive "hell" spaces are the palimpsestic traces of the old maps of Chinese immigrant lives in the United States. They follow the previous immigrant stories of the nineteenth century, like the labor workers and gold miners. Meanwhile, the hard labor burdens Wang and challenges the ideals of the American dream. One of the "hell" spaces Wang first encounters is the Chinese restaurant where he works. Figure 4.2 shows a medium shot of Wang washing dishes. The focal point, where the light shines on the mountains of bowls and plates in front of him, highlights the challenges posed to him. The mountain of dirty dishes is like the insurmountable hardship and pressure that immigrants face, a Sisyphean task indeed. His face is obscured by the dishes all around him, as if he were insignificant. His diminished image buried in heavy labor challenges his view of "home." This "home" has already departed from its original essence, one that implies comfort and belonging. This "home" becomes questionable, especially if he cannot find ease and security there. The harsh reality of immigrant life in the United States disappoints him and his family, and it seems difficult for them to achieve their American dream.

Beijinger deconstructs the preconceived American dream, which is often exemplified by money, nice houses, and facades. However, the show does not simply depict the American dream as dystopia. Instead, the TV series portrays it as an abstract and fluid space that is interpretive, constructive, and multivalent.

FIGURE 4.2 Wang Qiming washing piles of dishes in Ah Chun's restaurant. Source: *Beijinger in New York/A Native of Beijing in New York* (北京人在纽约), directed by Zheng Xiaolong (鄭曉龍) and Feng Xiaogang (馮小剛), aired on January 1, 1994, episode 2, 37:32, accessed February 22, 2023, DVD.

Instead of a static space or place, the show paints it as a fluid journey that involves all the ups and downs and changes. A static map would not be able to explain such complication and fluidity, but if we view it as a palimpsest, we can better explain the intersecting and complicated layers of the maps. In this show, both heaven and hell spaces are inevitable. However, while these opposing images are sometimes effaced to make room for the changes, their traces remain, just like palimpsests.

This is not just a spectrum, moving between heaven and hellish spaces: a few prominent spaces in the show embody both heaven and hell, such as the knitting factory, the hotel room where Wang has sex with a prostitute, and the casino. The textile factory has witnessed the economic ups and downs of the two immigrants of different ethnicities—Chinese immigrant Wang and Irish immigrant David. The TV series sets them up as competitors in many ways, primarily in business and their love for Guo Yan. When Wang sits in his office speaking to his employees proudly, he realizes his success. Through the course of his American life, he has endured a lot of discrimination, physical and mental difficulties, separation from his daughter, and endless sleepless nights of work. He represents a successful example of upward mobility and the possibility of achieving the American dream through hard work and persistence. In his first appearance, he wears a pair of jeans. Later, his attire changes into formal dress clothes and neckties when he goes to meet his clients on Fifth Avenue. Guo Yan also starts to wear fashionable clothes and jewelry. Wang gets used to being treated with respect and admiration, now being called "Boss Wang" (*Wang laoban*). The factory becomes the site of his upward mobility, as he grows from a humble worker sewing clothes to a successful, wealthy owner.

However, the factory also bears witness to the failure of businesses. Wang and David fight over the ownership and the space for the factory just as they fight for Guo Yan from the beginning to the end of the show, indicating that there is fierce competition among immigrants to get the resources and limited spaces left for them. Even a white Irish immigrant like David has to go through similar hardships as Chinese immigrants in the 1990s. Though Irish immigrants were by then no longer discriminated against (as they were a century ago), the fact that he still goes through hard times in the 1990s can be interpreted as a palimpsestic trace that is carried from earlier times. In episode 11, when David's business fails, a look of dismay can be seen on his face while he stands in the middle of the sewing room. This shot of David is quite familiar, as it mirrors the earlier zoomed-in shot of Wang when he is despondent. David, an Irish immigrant who made himself successful and wealthy in the fashion business, suddenly becomes bankrupt. Everything vanishes in one day. The next shot shows the staff taking the machines and clothes away and leaving. He is so devastated that he even hits his most loyal manager, Ms. Bai.

One could argue that individual successes and failures are common in many stories. Yet this story particularly criticizes American capitalism, with Wang as a victim of the dark power it holds over people. When Wang gets upset, he is seduced by an American woman on the street. He brings her to a hotel room, where she takes off her clothes and licks his body. Before going further, however, she asks him for money. He sarcastically says, "I give you money, then you are willing to do anything?" "Anything," she replies. Even though she might be a prostitute, and serving men is her job, this scene deliberately shows the power imbalance between the Chinese man and the American girl, at least initially. Figure 4.3 shows a super close-up shot of Wang, with half of his face highlighted in a hard light, whereas the other half is in the dark. The hard light shows the contours of his face, highlighting the wrinkles from his hard work, while his face expresses sarcasm and discontent. He looks down toward the white woman, who tries to seduce him to get money. The camera then zooms back a bit further, now focusing on the lady's half-naked back, covered with the dollar tips from Wang. She is trading her body for the money her customer offers. We can see half of Wang's face in the image with his crossed arms behind his head, showing his arrogance. The prostitute asks for more and more, gently saying, "Give me the last bit." Next, Wang turns from a level position with the lady to a higher position, pressing her under himself, forcing her to say "I love

FIGURE 4.3 Wang Qiming playing with an American prostitute in a hotel room after getting drunk. Source: *Beijinger in New York/A Native of Beijing in New York* (北京人在紐約), directed by Zheng Xiaolong (鄭曉龍) and Feng Xiaogang (馮小剛), aired on January 1, 1994, episode 16, accessed Feb 22, 2023, DVD.

you," as though she were his lover. This medium shot shows Wang in a position of power over the lady. She is pressed underneath, powerless, forced to say whatever he asks. The scene is filled with warm lighting from the lamp in the room, yet his face is dark. The picture seems to suggest he blends into the darkness of this capitalist society. Perhaps he has become, as his daughter calls him, a "stinky capitalist." While he becomes more like an American capitalist, he also subverts the stereotypical power imbalance between white and Asian. Wang's instant success and failure is a by-product of capitalism, or rather, Wang is portrayed as a victim of capitalism.

Just like the textile factory, the casino shown in the series embodies both heaven and hell. The fast material success Wang and his wife achieve, whether it is through business or relationships, is prone to disappear all at once. The story ends with episodes of the business failing and Wang gambling away his savings in Atlantic City (episode 20). The casino scene captures his tragic ending well. The scene first begins with a gliding view of the casino, and then the camera focuses on the blackjack table where Wang Qiming is playing. The camera first focuses on the matches he swipes, then a close up shot of his face, showing tension (see Figure 4.4). Then, the camera shifts between the gambling table and Wang against the backdrop of the casino lights. Behind him, lights flash like the streetlights of New York. The depth of field is created with a lower f-number, causing the lights to become blurry and starry, just like his mirage of America itself. Yet at this moment, he is soaked in sweat and tears, lost as to what he can do and on the verge of failure. A super close-up shot highlights the wrinkles on his forehead, his hair standing up, his weary eyes, and the sweat on his face. As these images show, at this moment, he is very tense and nervous. "Perhaps I shouldn't have come here," he says, suggesting both coming to casino and to the United States. He takes out the last five thousand dollars from his pocket, and gambles it all away. The music "hung hung" adds to the anxiety of the moment. Losing it all, he walks into the darkness of the casino, and the narrator says *ta shi le* ("steady"). When he walks out of the casino and gets into

FIGURE 4.4 Wang Qiming losing the last bit of his money and getting anxious in a casino. Source: *Beijinger in New York/A Native of Beijing in New York* (北京人在紐約), directed by Zheng Xiaolong (鄭曉) and Feng Xiaogang (馮小剛), aired on January 1, 1994, episode 21, accessed February 22, 2023, DVD.

his car, strangely, he does not seem very sad or disappointed; rather, he is relaxed. He is playing the fast-beat Chinese folksongs, which brings us back to the first scene when American music is playing, contrasting with his earlier expectations.

All in all, *Beijinger* paints New York and America as a palimpsestic map. One level on the palimpsest depicts the American dream as material constructs—good money, big houses, and fancy cars—the result of capitalism, as well as liberty and freedom. Even though the map of the American dream is overwritten, it still leaves some traces of this vision. The map that the TV series has drawn allows viewers to see but also question the preconceived American ideal. The series constructs and dramatizes New York as in-between spaces of heaven (such as Wang's mansion, Fifth Avenue, David's lake house, and the prosperous Manhattan) and spaces of hell (such as the basement apartment, the kitchen of the restaurant, and the street corner where the drummer stands). New York at one moment symbolizes the modernity and liberty that immigrants long for. The next moment, it is like a casino where one gambles their life savings away. In this manner, in New York, the traces of indenture (hell) and the American dream (heaven) are overwritten. They are replaced with a more complicated map that sketches the journey of immigrants' lived experiences in the United States, where things are not black and white, but immigrants must navigate the gray area that is bound by the expectations and pitfalls of the American dream.

While deconstructing the national American ideals, the story has reconstructed a map made up of personal, affective relationships—family, love, and a sense of belonging. At a deeper level, the old map of the American dream is nationalized, whereby ones who live it become quintessentially American, defined by materialism and capitalism. *Beijinger* creates a new map that redefines the American dream. This new version traces the emotional, affective trajectory of Chinese immigrants, their journey of searching for home and sense of belonging—and like the space between heaven and hell, it is not as simple as being either Chinese or American.

This new affective map recharts the emotional journey of these new immigrants in a new land. Unlike the physical map of their trajectory, which is simply from China to the United States, their emotional, affective map is much more complicated, filled with twists and turns. It does not present a map that is a single directional. Rather, it is multidirectional. The immigrants are pushed and pulled between two lands and two cultures, struggling with their sense of belonging. As Guo Yan says to her aunt in episode 15 of the show, "I cannot become American, but also forgot what it's like to be Chinese." Even older immigrants such as Ah Chun feel that "I find I am neither American nor Chinese." For her, America is a temporary home to immigrants yet immigrants are forever "foreigners" in this country, as David reminds Wang. Even with the success that Wang achieves, it is all but temporary. America is not heaven or hell, nor both or neither. The diasporic search for home is not a static one, but dynamic and always shifting, just like the maps that immigrants draw along their own journeys.

The Way We Were: A Palimpsest of the Chinese and American Dreams

Whereas *Beijinger* portrays those who come to America for economic opportunities and freedom, *TWWW* features those who come to further their education. The show quickly became one of the most popular idol dramas in 2018, directed by Liu Jiang and starring famous young actors and actresses such as Tang Yan (Tiffany Tang), Luo Jin, and Xu Lingyue. It was broadcast in mainland China, Malaysia, and Singapore. In China, it mainly aired in Beijing and Shanghai. On Dragon Television (its original name was Shanghai Television), Asia's largest open-press studio, this show has been consecutively ranked in the top five each time an episode was shown and was nominated for awards in several TV series competitions.

TWWW is based on a script written by Gao Xuan and Ren Baoru, a regular pair among scriptwriters in China. The story focuses on a few overseas Chinese students—Shu Che, Xiao Qing, Miao Ying, and Ning Ming—and their journey from China to the United States, particularly in California. Shu Che and Xiao Qing are affectionate and have been close friends since their youth. They both come from prestigious families—Shu's father is the mayor of a town in China, and Miao's father is a CEO of a big corporation. After being separated in two different places for six years, Shu Che and Miao Ying finally get together in the United States, and they almost get married. However, their parents' secret business has ruined their plan, as will be explained below. While at an elite college in China—Tsinghua University—Miao Ying had been pursued by many, including Ning Ming, who has secretly admired and protected her the whole time. He has hidden his love and enjoyed his own journey of pursuit. Xiao Qing is from a middle-class family, the daughter of a good, incorruptible prosecutor and a music teacher. She and Miao Ying meet on the plane to the United States, with both entering into one of the best universities there—Stenden University (a fictional name based on the real Stanford University). Unlike Miao's rich family, Xiao Qing works hard to sustain herself by getting jobs on and off campus. When hearing that Shu Che and Miao Ying are getting married, Ning Ming decides to come to the United States. Unexpectedly, he witnesses Miao running away on her wedding day and secretly protects her in her most vulnerable moment. In the end, he decides to stay in the States. While working lowly jobs, he takes joy in observing and protecting his love. When Shu Che learns that Miao Ying helps her father hide the secret of their fathers' collusion, they eventually break up. Shu Che and Xiao Qing instead get together as a couple. Miao Ying and Shu Che's father's collusion finally gets revealed, with Xiao Qing being an important witness. They both have to pay the price and get sentenced to prison at the end. After that, Shu Che exiles himself to Cambodia, far away from everyone else. Finally, Xiao Qing finds him and accompanies him for a time, but she is not able to convince him to return with her. Miao Ying and Ning Ming return to China to develop their business and build a family together. At the end of the show, Shu Che is interviewing as an intern in Xiao Qing's law firm in China, which draws her to tears. They finally reunite.

TWWW, with its title taken from the poem *gui qu lai xi, tian yuan jiang wu*,[22] implies a strong promotion of returning to homeland. The American dream is no longer a destination but only a path/step to the Chinese dream in service of the national discourse. It adds to the palimpsest we see in *Beijinger*, carrying now also traces of the earlier overseas Chinese students (*liuxuesheng*) as in the 1960s and 1970s, those who wanted to study abroad and return with glory, along with the American ideals of democracy, freedom, and justice. Meanwhile, this map re-creates the model of a new generation of Chinese immigrants who also question the purpose of studying abroad. The new layer of the palimpsestic map paints a story of personal romantic relationships between the four college students who came from China to the United States. While retaining the traces from the older-generation overseas Chinese literature in the 1960s and 1970s, this map overwrites some characteristics on the old map—the sense of loyalty and patriotism, for instance. Instead, painted on top is the new layer that maps the emotional, affectionate, and interpersonal trajectory, while also suggesting that a return to the homeland itself is possible.

This TV series could easily be interpreted as a bildungsroman, focusing on the moral and psychological growth of the protagonists. These overseas Chinese students, when faced with the reality of ethical and moral challenges, grow and change beyond their expectations. One example of this is another student, Chen Ran, who learns to stand on his own feet rather than being a *fu'er dai* ("second-generation rich kid") who relies on his father, and Shu Che, the *guan'er dai* ("officials' kid") who becomes independent in everything he does. If that is the case, the story could well happen in China. What then is the role of America and the American dream in this show? Why is it set in the United States, and what role do Chinese immigrants or overseas Chinese students play? To answer these questions, the following explores the geographical, ideological, and psychological maps drawn in *TWWW*.

Like *Beijinger*, this TV series represents, contests, articulates, and problematizes the American dream, writing over it with the Chinese dream but retaining its traces. It is reinvigorated and renewed: the old American dream that connects to the idea of prosperity and wealth remains, as presented in images of beautiful beaches and Stenden University. Yet, more so, this old idea is challenged: while some immigrants achieve upward mobility, others see and experience a different journey, enduring the most extreme hardships. Ning Ming, for instance, endures threats against his life and long shifts working in a motel. He is also in danger of being deported while working without documentation in a restaurant. Eventually, he achieves tremendous success in his field, but the terrible experience he has had is beyond what he would have had in China: "What's the next meal, where do I sleep next?" Ning Ming keeps shifting from job to job in order to survive in these low-paying, difficult working and living conditions. He does not know where he wants to go or where he will end up. The tumultuous path that Ning Ming walks mirrors the disastrous hardships the old immigrants experienced. As such, it can be said that the show has traces of an old map showing the tumultuous journeys of previous Chinese immigrants in the nineteenth and twentieth centuries that we also see in *Beijinger*.

However, the map reaches beyond the map of "heaven" and "hell" in America. Rather, it acts as an extension of the old map of Chinese immigrants, whose trajectories end in the States. The new map adds a link to the homeland. Interestingly, unlike *Beijinger*, which only presents one image of a "heavenly" America, *TWWW* shows idyllic pictures of the two countries. The parallel shots of the two cities in America and China, respectively, in Figure 4.5 (top and bottom) share many similarities—high-rises, the river, skyscrapers, a beautiful sky, and tightly connected, largely developed buildings, showing that China nowadays is as beautiful and developed, if not more than, the United States. Compared to previous immigrants who are eager to settle in the United States, for contemporary immigrants in this show, America becomes a stopping point rather than the final destination.

Yet, the return home does not mean that the characters themselves are unchanged. These new overseas Chinese students renew the meaning of the

FIGURE 4.5 Comparing the images of an American city and a Chinese city. Source: *Gui qu lai* 歸去來, *The Way We Were*, directed by Liu Jiang (劉江), aired on May 14, 2018, episode 48, accessed February 22, 2023, DVD.

American dream beyond prosperity. Especially for those who come from more privileged social and economic backgrounds, these immigrants pursue freedom. As the male protagonist Shu Che says to his parents in episode 31, "thanks for sending me abroad to study, to let me have my own right to choose and own freedom." As discussed previously, this sense of freedom is an essential part of the American dream. Shu Che grows up in a bureaucratic family in which his parents are always making decisions for him. He wants to resist the values his father imposes on him. America provides him with an environment to live his own life and make his own choices. He sets up his own company with his talents and connections in the United States. He continues on to get a degree in law after getting his MBA at Stenden University, hoping to pursue justice. To him, America serves as a midpoint for achieving his ideological independence. Even though Shu Che's parents criticize him for his excessive self-confidence and constantly making decisions without consulting them, in the end, his stubborn insistence on morality saves him.

Yet the show critiques the problems brought by these overseas Chinese students' active pursuit of America. Bereft of self-confidence, a lot of Chinese too often fall prey to the most negative consequences of American liberalism. For instance, Miao Ying's brother, Cheng Ran, adopts negative Western ideals and becomes obsessed with money. Before meeting and falling in love with Xiao Qing, he lives irresponsibly on his father's wealth. He accepts a marriage proposal as a business transaction with another Chinese immigrant character nicknamed "Green Card." The fact that he calls her Green Card, a mispronunciation of her real name, Lü Ka, is ironic, as the practicality of their marriage implies the stereotypical fake green card marriages of many U.S. immigrants.

Extending beyond the effects of America on these younger immigrant characters, the show zooms in to look at how these young generations of Chinese carry a stronger sense of justice and morality than older generations. From the beginning, Xiao Qing chooses not to lie to the police when Shu Che drives without a license and speeds. In the police station, the American police officers think that Chinese people take the blame for others because of *renqing* (literally "human feelings," but meaning "attachment" or "empathy") or the idea that lacking *renqing* is unacceptable in Chinese culture. This stereotype of the police (the symbolic standard American white people) proves how Westerners see Chinese as prioritizing *renqing* over law. Shu Che and Xiao Qing prove this wrong. Whereas in *Beijinger* a lack of *renqing* is seen as a bad trait, such as when the aunt leaves Wang and Guo Yan in a run-down basement apartment upon the couple's arrival in New York, and the aunt's lack of *renqing* is described as her losing her Chinese virtues, here, two decades later in *TWWW*, lacking *renqing* and not giving favors are highlighted as moral developments of the younger generation. This can be seen in Xiao Qing's refusal to lie to the police for Shu Che and when Xiao Qing becomes a witness and honestly confesses the truth in court rather than fulfill his *renqing*.

These situations show the character's "improvement of morality,"[23] which is one essential element of the Chinese dream. Indeed, instead of only demystifying the American dream, like *Beijinger*, this show adds the Chinese dream to the palimpsestic map by showing that America is no longer a final destination; rather, it is only one of the steps toward the Chinese dream.

Another example of how the show incorporates the Chinese dream centers on anticorruption, which as mentioned above represents one of Xi's major campaigns.[24] *TWWW* presents a typical source of conflict: collusion between a bureaucratic high official, Shu Che's father, who is the mayor of the fictional city Yan Jing and a businessman, and Miao Ying's father, Wei Cheng. Both of them have been planning to win a bid for a large railroad business behind the scenes. However, to complete this business, they sacrifice their employees' lives, their family relationships, and their children's marriages. Miao Ying and Shu Che become the victims of their family's power and collusion. The longing and love between the couple extend across the Pacific, yet they are initially broken apart by their families' business collusion.

Even though the older generation—the protagonists' fathers—violates the law, the younger generation, having received higher education in the United States, becomes aware of the social problems brought about by the privileges of their families. They become the "outsiders within," observing and judging situations from a new perspective. They reject the value systems of the older generation and rebuild their own. Indeed, they lead the older generation to realize their wrongdoings. In one scene, Shu Che writes *tianyuan jiang wu* (田園將蕪) on the blackboard in his American apartment, taken from the poetic line *gui qu lai xi, tian yuan jiang wu hu bu gui* 歸去來兮 田園將蕪胡不歸 by a famous writer from the Dong Jin era (317–420 CE), Tao Yuanming (陶淵明). The whole passage reads, "I am going home! My fields and gardens are choked with weeds. Why should I not return? My mind has been my body's slave; how sad and lamentable! I realize that the past is gone, but I can certainly rectify what is to come. I have not actually strayed too far from the path. I have awakened to today's rights and yesterday's wrongs."[25] This poem narrates Tao Yuanming lamenting on his official career of corruption and his choice to leave in peace. He realizes that officialdom easily leads to confusion, and therefore he returns to retreat. Similarly, after Shu Che's father visits him in the States and sees the poetic line written on his blackboard, he reflects on his actions and starts feeling guilty.

Eventually, the younger generation builds up their privileged careers and families not based on their inherited corruptive system and values but through the new values combining Eastern philosophy and Western ideology. In the end, Shu Che's father and Miao Ying's father are punished by the Chinese legal system. The younger generation achieves their Chinese dream through their adopted environment, a developed society that has justice and law. Their parents' arrests for bribery become a vivid example of the purer political environment in China. Meanwhile, contemporary Chinese businesses, unlike before, promote "independent intellectual property rights." As Mayor Shu tells Cheng Wei, that is his only key to success, distinct from others' strategy of "Made in China, but made by Germany/made by Japan."[26]

This TV series presents a new palimpsestic map, one overwritten by the Chinese dream, but with some traces of the ideologies from the American dream still remaining. Yet it also creates its own set of values distinct from the American dream. When President Xi first brought up the idea of the Chinese dream in 2012, he stated that the effort is to "push forward the great cause of socialism with Chinese characteristics, and strive to achieve the Chinese dream of great rejuvenation of the Chinese nation."[27] The TV series advocates some Chinese virtues, like when Xiao Qing says to her professor, "Chinese can survive under any condition, even with adversity and desperation."[28] Xiao Qing is portrayed as a perfect, young, aspiring girl who is strong and upright, embodying the Chinese dream.

TWWW explores how the American and Chinese dreams relate on the palimpsestic map through the key dilemma of whether "to stay or to return." The title *Gui qu lai*, aside from being taken from Tao Yuanming's aforementioned poem, also alludes to Han Shaogong's "Gui qu lai" (1985), which is a story revealing how "self-identity" is constructed through memory. Han's narrative is a first-person account of a visit to a village, where he is called by the name "Ma Yanjing." The title of this story represents this paradox in which the question of "who goes or comes" is projected. The whole story is inseparable from the contradiction of the two selves. The image of Ma Yanjing constructed through villagers' memories makes the narrator at once the embodiment of this legendary figure. At the same time, his own memory tells him he is not Ma but Huang. As a typical work of root-seeking literature, it seeks cultural identity through literature, which offers us an insight into the construction of self through memories in a historical context. These two forces come into being in his heart, which helps him reconstruct his self-identity. Although it involves confusion and torture, the conflict of two selves constitutes a powerful combination—one that helps him redefine his identity.

The overseas Chinese students in this new *Gui qu lai* share a similar dilemma of conflicted selves. However, unlike Han Shaogong's "Gui qu lai," this show reflects identity conflicts between the past and the present, between homeland and the new land. These layers of the palimpsestic map are not easy to navigate, and the TV series features a lot of "in-between" characters who are stuck between China and America, old lovers and new lovers, personal ambition and collective, family, or national obligations. The show portrays the perplexity and confusion of these various figures. Regardless of their issues, they are all marked by togetherness and separation. The scenes of separation are all dramatized, such as Ning Ming's family standing on the street, sending him off, and Miao Ying sending off Ning Ming at the airport. These partings and gatherings are symbolic of the struggles that diasporic communities and overseas Chinese students face.

Among all the "in-between" characters, the most interesting one is Liu Caiqi, the mistress of Shu Che's father, who is later sent to America. Liu Caiqi becomes the victim of the business between Cheng Wei and the mayor. She first is forced to deny her relationship with the mayor, and then her child with the mayor is killed. After she marries an American, the businessman Cheng Wei frames her new husband for his felony. Her relationship with Shu Che's father is never acknowledged, and her relationship with the American who she later marries, Roonie, is never complete. She emphasizes many times that she wants nothing else but to be admitted. As a hidden lover, she often feels neglected and wants to be noticed. Her status in some way symbolizes the in-between diasporic community that has been stuck between the original land, hidden and unnoticed, and the new land, where its members are not fully accepted or loved.

These in-between characters and the hardships they experience in the United States are nothing new in the Chinese immigrant history. Just as in *Beijinger*, we see traces of old American dreams but also nightmares. From the labor immigrants in the nineteenth century to the earlier overseas Chinese students in the 1960s and 1970s, who were doubly exiled from mainland China to Taiwan, then to the United States, all are hoping to be free in America. Yet they pay the price of being alienated, displaced in the new land. In contrast to those earlier immigrants, these new overseas Chinese students are more attached to their homeland and their family back home—as demonstrated by Xiao Qing calling her parents in China frequently, Miao Ying and Shu Che's parents visiting them in the States often, and Ning Ming longing for and hoping to take care of his family. Their close connections to their family and the rise of China give them more motivation to return to their homeland after they graduate.

Using the title of *Gui qu lai*, this TV series brings us back to the question "Who goes/comes?" Overseas Chinese students face significant decisions. Surrounded by the memories of their homeland, their families and the past are now mixed with their new ideologies, knowledge, and experience shaped in the United States. In *Beijinger*, we have seen traces of the hardships that Chinese immigrants experience; in *TWWW*, we still see traces of the sacrifices these students make when they leave their homes for life abroad. This is especially true in the cases of Xiao Qing not being able to be around her mom when she gets into accident and stays in the hospital, and working-class people such as Ning Ming, who worries about his family back home. Those sacrifices, along with the hardship they experience abroad—displacement and alienation—still play a crucial part in their sojourn. This is a covered-over but always-present layer on the palimpsestic map.

On top of this layer, however, is a new trajectory, one that is much different from *Beijinger*, which was produced two decades earlier. Unlike the earlier immigrants from before the 1990s, who see America as their destination, the new immigrants see America as a stopping point on their path, with the new China becoming their final destination. Indeed, Tao Yuanming's poem *Tian yuan jiang wu hu bu gui* ("My fields and gardens are choked with weeds. Why should I not return?") and the English title, *The Way We Were*, seem to suggest a need to return to the past. "To stay or to return" becomes everyone's choice or dilemma after graduation. When the students first come to the United States, the decision is not so clear. "This is America, it's her sojourn in the future three years, it's a place where she wouldn't know to stay or leave, or perhaps it's her forever hometown."[29] In Ning Ming's case, his professor tries to persuade him to stay in a high-tech company such as Facebook, Google, or Apple, where he would have a stable middle-class income and a work visa. His professor says, "It's a dream that you come from a working family that can't even afford to pay you to study abroad to your current achievement." In terms of China, he asks, "If you go back to China, will you have a stable income and free market?" Yet Ning Ming gives up on attractive opportunities in the United States and chooses to return to China with his lover Miao Ying. Xiao Qing is also given an attractive offer by the law firm where she is interning. However, Miao Ying chooses to go back to rescue her father's enterprise. Similarly, Xiao Qing chooses to return to China to work in a law firm, and her lover Shu Che eventually returns to China after staying for a period of time in a remote village of Cambodia.

These characters are all presented with stable incomes and upward mobility, aspects of the old American dream. However, they all reject it. As Shu Che explains in episode 42: "If I stay in the U.S., I can see my foreseeable future, no matter in life or work, a gradual path towards the ceiling of one's life. It seems there won't be too many big breakthroughs; life would really become boring." He continues to talk about the alternative, returning to China: "Returning to the motherland is full of uncertainty, but it is that uncertainty that gives a promising space for us to develop. Going wherever we are needed would give us more opportunities to realize ourselves." He further explains his possible choice: "If I want to pursue a stable life, I would possibly stay in the States; but if I want to break through my ceiling, to pursue an unlimited life of wherever we want to go, or to realize, even surpass our dream, I would choose to go back to China." They all choose to leave—whether it is to be with or look for their love—and carry on their duty to their families. Near the end of the drama, Ning Ming wears a nice suit, comes out from a fancy car, and walks into his nice mansion, just like the nice houses in the United States. Similarly, the drama ends with Xiao Qing and Shu Che reuniting in a beautiful forest in China. These overseas Chinese students give compelling answers to the central question *Hu bu gui* ("Why don't I return?") in the TV series by returning to their motherland. The show portrays a blissful picture of the two couples' lives in China in the end—almost of the same quality, if not more, than in the United States.

However, the map that leads to their return home for these diasporic subjects is another layer that we must see as covering over, contrasting, and contradicting the map of earlier overseas Chinese students in the 1960s and 1970s. Nationalists, who are often called *waishengren*,[30] describe mainland China as *dalu* (大陆, "mainland") and as their motherland.[31] Their goal is to redeem the mainland and "extinguish the all-evil Communist bandits and rescue mainland fellows from the same womb."[32] Therefore, in David Der-wei Wang's words, in the 1950s and 1960s, mainland China became the imagined "native soil on paper" (*zhishang xiangtu* 紙上鄉土).[33] This supports the China-oriented discourse created by the nationalist government, and its obsession with an imaginary homeland. Most of the *waishengren* later came to the United States and were referred to as overseas Chinese students (*liuxuesheng* 留學生)—with *liu* meaning "remaining." They did not choose to go to Taiwan but came with their family for political and cultural reasons they had no control over. They still have a strong obsession with their imaginary homeland, the nationalist regime of mainland China. Therefore, overseas Chinese student writers during that time, including Pai Hsien-yung (1937–), Nieh Hualing (1925–), and Yu Lihua (1931–2020), show the rootless state of overseas students, as well as their longing for a glorious past of China, in their works.

Interestingly, the new immigrant stories after the 2010s portray a similar trace of a China-oriented discourse in their own ways, echoing the "rejuvenation of the nation" raised by President Xi. However, compared with the ones in the 1960s and 1970s, whose sense of national obsession came from their own personal backgrounds, the nostalgia for the past glorious China is from the official discourse. Therefore, an interesting tension between the government and the personal, between the official and individual discourse, exists in these narratives. In *TWWW*, the return to China and promises of justice and economic success paint a rosy picture of the Chinese dream. In the end, however, the pictures show that these recent overseas Chinese students return not to search for roots like earlier ones did. Rather, their return is for personal, affectionate relationships and goals. Even if America is not the endpoint, their journeys navigating the different layers of the palimpsestic map in America have changed them, allowing them to seek individual self-identity that is not bound by the collective. Figure 4.6 shows Miao Ying and Ning Ming's nice house in China. In the final scene, the viewer is led inside the house from the front overview of the house. The camera then zooms into a table, showing a picture of the couple together next to a Chinese flute (*tao di*), symbolizing their love. Figure 4.7 depicts a scene from the very end of the show, when Shu Che finally returns to China and joins Xiao Qing's law firm. They walk between beautiful lines of trees together. The camera focuses on the couple reuniting, smiling to each other. It then zooms out to show them walking away from the camera, painting a typical "happily ever after" picture, as in many movies. This makes a strong contrast to Yu Lihua's famous character Mou Tianlei, who typifies the "rootless generation," walking along lines of palm trees alone, lonely and lost.[34]

Compared with *Beijinger*, in which the characters' ultimate destination is the United States, this show complicates the overseas Chinese students' map by featuring the transition between homeland and new land. The journey begins with students graduating and leaving school (some leaving their country), to the

FIGURE 4.6 A zoom-in shot of Ning Ming and Miao Ying's picture and her flute he cherishes in their beautiful house in China. Source: *Gui qu lai* 歸去來, *The Way We Were*, directed by Liu Jiang (劉江), aired on May 14, 2018, episode 50, accessed February 22, 2023, DVD.

FIGURE 4.7 Shu Che unexpectedly returns to China and reunites with Xiao Qing; they are walking in between the trees, suggesting a happy reunion at the end of the TV series. Source: *Gui qu lai* 歸去來, *The Way We Were*, directed by Liu Jiang (劉江), aired on May 14, 2018, episode 50, accessed February 22, 2023, DVD.

airplane flight to the United States, to their study in the States, to their journey back home (to China). The show does not just anchor in one locale. It rather traces the trajectory/journey of multiple locales, ending in their return to their homeland. Along with this newly established geographical map, the show has also drawn an ideological map that presents the incredible individual wealth and personal success in China, which is now as achievable as in the United States. While the image of the Chinese dream follows the promises of the American dream, including personal freedom and justice, *TWWW* shows the promises of a new China. In this sense, America is more of a comparison point. Both the geographical and ideological maps seem to advocate the Chinese dream. Yet *TWWW* presents the aspirations and desires for individual dreams to be fulfilled, particularly love and reunion with one's family.

Furthermore, this newer TV series reinscribes the traces of the earlier overseas Chinese students by portraying their sense of alienation and displacement, all while erasing the national and collectivist traces. Instead, it paints a new map that poses the question of whether one will stay or return, the reasoning for returning, and questions of the American dream and the new Chinese dream. On one hand, it shows the collective ideal spaces of a new China, but on the other hand, it shows that individual dreams draw the trajectory of the new immigrants. This show charts a new map in which we can see traces of the maps of earlier immigrants and overseas Chinese students. With newer immigrants, we are presented with a more complex, refreshed map that demonstrates the tension between collective ideal of the Chinese dream and individual pursuits.

In sum, *Beijinger in New York* creates a palimpsestic map that writes over the traces of the American dream, and *The Way We Were* adds a new layer that extends the notion of the Chinese dream. This chapter reveals a new map for the diasporic subject, one where a return to home is not a paradox but seems to be a real possibility. At the same time, it shows that the journey itself, and the maps one creates along the way, transform that home, so that when one returns, one does not enter the past, but forges a new identity. In other words, it shows that even if a diasporic individual returns to the home(land) physically, they must use the same strategies we have seen throughout the book to create a home that feels like a home that is not bounded by the government or local and traditional customs—not a physical home but one in the imagination.

Coda

●●●●●●●●●●●●●●●●●●●●●●

Charting an Online Chinese
Diasporic Literary Map

The Chinese diasporic narratives discussed in this book suggest that the concepts of nation, family, or even acts of love are all contested sites to the Chinese diaspora. This monograph examines an atlas of "home" that these storytellers create through literature, whether it is national or familial, affective or creative. For example, chapter 1 on Ha Jin has shown that geographical locales and physical maps cannot fully explain this concept, as the characters in his stories strive to locate their own personal sense of belonging. These immigrant writers rely on their literary efforts to create this sense. All the literature and TV series discussed in this book attempt to cross borders—physically, emotionally, and creatively.

Previous chapters have outlined "home" as a spatial construction of the diasporic subject's social relationships with nation, family, and self. Closer attention must be paid to the material forms, sites, and tactics authors use when forming a "home." The process of world building requires making, unmaking, or remaking Chinese and American sites and works. Storytelling is their medium to navigate various sites and spaces, whether they are physical, ideological, or emotional. The trope of "home" is more than a sense of belonging that these authors portray in their diasporic characters; it is a trope that focuses the reader on the way that the characters navigate their world, offering strategies to manage their diasporic experiences. We have explored how "home" is represented at various sites and spaces in these Chinese diasporic narratives—including national, familial, affective, and personal ones. Rather than physical sites, we have seen how the characters in their stories map "home" as cultural, ideological, and emotional.

In this coda I look at a new but particularly powerful form of literary mapping: internet-based writing.[1] I contend that the internet is a new material form of transpacific cartography in both response to and reaction against global capitalism. On the one hand, these writings present global capitalism as an inherent part of the mapping practice that connects various transpacific spatial and temporal sites; on the other hand, they portray the problematics of global capitalism and advocate for universal humanitarian values and love. Terence Chong asserts in *Worlding Multiculturalism* that "the Worlding of multiculturalism is an innovative process that sees the utilization of cultural capital towards the everyday objective of rootedness, belonging, and solidarity."[2] In the following pages, I examine how these online Sinophone writings have become "modes of world-making that ultimately make people (us) worldless," allowing people in diaspora to transcend the boundaries that restrict them—whether they be political, culturally, or personally.[3]

Previous scholars have pointed out the power of cyberspace in engendering a home in diasporic communities. For instance, Loong Wong posits that cyberspace allows diasporic communities to create a home that is "experienced, recreated and experienced, enabling a sense of continuity, familiarity, communality and community."[4] The internet does so, he argues, by both transcending the sentiments of isolation and displacement and forming connections culturally and politically. Wong contends that the relationships formed online are "simultaneously local and global." Similarly, the volume *Global/Local: Cultural Production and the Transnational Imaginary* (1996), edited by Rob Wilson and Wimal Dissanayake, presents contemporary cultural productions that map a "new world space" that is more "globalized and localized" than before.[5]

It is worth mentioning, however, that the contemporary internet is significantly different from a couple decades ago, when it was mainly used to connect strangers and create new imaginary personas. The transition from Web 1.0 to 2.0, as Jessa Lingel asserts in her case study of Craigslist, has "moved from an internet of messy serendipity to one of slick commercialism."[6] Today's Web 2.0, which took form in early 2000s, is characterized by interactive experiences and social networks. The everyday use of Facebook, Twitter, and Instagram has proven this. This widely connected network enables people from all over the world to connect. Today, my students are often impressively well-informed of the trendiest YouTube videos, anime, K-pop, and other forms of popular culture. They also tend to read literature and scholarly works online rather than acquiring physical books. Online immigrant writings, like other media productions, make up parts of the map of contemporary globalized cultural productions.

In some ways, because these contemporary authors grew up in a more globalized China and open economy, their experience in the United States is less exotic or shocking to them than it might have been to immigrants before them. One can argue that the turn we see in Chinese diasporic literature toward the individual is a natural result of this more globalized upbringing. But this observation leads us to some interesting questions: Given that diasporic writers' sense of home is already less nation-centered and more affect-driven during the course of their immigration, how do new forms of technology and digital writing further transform their sense of home? Do they enable them to further unveil their transpacific mapping of home? In looking to answer these questions, I offer some meditations on how these diasporic writers utilize the internet to form a new world map of cultural identity and immigrant route.

Chinese Diasporic Writers in Pandemic Times

The global crisis during which I wrote this book exacerbated even further the effects of these technologies. The COVID-19 pandemic has posed severe challenges to globalization—specifically, to the free flow of goods, capital, and people across borders—closing borders and pushing the world onto a virtual network. In addition, the China-U.S. trade war that preceded the pandemic created a great deal of tension between the two superpowers. Donald Trump's administration added fuel to this fire, hardening American biases against China by describing the coronavirus as the "Chinese virus" and, subsequently, the "China virus." These slurs inflamed stereotypes about China and Chinese and Asian people in general, leading to physical and verbal attacks against them all over the world. The Trump administration's relentless attacks against China even led to suspicion against digital apps and social media that Chinese people and others use to connect with friends and family. Attempts to ban TikTok and WeChat in the United States have made many Chinese in America worry they will not be able to connect with their families in China. And the current rise in anti-Asian hate crimes in the West has brought back some of the discrimination and mistreatment of Asian people that took place in the mid-nineteenth and twentieth centuries. This all has resulted in a unique challenge to the general trends of the past twenty to thirty years: just as borders and concepts of nationality were beginning to melt, the pandemic and rising isolationist tendencies among countries and governments around the world have seemingly shoved them into the freezer, hardening them once again.

The pandemic and the Sino-American tensions have put subjects of the Chinese diaspora in more of a limbo state than ever before. Because of this conflict, they are no longer free-spirited cosmopolitan subjects and worldly citizens who enjoy traveling back and forth with ease. Instead, they encounter difficulties navigating double identities and homes. Some who have considered America to be their home find themselves no longer welcome in China; they are even seen as traitors. Chinese American writer Sheng Lin, based in

Houston, graduated from the Department of Chinese in Hangzhou University and served as a journalist and editor in China. She has published several novels and collections of essays. Since the start of the pandemic, she has published her pandemic journal and others' works on her public WeChat channel. In April 2020, she published a story in the *Peng Pai News* about her journey back to the United States during the pandemic.[7] But it was her reference to America as her second "home" that offended some Chinese nationals, who attacked her by saying, "Don't ever come back, you Chinese diaspora [*huaqiao*]." She quickly discovered that some Chinese nationals expect her sole loyalty and deny her dual identity as a Chinese immigrant in America. Meanwhile, in the United States, she is mainly active in the Sinophone circles with other Chinese immigrants, but not known in the American literary circle. She represents the limited circle of Sinophone writers and the dilemmas they face in the United States. On the one hand, they are readily treated as traitors by overzealous Chinese patriots, and on the other hand, they are locked out of the mainstream American literary circle. Writers like Sheng Lin walk in the chasm between the two lands, struggling to define themselves in the widening gap between the two cultures.

Despite these widening gaps, these writers do enjoy the privilege of their special in-between position. They are overseeing, witnessing, and narrating two cultures from their unique perspectives. This is what Homi Bhabha describes as a "third space," which derives from being in a place that simultaneously is and is not one's home. Artists in this position can create works that highlight cultural hybridity, which "gives rise to something different, something new and unrecognizable, a new area of negotiation of meaning and representation."[8] Chen Ruilin, a pioneering critic in Chinese diasporic literature, summarizes two main contributions of these writers: writing about the cultural conflicts in their lives abroad, and writing about China from their unique diasporic perspective.[9] Both contributions are mainly attributed to their position as "participant observer" in both their homeland and new land.[10] Despite the unease and difficulties this in-between position can bring at times (as with the example of Sheng Lin), these authors take advantage of this situation to form a unique perspective in their writings.

Indeed, these Sinophone writers go beyond the "third space" and "in-between" position in Homi J. Bhabha's analysis, which is based on a binary between South Asian colonized and British colonizer. Comparatively, these writers and their works disrupt the binary, as they are not criticizing or overcoming any colonial relationship. Rather, they use their special position to inform readers from another shore. For instance, after mainland Chinese writer Fang Fang documented lockdown life in Wuhan in the early days of the coronavirus outbreak, many overseas Chinese writers followed her lead in documenting life in the pandemic all around the world, through online blogs, websites, news, public WeChat channels, and more. Early on in the pandemic, many in the public experienced high levels of stress, and some felt the need to record the unusual time. One Chinese writer, Shen Fuyu (申賦漁), who used to be a journalist in Paris, wrote *Fengcheng Bali* (封城巴黎, *Lockdown Paris*), which was first published in his own public WeChat account, and soon afterward forwarded to media outlets in China. Similarly, the Chinese writer in England Zhong Yilin (鐘宜霖) talked about the early pandemic life in London in her vlog, *Zhong Yilin Lundun bobao* (倫敦播報, *Zhong Yilin's London Talk Show*), which attracted a good deal of attention. In Italy, another area strongly impacted by the pandemic, immigrant journalist Wang Qinbo wrote a diary about life in those hectic times.[11] These Sinophone writers, though having a hard time returning to their homeland or being accepted in mainstream society, spoke out, and their stories reached the widespread Sinophone communities within and outside China.

As such, these writers are an example of connecting in a virtual world and creating new identity in times when meeting in person is impossible. To that end, Hongwei Bao argues that "writing is simultaneously a subjectivising and de-subjectivising process; the self is created at the same time it is broken down. . . . I become more-than-and-other-than-myself. In this process, bodies and affects have started to connect, entangle, and disentangle."[12] To creative writers like Bao and other artists, creative production energizes them and connects them to the world amid isolation, transcending the boundaries of the self in order to unite with others. Writing becomes a medium to "connect with and care for each other in words, on digital media, and through difficult times."[13] For academics, many open-access literary journals and blogs have provided a new platform for us in the current age to voice our opinions and connect with the intellectual community.

Some literary channels like Twitter journals emerged during the pandemic for writers to express, embrace, and create identities.[14] Yet, different writers had different experiences in those troubled times. On a panel with five Asian diasporic writers, some expressed that writing was a form of survival during the pandemic, and death makes them think about legacy, such as who and how they loved. Some, however, demonstrated frustration about how the pandemic blocked their writing and communication. Yet they all acknowledged a surge of flash fiction (fictional work of extreme brevity that still offers character and plot development) during the pandemic, as it gave them a sense of speed and urgency that allowed more possibilities for the present moment. One of the writers, Jireh Deng, said, "The reason why I think that Asian American writers (and writers of color in general) particularly thrive in the blend of genres like flash fiction is because we're living compressed histories."[15] I want to highlight the plurals he uses here, which symbolize the different histories Asian Americans are part of, including both Asian and American histories. And it is living in the midst of these histories that pushes them to find innovative ways to define themselves, therefore making them particularly good at genres like flash fiction. This quote reaffirms the "privileged and vulnerable" dynamics Asian American writers embody—that they could incorporate "wildly diverse histories, homelands and literary traditions" into their writings, yet struggle to find words and phrases that could express their identities.

As a subgroup of Asian American writers, online Chinese diasporic writers also lived in compressed histories and expressed themselves in compressed spaces during the pandemic. They embodied a position that gave them a voice but also made them a target in the face of intensified Sino-American tensions. To fully understand how the online Sinophone literary community in North America has developed, we will trace its history.

Historicizing the Online Sinophone Literary Community in North America

It is worth mentioning that the online Sinophone literary community in the United States is not only a pioneer but also plays a significant role in the online Sinophone literary community in the world.[16] However, there is no one confirmed date for the origin of this kind of literature. One of the first recorded internet journals on this topic is *Huaxia wenzhai* (華夏文摘, *China News Digest*) (http://www.cnd.org), founded on April 5, 1991, in the United States. Although it was not a purely literary journal at the time of its founding, it was the first platform for online Sinophone writers. Shao Jun (少君, Qian Jianjun) published his first novel, *Fendou yu pingdeng* (奮鬥與平等, *Struggles and Equality*), in this journal. Prior to that, Zhang Langlang's (張郎郎) *Buyuan zuo erhuangdi* (不願做兒皇帝, *Not Willing to Be Small Emperor*), published in the third issue of *Huaxia wenzhai*, was considered to be the first Chinese internet literary work. In 1994, Fang Zhouzi and others founded the first internet literary magazine, *Xin yusi* (新語絲, *New Threads*), a year after the first internet poetry magazine, *Gan lan shu* (橄欖樹), emerged. The earliest writers who founded or participated in publishing these internet magazines were overseas Chinese students at the time.

Ouyang Ting has divided the history of North American online Sinophone literature into three periods. Ouyang first identifies the years 1991 to 1993 as the origin of this movement. The second period, from 1994 to 1997, marks the unprecedented development of internet literature. This period saw the emergence of literary blogs, Chinese literary e-magazines, databases, internet literary awards, and more. Finally, from 1998 to the present, this type of online Sinophone literature has extended and returned back to mainland China, Taiwan, Hong Kong, and other Sinophone regions.[17] The twenty-first century is seen as the golden age of online Sinophone literature, as there has been an overall boom in new writers. Along with the new Chinese online literary community and websites in China, such as the well-known *Rongshuxia*[18] (榕樹下, *Under the Banyan Tree*), (founded in 1998), members of the North American Sinophone community started to immerse themselves in the online literary community within China, reconnecting with their homeland through writing. One of the earliest popular Sinophone internet novels was Cai Zhiheng's (蔡智恆) *Diyici de qinmi jiechu* (第一次的親密接觸, *The First Intimate Contact*), published in a serialized format in a forum in 1998. From then on, internet literature in mainland China, Hong Kong, and Taiwan has developed at an unprecedented pace. In the early 2000s, Sinophone internet literature began turning more commercialized. The Chinese internet writer Chen Cun (陳村) said in 2004 that "the best time of internet literature has already passed,"[19] indicating that commercialization lowered the quality of internet literature. The financial systematic support of Sinophone literature in China well exceeded the overseas market in the twenty-first century. In the 2010s, internet reading culture reached its peak, and it has since become a part of everyday life for mainland Chinese. Comparatively, internet reading and writing in the United States has remained within a small circle, unable to reach larger audiences at home and abroad.

Even though online Sinophone literature in North America has not thrived in a commercial and economic sense as it has in China, the Sinophone literary communities in America developed for themselves. One could say that these writers need writing and the writing community more than money; often, they write not for commercial value, but to make friends with those who share similar interests and also form a community through language and writing. One of the most impactful organizations is Haiwai Wenxuan (海外文軒) (http://www.overseaswindow.com), founded by a New Jersey–based Sinophone writer, Hai Yun, in 2009. Open to Sinophone communities around the world—including the United States, Canada, Europe, Africa, and mainland China—Haiwai Wenxuan allows writers to self-publish works across genres, including novels, poetry, essays, and travelogues. During the past decade, it gained over a thousand active writers and tens of thousands of readers. The Haiwai Wenxuan website was selected as the best Sinophone literary website in 2012. Most of these organizations, including Haiwai Wenxuan, are self-organized nonprofits that manage websites, publish magazines, and self-publish books.

Connections are one of the most important aspects of the internet writing for this community. Their readership circle is relatively small compared to Sinophone writers in Southeast Asia and China, be it in print or online. Some who have connected to the publication and literary network in China and Southeast Asia have a larger audience, like Chen Ruilin and Yan Geling. However, many have self-published their works in the United States, circulating within Sinophone communities within the country. I have participated in some social gatherings of the Chinese Writers' Association in Houston, where members gather to share their works with each other. Some writers gained notoriety after their online publications became more popular during the pandemic. As such, writing provides members of this community a great sense of connection and satisfaction.

Compared to traditional forms of writing, online Sinophone writings span multiple genres, but short forms are popular among them. In general, flash fiction, essays, and poetry have become more popular, as they are quicker to write and to read. One survey revealed that among the literary genres in the online Sinophone community, essays make up about 34 percent of the total publications, followed by poetry (17 percent), novellas (18 percent), and long novels (16 percent).[20] In many cases, the writers need to compose shorter works, as they mostly write part-time while working full-time elsewhere, mostly in STEM fields, or are homemakers. Either scenario would not give them enough time to dedicate themselves to full-time writing.

Some writers wrestle with themes found in overseas Chinese literature as well, such as "rootlessness." Shi Yu, one of the most well-known contemporary Sinophone writers, describes the ambiguous relationships immigrants have with two lands: "We are living, but spend time in another place; we are living, but forever faceless; we are living, hoping to live like humans; we are living, though saying we are in our own land, but who can claim as real locals?"[21] Literary works like this have echoed one constant theme in earlier immigrant literature: root seeking. Like the so-called root-seeking literature in the 1980s in China, new immigrant literature has followed this tradition by searching for immigrants' self-identities, as well as their cultural and literary connection with their homeland. However, unlike the desolate "rootlessness" portrayed in earlier overseas Chinese literature, as in Yu Lihua's works, these more contemporary immigrant literary works present a more forward-looking, optimistic view of this identity. Their view of their homeland is also nostalgic but not sad, profound but not inevitable. Rather than the sadness of departure and disconnection, new immigrants are more concerned with Chinese culture and the new changes China undergoes in the contemporary age. Their works can be said to contribute to the creation of a "new China" image in the global, transnational era.

(Un)Elitism

The ability to write and connect through the digital media network enabled writers to be privileged citizens during the pandemic, working and living from home while others faced homelessness, joblessness, or a lack of a stable internet connection. We could say that what these writers and scholars did during the pandemic was a new type of act by elites, to use the "intellectual reality" of their diasporic stories.[22] And it is their social status and educational background that allowed them to create during difficult times like this.

Educational privileges has been a common trait of overseas Chinese writers since the beginning of *liuxuesheng* literature in the 1960s and 1970s. The earlier overseas Chinese student writers were largely elites who were exiled from mainland China to Taiwan, such as Pai Hsien-yung and Nieh Hualing. Critics have called into doubt their self-representation as a "rootless" generation, since they themselves are cultural elites. Sheng-mei Ma argues that immigrant and minority writers have contradictory feelings; they are "nostalgic for China while eagerly Westernizing themselves, busily putting down roots on American soil yet apathetic to their own marginalized status."[23] He thus criticizes overseas student writers for being assimilationists and elitists.[24] Xiao-huang Yin, in his *Chinese American Literature since the 1850s* (2000), has also pointed out the elite status of the Chinese immigrant student writers whose writings have been largely shaped by academic settings.[25]

While it is true that education and literacy enables contemporary writers to form a culture and community online, their online writings also break down the preconceived class barriers in diasporic writings. Many of the writers we have discussed are not trained professionals. To many Sinophone writers in this book, literature is a luxury. Some have their own professions, such as in the medical or engineering fields, and only write on the side or for fun. Many of them write op-eds and blogs on the Chinese Writers' Association's website and other online media. While wanting to share their immigrant stories with readers back in their homeland and in the Sinophone community, they also want to create a literary community with other Sinophone writers. From their writing, they can further build connections with others, presenting and sharing the transpacific maps that they create in their fictions. According to a renowned Chinese immigrant web writer, Shao Jun, the major contemporary Chinese immigrant writers include the working class, housewives who have free time to write part-time (with most of their writings focusing on love and family), and the intellectual elites who write as a hobby.[26] These writers challenge the idea of homogeneous class makeup and demonstrate new communities for Sinophone writings. Blogs and online journals have captured immigrant stories and current events, engaged the public outside elite writing communities, shone light on the immigrant lives in the United States, and inspired community building. Contributors to these media form a global network of literary production and sense of community, whether they live in Southeast Asia, Europe, or North America. Technological tools allow this to happen. These writers create an online community that contrasts with the elite culture that dominated the previous Chinese diasporic literary scene.

Technology has helped this literary community in several ways. First, these web-based platforms allow writers to share their works more easily. Unlike in the traditional publishing industry, which is hierarchical and restrictive for writers, the internet allows many more to writers to publish freely. As Da Wei notes, "Each terminal of the internet is not only equal in technology, but also in spirits. There is no authority in the internet world, only communication and interaction of individuals regardless of their class and status."[27] Online works increase authors' visibility among their literary community, even if they are not widely shared beyond Sinophone and immigrant circles (except for some bilingual writers or works that are translated). The official website for the Chinese Writers Association of America features several individual writers and gives them opportunities to set up their own pages.[28] Although they may not have a literary background, these authors are still passionate about writing and literature. Most of them have published novels, poems, or essays online. This website presents a large pool of new immigrant literature by a variety of Chinese diasporic writers from different walks of life, bringing value to both the authors and readers. It gives authors an outlet for their literary works and personal interests that a traditional literary journal could not, and it gives readers the opportunity to read different perspectives and styles by a diverse group of emerging immigrant writers.

Second, writers and readers can interact in even more ways than before. Though online journals and blogs existed in the early 2000s, social media sites such as Facebook have gained large usership in the past two decades. With these kinds of platforms, there is a greater chance for connection within the community. For instance, earlier websites with writings from overseas Chinese, such as New World Poetry, collected poems in a traditional journal form in the 1990s.[29] The website is a great resource for scholars and writers who want to look for the poetry and criticism published by previous generations of overseas Chinese and scholars, but it does not have a venue to interact with the authors, comment on the poems, or provide feedback. It reads more like a traditional companion to the poetry collection than a true community. In contrast, today's online literary platforms provide enough spaces for readers and writers to interact. Often, the writers write and publish at the same time, and they replenish with new material after reading readers' responses. The website Overseas Window (*Haiwai wenxuan*),[30] which was founded two years after the founding of the organization Haiwai Wenxuan in 2009, provides a platform for thousands of users to read, comment, and share the newest literary works.

Meanwhile, in the academic world, open-access journals, which have become more popular in recent years, have made scholarly works more widely accessible to the public. MDPI, the largest open-access publisher in the world, started in 1996 as a chemical sample archive. The publishing institute was not founded until 2010, but its popularity has grown significantly over the past few years.[31] I myself published a couple of online articles during the pandemic,[32] which I believe are much more widely read than my other articles in traditional journals.

Third, open-access journals and largely accessible online communities shorten the distance between the so-called elite academics, writers, and the public. These online Sinophone journals, websites, and blogs in North America are more accessible. They do not have subscription fees, unlike many online literary websites from mainland China, which require membership fees or subscription points. Even though the free, democratic online platforms in the West create a space of freedom, some scholars, like Ouyang Ting, critique how they ignore the commercial aspect of literature. She argues that Sinophone literature websites in North America are unable to form their own market, and writers often limit themselves to their own circle, perpetually staying within the margins. In addition, she points out the "unprofessional" nature of the North American Sinophone literary community in the sense that it does not offer any motivation for writers to connect with the wider literary market or improve their writing abilities, affecting the quality of their works.

It is true that online platforms enable more writers and readers of more middle-class backgrounds to participate. The diversity of the writers and the literature they create testifies to the democratic nature of this online form. Some of the popular websites that have longer histories and are regularly visited by overseas Chinese have drifted away from the traditional forms and contents of literature; instead, they focus on more popular subjects. Wenxuecity is a popular website that started in California in 1997. Today, we would find the translation of its name "literature [*wenxue*] city" ironic, as there is only a small section of overseas Chinese writings hidden under the forum section. Comparatively, other sections like news, education, finance, food, fashion, travel, and movies make up a majority of the content on the website. The media section, however, does introduce a variety of popular movies and TV shows currently broadcasted in China. Rather than relate information and knowledge about literature, this "literature city" website offers news and useful information on everyday life to diasporic Chinese. The site's "About Us" page proclaims its goal to "continue [its] focus on enhancing our Chinese online community and creating more products/venues to meet the changing needs of overseas Chinese."[33] This suggests that the site administrators are seeking to broaden the literary community beyond fiction and drama. With websites like this, real-life stories can be told and practical information can be offered to a wider public audience. These writings, more journalism than literature, could speak to a larger audience that is more interested in everyday life instead of fiction.

Moreover, the themes of the new Chinese immigrant literature are much more diverse and fragmented than in earlier diasporic Chinese literature. *Liuxuesheng* literature in the 1960s and 1970s is known to portray the "rootless" generation at their time. Besides writing about root seeking and nostalgia, they also address a broad range of topics—from the immigrant experience to Chinese stories to imaginary historical fiction. Comparatively, they are more interested in the trivialities and realities of immigrant lives, romance, politics, travels, and more. As previously discussed, the online journals and blogs cover an even wider range of topics. Even though there is a tendency to apply their own experience of immigration and cultural conflicts into their works, there is not necessarily a coherent theme in these writings. They strive to explore the fragments and divergence of diasporic life. Therefore, some scholars summarize their main characteristics as "hybridity" (*hunza*) and "diversity" (*duoyuan*).[34] Everyone has their own piece of map, but it is when we bring all the pieces together on the internet that we generate a sense of home. The digital community, though seemingly fragmented, helps connect the pieces of a more comprehensive map of the Chinese diaspora.

"Diversification" is definitely a key word to describe the contemporary Chinese immigrant literary scene. Websites, blogs, online journals, and other web-based channels enable diverse voices in the immigrant community to become writers. The web becomes a medium for decentering the elite culture found in earlier Sinophone immigrant writings. Meanwhile, the accessibility of these online writings helps immigrants form a widespread community based on their linguistic commonality. Their Sinophone writings also reconnect them with the literary world and community back in their homeland. Although their works are so far not widely accessible in the mainstream Western market, they bring new perspectives to the Chinese audience at home and abroad, challenging the notions of Chinese literature and Sinophone literature.

Technology and the internet do not automatically turn us all into global citizens, but they affect literary mapping to some extent. As discussed earlier, the literary mapping created by the digital community hardly breaks down the boundaries of the countryside and cities, as urban and rural places would have very different accessibility to technology. Yet technology does allow for maps to be drawn by common citizens rather than governments or intellectual elites, a democratization of the mapping process that allows readers to also be literary cartographers in a way that was not possible before the internet. The internet allows democratization of writing and publishing to happen, people have access to creating information in a way that they did not before, and part of that is to create literary map with online writing.

Shao Jun

I now turn to a discussion of one author who is a representative Chinese diasporic online writer and in fact a trailblazer for the online writing community, becoming a known and published writer. Shao Jun is one of the earliest and well-known online Sinophone writers. Shao Jun's original name is Qian Jianjun (錢建軍, with *jian* meaning "build" and *jun* meaning "military"); like his name indicates, he comes from a military family. He attended Beijing University, a top university in China, and majored in physics. He had always been passionate about writing since he was young and had a wide range of experiences, including as a student, worker, engineer, journalist, researcher, professor, manager, and CEO of a transnational company. He came to the United States in 1988 for his studies and started writing online in 1991. His novel *Fendou yu pingdeng* (*Struggles and Equality*, 1991) is said to be the first Sinophone internet novel.

Many critics have argued that his various experiences have shaped his writing, but Chen Ruilin believes Shao Jun's writing comes from a yearning for spiritual release. She quotes his words, "I cannot not write; writing relieves me from the suppression due to money games; writing makes me realize the life value in alienated life abroad."[35] Because Shao Jun sees writing as a relief from his business profession, "letting out frustration with words [*yi wen xie qi*],"[36] it makes sense that he cares little about submitting to major publications because of the tedious process and fierce competition. Writing for him is more about expressing his works and feelings. Therefore, he chooses online forums, magazines, and websites as his writing platforms.

Shao Jun's most well-known work is *Rensheng zibai* (人生自白, *Life Portrait*), which is made up of one hundred short stories. First serialized from January 1997 to February 1999 in *Dallas News* (a Chinese newspaper), these stories subsequently got republished in a few famous online newspapers like *Xin yusi*, *the World Daily*, *People's Daily*, and *Shijie huawen wenxue*. These stories reflect not only his colorful experiences from working in different professions but also his interests in human relationships and human spirituality. In this collection, Shao Jun presents and extends his concerns as a new immigrant writer. Rather than focus on immigrant experience, he shows deep concerns for universal human subjects like love, marriage, and growth. He also imagines many characters in the new China as it has changed after the Cold War, including an actor and director, boss, headmaster, teacher, singer, construction worker, journalist, lawyer, nanny, dancer, model, guide, and others. The portrayal of these characters and their complicated relationships demonstrate the problems of the new China in the 1990s when there was a moral decline with the craze of economic pursuits. Using an intimate tone and colloquial writing style, as well as the first-person narrative, Shao Jun shortens the distance between the narrators and the readers, relating to his audience the social, moral, and humanistic concerns he has had for Chinese society and Chinese people abroad.

Meng Xingyu has argued that Shao Jun has incorporated "individualism" and "religious humanism" of American culture in his writings. Meng claims that the individual characters Shao Jun establishes show clear individual, unique characteristics, reflecting the "individualism" that Shao Jun advocates. Some characters, though disobeying the moral standards in Chinese traditions, pursue their happiness at their own will. Rather than focus on the struggles between traditional family values and Western values, like many other diasporic writers, Shao Jun is more interested in intricate relationships of family and complicated emotions of individuals, which, to Meng, is insufficient in contemporary

Chinese literature. While Meng criticizes the narrative of eroticism in contemporary Chinese writings, claiming it is "writing with the lower body" (*xiabanshen xiezuo*), Meng argues that Shao Jun's writing distinguishes itself from this style and spotlights innocent and beautiful love due to his Christian beliefs. Although there may not be a direct connection between Shao Jun's religion and his writing about love, Meng's focus on individualism and human relationships are worthy of study.[37]

Web journals, online platforms, and literary associations create a space for Shao Jun to freely develop his literary identity beyond his multiple professions. According to him, the internet is a platform "without any restrictions from rules and control from editors,"[38] which motivates him to write without fear of rejection. Internet writing also enables a much larger audience of his works compared to traditional publications. His experience and writings also illustrate the boundary-crossing I have previously discussed: not only does he cross boundaries from a scientist to be a writer, but his works also constantly get published first online and then turn into traditional publications. Furthermore, his love for photography also influences his prose; his ability to describe scenes in his works is quite picturesque. In *Yinxiang Chengdu* (印象成都, *Impression of Chengdu*), he paints an attractive picture of Chengdu to outsiders from above.[39] To him, when he has reached financial goals, writing and publishing online in his mother tongue re-creates for him a virtual space of home, while sharing his unique perspectives and experiences with his fellow Chinese at home and abroad.

Unsettled Sites of Home

Previous chapters in this book show that contemporary Chinese immigrants' sense of home mostly generates not from physical sites and geographical locales but rather from affective and emotional relationships. But the sense of community and home is not completely placeless; rather, it is often place- and space-oriented, like the American residence in *Notes of a Couple*.

This book has examined how different Chinese diasporic storytellers and their characters navigated their experiences through mapping their sense of home. With technological advancements and pandemic lockdowns, we have moved away from physical spaces and turned to virtual communities. Literary WeChat groups, virtual book sharing and events, online conferences, and open-access blogs and journals all constitute new kinds of spaces—akin to the dance hall in *Beijinger in New York*—where community and home are formed. No matter what background they come from and what writings they produce, what is important is that they utilize the online social media platforms to create a community and an identity that they wish to envision.

Many scholars have considered migrant spaces in cities to be "liminal space[s]."[40] The word "liminality" has more complicated meanings than simply "marginalized." Originating from the Latin word *limen*, "a threshold," liminal refers to the middle stage of a rite of passage, as Arnold Van Gennep coined initially in his 1909 *Rites de Passage*. Van Gennep divides the process of shifting from one social status to another into three stages: disengagement, liminal stage, and reengagement. British anthropologist Victor Turner further developed the theory of liminality.[41] A liminal space has the potential to push against the static state and enable movements and fluidity by highlighting the state on the verge of the transformation of social status and cultural identity.

By reading these Chinese immigrants' online creative spaces as "liminal space" in this sense, we can see the nature of these spaces as moving, experimental nodes on the diasporic "map." These writings, from their outset, are at a transitional stage. Some of them are put online for their closest readers, those who share similar interests and talents, before their works become known and are included in more "official" publications. For instance, Shi Yu, one of the Sinophone writers I discussed in chapter 3, serialized her *Daofeng xia de mangdian* in *Xiaoshuo yuebao* (小說月報, *Short Story Magazine*) in 2006, which was subsequently published by Zhongguo Huaqiao Chubanshe in 2011. Or at times, they publish genres online other than what they normally publish in print. Su Wei, for instance, has posted a series of poems online,[42] while he publishes novels and essays in print. Regardless of the style, medium, or genre of the works, the experimental and fluid nature of these writings match their authors' identity in flux, and their state as a "liminal space."

The virtual space also serves as the passage across the threshold—the *imen*—in which transformations are generated. The shared identities of these writers as Chinese diasporic subjects connect them in this liminal space: those who have firsthand experience of their homeland and have the experience of uprooting from the old land and rerooting in the new land. To some extent, the threshold image has represented a visual transition from one land (homeland) to another (the new land). As the threshold suggests a point where something starts, the virtual space for Chinese immigrants implicates a point where they start building their networks through their own language and writings. Even more, they reach beyond their own homeland, to connect all the Sinophone communities around the world. These virtual communities, online blogs, and journals are a threshold because these immigrant writers are in a liminal state, "separated from [their] homeland culture and yet not incorporated into the host culture."[43] The website of the Chinese Writers Association of America summarizes the characteristics of Chinese diasporic writings as "filled with nostalgia for homeland, but show[ing] progressive courage."[44] This evaluation points out the mixed, transitional nature in Chinese immigrants' works: while they demonstrate a connection to homeland culture, they boldly move beyond Chinese culture and writing styles.

Despite Chinese diasporic subjects being in a liminal space, the internet enables us to connect with each other and generate a sense of home. Perhaps in the pandemic lockdown, the concept of diaspora no longer existed, or we could say that everyone was in a diaspora. During the pandemic, I met and mingled with many writers and colleagues online. Meetings with friends in China, scholars from Europe, and colleagues from the East and West Coasts have all become more common, sometimes on the same day. Sitting in a box of the gallery view of a Zoom or Teams meeting, I feel like I am riding with other participants in a railroad train car.[45] Like the naturalist John Muir said of the transcontinental railroad annihilating time and space, when you are sitting in a railroad car, you experience the world differently. Today, at a multitude of Zoom conferences, we forget when we are and where we are. We connect instantly and momentarily. The moment is captured in this little computer or phone screen as "home." One moment, we gather with people we care about and love; the next moment, we are teaching in an academic classroom, discussing and sharing academic ideas, or reading and sharing our works through online platforms. It is amazing that technology brings us together into a virtual room even though we are physically at different places. It condenses the meaning of space and time, but highlights the sense of "the moment."

We are finally home, whether it is a small apartment or a big house, an American home or Chinese home, our family's home or our vacation home; we are HOME, in front of the camera, in the numerous Skype and Zoom meetings. We are home, we are home, we are home. The lockdown and stay-at-home policies kept reminding us of that. Yet, the emotional and existential distress caused by the pandemic, racism, turbulent political climates, and environmental and climate change make us feel we are homesick and homeless while stuck at home. Meanwhile, we all know the sense of home that is created in these online platforms is fleeting, like the dance hall in *Beijinger in New York*. Eventually, we will need a physical base. It is a new form of nostalgia and distress caused by the societal changes during the pandemic.

Yet one cannot be too optimistic and idealistic about how social media and the online community help us create a virtual sense of home. I acknowledge that the ability to develop a sense of home online is as elitist as the online communities I criticized in the preceding pages. Our online accounts give us a space of life, an identity that we can envision without having to be it, a space that we could imagine without having to be in it. Yet online, people are vulnerable to the threats of scams, privacy invasions, and identity loss. And once an account is blocked, the space of life disappears immediately. For some, online platforms open up new work spaces, innovative teaching methods, and more. For others, this is only a forced way to mingle and create community when there is no other choice. It is only the "threshold" toward a newer, hopefully better, way to reconnect after the pandemic.

The virtual home we are embracing now, like the virtual community set up by these Chinese diasporic writers, is not always pleasant, but is often filled with contradictions and complexity. But no matter what, this new sense of home is a new form of the "reproduction of art,"[46] as Walter Benjamin describes it. As he proposes, the photographic reproduction of an artwork has more significant social value than the original, as often the reproductions of the original artwork, such as postcards and posters, are much more appreciated in specific situations. This goes in line with the example of the vessel in his "The Task of the Translator,"[47] which proposes that the original text and translations are like fragments of a vessel, not resembling each other, but to be glued together to form a greater language. If we read the technological home through Benjamin's notion of reproduction of art, the original notion of home is further challenged. The transpacific mappings in the multiple media this book discusses—from novels to TV series to internet writings and social media—have created new meanings of home that fit various situations of the Chinese diaspora, exceeding the possible values of the original. In fact, the original sense of home begins to lose it relevance; rather, it is the cartographies of home in these various diasporic narratives that make up the pieces of a richer map than one determined by political or physical boundaries alone. This map is not static, either, but is constantly evolving and renewed by the perpetual remapping through Chinese diasporic narratives that we call transpacific cartographies.

Acknowledgments

I owe a great deal of thanks to the institutes and mentors who have cultivated my academic interests and experience for many years, tirelessly providing support from afar. The University of Hong Kong, where I started my academic pursuits, is filled with talented professors whom I have gratitude and admiration for. Joseph Hon Kwong Poon is a great combination of a dear friend and a reliable and strict mentor. Isaac Yue generously took on the role of my main advisor when I was a master's student and has continued to give me advice in my academic career, including for this book.

Faculty and friends at Washington University in St. Louis welcomed me with open arms when I started my PhD and provided me with a sense of home. I am immensely grateful for the support and encouragement of my dissertation committee members, including Lingchei Letty Chen, Robert E. Hegel, J. Dillon Brown, Lynne Tatlock, and Zhao Ma. My primary advisor, Letty Chen, has been a great friend and mentor who has fostered a great family for us overseas students. Patiently and persistently, Robert Hegel has labored to add substance to the breadth of my knowledge and has been a source of inspiration and support over the past years. Lynne Tatlock, the director of the comparative literature program, has been a wonderful resource and always comes to my rescue without any hesitation. Besides my home department and advisory committee, the McDonnell Academy was a precious home to me at Washington University. I not only learned leadership and communication skills there but also had the best, memorable experience I could never find elsewhere—from the welcoming Thanksgiving family dinners with academy mentors and directors, including James Wertsch, Nancy Morrow-Howell, Stephen H. Legomsky, Henry Biggs, and Laura Benoist, to leadership trips with the chancellor to Washington, DC, and New York. Those experiences have helped shape my global visions and cultural awareness in my diasporic projects. At Wash U, I

136 • Acknowledgments

also had the great opportunity to work with the Writing Center, and Steve Pijut provided tremendous help and advice on improving my academic writing early on.

The Department of Comparative Literature at Harvard University also graciously hosted me as a visiting fellow from 2015 to 2016, where I received insightful thoughts and invaluable knowledge from Karen Thornber, David Der-wei Wang, and many other scholars. I especially benefited from Thornber's seminar on diaspora and Wang's seminar on Sinophone literature. I am indebted to the Harvard-Yenching Library for some of the newer Sinophone immigrant literature I discovered.

At conferences, talks, and academic programs, the sharp intellectualism of many scholars inspired me to keep working on new topics and reviewing my existing research: Sheng-mei Ma, Weijie Song, Christopher Lupke, E. K. Tan, Brian Bernards, Haun Saussy, Shu-mei Shih, Madeline Hsu, Tina Chen, Jiami Yan, Stephen Lee Field, Lai-kwan Pang, Liang Luo, Emily Wilcox, and Ping Qiu, among many others. I am also grateful to be part of the School of Criticism and Theory at Cornell University during my MPhil time and Timothy Murray's seminar as well as the American Studies tour led by Prof. Wing-kai To, which initiated my interests in pursuing academic studies in the United States.

My home department, Modern and Classical Languages, at the University of Houston has provided fertile soil for my scholarship. UH not only has been a supportive space for my intellectual growth but also has offered me productive environments, opportunities, and grants that have helped me develop my project, among which include the CLASS Research Grant, UH Small Grant, New Faculty Grant, faculty café, and UH Residential Life. Two successive department chairs, Hildegard F. Glass and Emran El-Badawi, have provided me with tremendous support. I am also grateful to other colleagues in the department for their friendship, encouragement, and generosity—particularly Duy Ngyuen and Julie Tolliver, who read early drafts of my manuscript and generously provided helpful comments. Conrad James, Richard Armstrong, Casey Due Hackeny, Alessandro Carrera, Francesca D'Alessandro Behr, Julia Kleinheider, Sharon Xiaohong Wen, Jing Zhang, and Marshall McArthur, among many, whose friendship and support motivate me. Some other colleagues at UH have also been great inspiration and academic models for me with their scholarship and contribution to UH and the community, including Yali Zou, Karen Fang, Xiaoping Cong, Jose Longoria, Guadalupe San Miguel, Theresa Chapman, Chatwara Duran, and Hosam Aboul-Ela. One person I would like to specially mention is the late Michael A. Olivas from the UH Law Center, who was the first reader of my book proposal and had given me confidence when I did not believe in myself. I think he would be happy knowing this book came to fruition.

I owe special thanks to some mentors I have had over the years outside of my institutes. I am especially grateful to Rob Sean Wilson, whose erudition, critical acumen, and sense of humor have played an important part in the formation of my intellectual makeup. A big name in literary geography, Robert Tally is a respected professor whose profound influence and compassionate toughness of mind led me to undertake this project on literary cartography in the first place. Andy Wang, whose scholarship on Asian Americans inspires me greatly, generously read and commented on earlier drafts of my chapters. Timothy August, a Vietnamese American specialist, provided me with insightful comments on the project.

The final production of this book demonstrates in many ways the good fortune of benefiting from the help of editors. My friend and editor Brad Allard tirelessly helps me with my projects and provides me with instant feedback and copy-edits. I am also obliged to Steve Pijut, Nick Geller, Colleen Berry, Kathleen Vacek, and Noah Weber for their editorial assistance.

Many thanks are due to the writing groups I have been part of, which make writing less lonely: my NCDFF writing group, including Albert Y. Kim, Kristin Kan, and Katherine Arlinghaus; my faculty café writing group organized by Leslie A. Coward and Jebreyah A. Chevis; and my Skype writing group during the pandemic, including Mary Manning, Caryn Tamber-Rosenau, Rose Barbara Lange, Willa Friedman, Lea C. Hellmueller, and Sandra Zalman.

Thanks also go to the Chinese diasporic writers community for sharing their works and inspiring my book project. Particularly, Ha Jin, one of the first writers I studied in my academic career, has kindly offered support and friendship over the past decade. His works are a major source of inspiration for this and many of my other projects. The Houston Chinese American Writers' Association has introduced me to numerous local and nonlocal contemporary Chinese diasporic writers. Its leader, Ruilin Chen, generously provided me with numerous materials that are hard to obtain. As a pioneer in the field of new immigrant literature, Chen has inspired many younger scholars like me to delve more into this area, of which this book is a product. Others associated with the group, like Wu Tong and Raymond Douglas Chong, have been sharing their interesting works and events with me. Furthermore, through Chen and this group I have gotten to know some of the writers and other Chinese diasporic writers' groups in other cities, including Chen Qian, Shi Yu, Rao Lei, and Su Wei. Jennifer Stephan Kapral from the Asia Society Texas Center has offered me opportunities to attend many inspiring community events.

I owe so much to the loving care of many friends who have had faith in me, even when I doubt myself, and have loved me despite all my mistakes and faults, including Ronnie Littlejohn, Fang-yu Li, Cynthia Ma, Kyle Miao Dou, Jerry Lin, Chris Born, Laura Wen, Shihui Dou, Gary Wang, Floyd Vaughn, Greg Stark, Anthony Tompras, Angela Zhang, Shuxiang Ruan, Ashley Zhang, Anjulena Renee, Sylvia He, Vicky Tang, Tanya Tan, Miriam Bautista, Tania Wu, and Victor Lim.

Many thanks to Rutgers University Press and its Asian American Studies Today series for providing a home for my monograph. I also want to give special thanks to the series editor, Huping Ling, for her trust in my project. The previous editor, Jasper Chang, has been trusting my work and was immensely encouraging from the start. The current editor, Carah Naseem, took over graciously and generously toward the end.

My husband, Luis Guerrero, who is a hardworking, smart handyman and a loving partner, has stayed by my side through ups and downs since I came to Houston. He has provided me with calmness and compassion while writing this book.

I am deeply indebted to my mother, Yuefen Li, whose loving care never fails me. My mother embodies for me endurance, persistence, and unconditional love that I always admire. I have learned a great deal from her. She has been a constant source of cheer and support through all the variables throughout my academic and immigrant journey. This book is dedicated to her, along with my grandparents, who I grew up with, with respect and affection.

Notes

Introduction

1 Ha Jin, *A Free Life* (New York: Pantheon Books, 2007), 649.

2 Ha Jin, *A Free Life*, 650.

3 Salman Rushdie, *Imaginary Homelands: Essays and Criticism, 1981–1991* (New York: Viking, 1991), 10–11.

4 I use "writer" broadly in this manuscript as a synonym of author, including those who write books or TV drama script/producer, and online literary content creators.

5 These terms have been popular among Chinese American studies in the past two decades. Numerous research on Chinese American literature and culture have focused on the "hybridity," "in-betweenness," and "Chineseness." I am only listing a few comparatively recent ones as examples here. Yuechan Wang, "An Experience of In-Betweenness: Translation as Border Writing in Gene Luen Yang's *American Born Chinese,*" *Neohelicon* 48 (2021): 161–178; Serena Fusco, *Incorporations of Chineseness: Hybridity, Bodies, and Chinese American Literature* (Newcastle upon Tyne: Cambridge Scholars Publishing, 2016).

6 Ian Johnson, "Biden's Grand China Strategy: Eloquent but Inadequate," Council on Foreign Relations, May 27, 2022, https://www.cfr.org/in-brief/biden-china-blinken-speech-policy-grand-strategy.

7 Sheng-mei Ma points to this as déjà vu, similar to what happened after Japan's attack on Pearl Harbor—all Japanese Americans, whether they were Japanese immigrants in the United States or Americans of Japanese descent, were interned. See Sheng-mei Ma, *The Tao of S: America's Chinee and the Chinese Century in Literature and Film* (Columbia and Taipei: University of South Carolina Press & the National Taiwan University Press, 2022), 26.

8 See Yao Li and Harvey L. Nicholson Jr., "When 'Model Minorities' Become 'Yellow Peril'—Othering and the Racialization of Asian Americans in the COVID-19 Pandemic," *Sociology Compass* 15, no. 2 (2021): e12849. Earlier, I pointed out that the "model minority" and "Yellow Peril" are both stereotypes employed in mainstream discourse. See Melody Yunzi Li, "'We Are Not a Virus': Challenging Asian/Asian

139

140 • Notes to Pages 4–7

American Racism in the 21st Century," *U.S. Studies Online* (blog), March 22, 2021, https://usso.uk/we-are-not-a-virus-challenging-asian-asian-american-racism-in-the-21st-century/.

9 I use "we" (first-person pronouns) here because as someone originally from China, I identify myself as a member of the Chinese diaspora who has been experiencing the same struggles.

10 Melody Yunzi Li, "Rebuilding Home around Hardened Borders," *British Journal of Chinese Studies* 10 (2020), https://bjocs.site/index.php/bjocs/article/view/77.

11 "Extraterritorial domination" is a political concept and is grounded in the ideology of loyalty. Ling-chi Wang, "The Structure of Dual Domination: Toward a Paradigm for the Study of the Chinese Diaspora in the United States," *Amerasia Journal* 33, no. 1 (2007): 144–166. This article first appeared in *Amerasia* in 1995.

12 One scholar who particularly contributes to the study of *liuxuesheng* in Asian American studies is Chih-ming Wang. See Chih-ming Wang, *Transpacific Articulations: Student Migration and the Remaking of Asia America* (Honolulu: University of Hawai'i Press, 2013).

13 Cynthia Wong notes the importance of Sinophone works in the formation of the Chinese American canon in the late 1990s. She writes, "As translation can play, has played, and will continue to play a decisive role in the formation of Chinese American canon, important Chinese language works will be noted as well." See Cynthia Wong, "Chinese American Literature," in *An Interethnic Companion to Asian American Literature*, ed. King-Kok Cheung (Cambridge: University of Cambridge Press, 1997), 41. Shan Te-hsing redefines "Chinese American literature," which he calls *Huawen Meiguo wenxue*. He emphasizes that it is not limited to any particular ethnic background, and it includes Chinese diasporic works written in Chinese. See Shan Te-hsing, "An Emerging Literature/Research: Taiwan's Asian American Literature and the Literature of Native American Residents" 冒現的文學/研究: 台灣的亞美文學研究—兼論美國原住民文學研究, *Chung-Wai Literary Monthly* 中外文學 29, no. 11 (2001): 19.

14 In an interview, Maxine Hong Kingston insisted that the hyphen in "Chinese-American" must be deleted because of the equivalence of each part of the phrase. Maxine Hong Kingston, "Cultural Mis-readings by American Reviewers," in *Asian and Western Writers in Dialogue*, ed. Guy Amirthanayagam (London: Palgrave Macmillan, 1982), 55–65.

15 This definition follows the one found in Wanhua Huang (黃萬華), "*20 Shiji Meihua wenxue de lishi lunkuo*" 20世纪美华文学的历史轮廓, *Huawen wenxue* 华文文学 (2000), 4. There are some alternative definitions of the term by other scholars. Similarly Xianmao Chen (陳賢茂) has specified "new immigrants" in Sinophone literary history as those coming from mainland China to the United States in the late 1970s and early 1980s. He has explained the different histories of Hong Kong, Macau, and Taiwan and why they are not included in his definition of the "new immigrant." See Xianmao Chen, *Haiwai huawen wenxueshi* 海外华文文学史 (Xiamen: Lujiang chubanshe, 1999). There is also a recent tendency to adopt a more inclusive definition by scholars such as Liqiu Ni, who does include immigrants from Taiwan, Hong Kong, and Macau in his use of "new immigrants"; see Liqiu Ni 倪立秋, *Xin yimin xiaoshuo yanjiu* 新移民小说研究 (Shanghai: Shanghai Jiaotong daxue chubanshe, 2009). Even though I am inclined to use a more inclusive definition, my goal here is not to argue for a definition but to prove how difficult it is to categorize these writers.

Notes to Pages 7–12 • 141

16 See Lei Zhang, "The Chinese Student Protection Act of 1992: Student Immigration and the Transpacific Neoliberal Model Minority," *Journal of Asian American Studies* 24, no. 3 (October 2021): 443–470.

17 For the detailed data, see Carlos Echeverria-Estrada and Jeanne Batalova, "Chinese Immigrants in the United States," Migration Policy Institute, January 15, 2020, https://www.migrationpolicy.org/article/chinese-immigrants-united-states; and "2017 Sees Increase in Number of Chinese Students Studying Abroad and Returning after Overseas Studies," Ministry of Education, People's Republic of China, April 3, 2018, http://en.moe.gov.cn/News/Top_News/201804/t20180404_332354.html.

18 For example, Yu Lihua's most famous novel, *Again the Palm Trees (Youjian zonglü, youjian zonglü* 又見棕櫚, 又見棕櫚, 1967), focuses on the sense of rootlessness people felt after leaving their homeland, mainland China, for Taiwan. Similarly, Pai Hsien-yung's short story collection *Taipei People (Taibei ren* 臺北人, 1971) describes those who went from mainland China to Taiwan and their nostalgia for their homeland.

19 Belinda Kong, *Tiananmen Fictions outside the Square: The Chinese Literary Diaspora and the Politics of Global Culture* (Philadelphia: Temple University Press, 2012), 2.

20 See Lei Zhang, "The Chinese Student Protection Act of 1992," 443.

21 This term was coined by Madeline Hsu in *The Good Immigrants: How the Yellow Peril Became the Model Minority* (Princeton, NJ: Princeton University Press, 2015).

22 Wang, *Transpacific Articulations*, 140.

23 The term *haiwai huawen wenxue* usually includes overseas Chinese-language literature (*haiwai huawen wenxue*) and overseas non–Chinese-language literature (*haiwai fei huawen wenxue,* 海外非華文文學). See Laifong Leung, "Overseas Chinese Literature: A Proposal for Clarification," in *Reading Chinese Transnationalisms: Society, Literature, Film,* ed. Maria N. Ng and Phillip Holden (Hong Kong: Hong Kong University Press), 117.

24 Sau-ling Cynthia Wong, "Global Vision and Locatedness: World Literature in Chinese/by Chinese from a Chinese-Americanist Perspective," in *Global Chinese Literature: Critical Essays*, ed. Jing Tsu and David Der-wei Wang (Leiden: Brill, 2010), 68.

25 Wong, "Global Vision and Locatedness," 68.

26 Wong, "Global Vision and Locatedness," 68.

27 This push-and-pull dynamic follows the idea of "routed identity" by diaspora theorists like Avtar Brah and James Clifford.

28 In her study of the memories that diasporic subjects carry in Sinophone fiction, Chen argues that "'diaspora' never ends even when 'Sinophone' begins." See Lingchei Letty Chen, "When Does 'Diaspora' End and 'Sinophone' Begin?," *Postcolonial Studies* 18, no.1 (2015): 53–54.

29 See William Safran, "Diasporas in Modern Societies: Myths of Homeland and Return," *Diaspora* 1, no. 1 (1991): 83–84.

30 As John McLeod observes, "Conventional ideas of 'home' and 'belonging' depend upon clearly defined, static notions of being 'in place,' firmly rooted in a community or particular geographical location. But these models or 'narratives' of belonging no longer seem suited to a world where the experience and legacy of migration are altering the ways in which individuals think of their relation to place." John McLeod, *Beginning Postcolonialism* (Manchester: Manchester University Press, 2000), 214.

142 • Notes to Pages 12–17

31 Stuart Hall, "Cultural Identity and Diaspora," in *Identity: Community, Culture, Difference*, ed. Jonathan Rutherford (London: Lawrence & Wishart, 1990), 222.

32 In the context of the trans-Atlantic Black slave trade, Paul Gilroy points out the problems of previous diasporic studies: "Modern black political culture has always been more interested in the relationship of identity to roots and rootedness than in seeing identity as a process of movement and mediation that is more appropriately approached via the homonym routes." Paul Gilroy, *The Black Atlantic: Modernity and Double Consciousness* (Cambridge, MA: Harvard University Press, 1993), 19.

33 They celebrate both the hybridity and multiplicity of diaspora as a means of understanding the globalized world, and they consider diaspora to be a process. See Avtar Brah, *Cartographies of Diaspora: Contesting Identities* (New York: Routledge, 1996); and James Clifford, *Routes: Travel and Translation in the Late Twentieth Century* (Cambridge, MA: Harvard University Press, 1997).

34 I have brought up this point in my case study of Ha Jin's *A Free Life*. See Melody Yunzi Li, "Home and Identity En Route in Chinese Diaspora—Reading Ha Jin's *A Free Life*," *Pacific Coast Philology* 49, no. 2 (2014): 203–220.

35 Wendy W. Walters, *At Home in Diaspora: Black International Writing* (Minneapolis: University of Minnesota Press, 2005), xvi.

36 Helena Grice, "Homes and Homecomings," in *Negotiating Identities: An Introduction to Asian American Women's Writing* (Manchester: Manchester University Press, 2002), 31.

37 Rey Chow, *Writing Diaspora: Tactics of Intervention in Contemporary Cultural Studies* (Bloomington: Indiana University Press, 1993), 142.

38 Alison Blunt and Robyn Dowling, *Home* (New York: Routledge, 2006), 199.

39 Xuechao Chen, "Ta xiang, gu xiang, jia yuan" (他鄉, 故鄉, 家園), in *Honeymoon Paris* 蜜月"巴黎: 走在地球經緯線上 (Tianjin: Baihua wenyi chubanshe, 2003), 1–3.

40 See Bai Juyi, "Chu chucheng liubie" 初出城留別 [Parting with Friends outside the City], in *Bai Juyi ji* 白居易集 vol. 1 (Beijing: Zhonghua shuju, 1999), 149.

41 Sam Hamill, "Translator's Introduction," in *The Narrow Road to the Interior and Other Writings*, by Matsuo Bashō (Boston: Shambhala, 2000), xx.

42 See Tally's detailed description of literary cartography. See Robert T. Tally, "On Literary Cartography: Narrative as a Spatially Symbolic Act," *New American Notes Online*, no. 1 (January 2021), https://nanocrit.com/issues/issue1/literary-cartography-narrative-spatially-symbolic-act.

43 Martin Heidegger, *Being and Time*, trans. John Macquarrie and Edward Robinson (New York: Harper & Row, 1962), 233.

44 Robert T. Tally, "On Literary Cartography: Narrative as a Spatially Symbolic Act."

45 Frederic Jameson, *Postmodernism, or, The Cultural Logic of Late Capitalism* (Durham, NC: Duke University Press, 1991), 51–53.).

46 Robert T. Tally, *Spatiality* (London: Routledge, 2013), 47.

47 Peter Turchi, *Maps of the Imagination: The Writer as Cartographer* (San Antonio, TX: Trinity University Press, 2004), 11.

48 Turchi, *Maps of the Imagination*, 113.

49 Karen Kelsky, *Women on the Verge: Japanese Women, Western Dreams* (Durham, NC: Duke University Press, 2001).

50 Tina Chen, "Global Asias: On the Structural Incoherence of Imaginable Ageography," *Asian American Literature in Transition*, vol. 4, edited by Victor Román Mendoza and Betsy Huang, 318 (Cambridge: Cambridge University Press, 2021).

51 Flair Donglai Shi, "Reconsidering Sinophone Studies: The Chinese Cold War, Multiple Sinocentrisms, and Theoretical Generalisation," *International Journal of Taiwan Studies* 4, no. 2 (2021): 324.

52 Chih-ming Wang, "The Sinophone (and) 1949: The Chinese Dream Rearticulated 華語語系 (與) 一九四九: 重新表述中國夢," *Sun Yat-Sen Journal of Humanities* 中山人文學報 42 (2017): 23.

53 Chien-hsin Tsai, "At the Crossroads: *Orphan of Asia*, Postloyalism, and Sinophone Studies," *Sun Yat-Sen Journal of Humanities* 35 (2013): 39.

54 Shu-mei Shih, *Visuality and Identity: Sinophone Articulations across the Pacific* (Berkeley: University of California Press, 2007), 4. "Sinophone" has been used in various contexts before. For instance, Ruth Keen defines "Sinophone communities" as "the Mainland, Taiwan, Hong Kong, Singapore, Indonesia and the US"; see Ruth Keen, "Information Is All That Counts: An Introduction to Chinese Women's Writing in German Translation," *Modern Chinese Literature* 4, no. 2 (1988): 225–234. Geremie Barmé describes the "Sinophone world" as "one consisting of the individuals and communities who use one or another—or, indeed, a number—of China-originated languages and dialects to make meaning of and for the world, be it through speaking, reading, writing or via an engagement with various electronic media." See Geremie Barmé, "On New Sinology," *Chinese Studies Association of Australia Newsletter*, no. 31 (May 2005): 5–9, http://rspas.anu.edu.au/pah/chinaheritageproject/newsinology/.

55 Shi, "Reconsidering Sinophone Studies," 330.

56 Rob Wilson, *Reimagining the American Pacific: From South Pacific to Bamboo Ridge and Beyond* (Durham, NC: Duke University Press, 2000), 15–16.

57 Mary Louise Pratt introduced the concept of "contact zone" in a 1991 keynote address to the Modern Language Association. She defines it as "social spaces where cultures meet, clash and grapple with each other, often in contexts of highly asymmetrical relations of power, such as colonialism, slavery, or their aftermaths as they are lived out in many parts of the world today." See Mary Louise Pratt, "Arts of the Contact Zone," *Profession* (1991): 33–40.

58 Lisa Lowe, "The Trans-Pacific Migrant and Area Studies," in *The Trans-Pacific Imagination: Rethinking Boundary, Culture and Society*, ed. Naoki Sakai and Hyon Joo Yoo (Singapore: World Scientific, 2012), 71.

59 Scholars who have contributed to the development of the idea of the transpacific include Yunte Huang, Jonathan Stalling, Naoki Sakai, Janet Hoskins, Viet Nguyen, Steven Yao, Erin Suzuki, Chih-ming Wang, and Lily Wong, among others.

60 Yunte Huang, *Transpacific Displacement Ethnography, Translation, and Intertextual Travel in Twentieth-Century American Literature* (Berkeley: University of California Press, 2002), 3.

61 Yunte Huang, *Transpacific Imaginations: History, Literature, Counterpoetics* (Cambridge, MA: Harvard University Press, 2008), 2.

62 Wendy Cheng, "Transpacific Articulations: Student Migration and the Remaking of Asian America by Chih-Ming Wang (Review)," *Journal of Asian American Studies* 17, no. 3 (2014), 382.

63 D. Nonini defines Pacific Rim discourse as a "trope for a set of economic political, and cultural processes creating relationships within a supraregion of Asia and the United States that have been under way since approximately the mid-1970s." See D. Nonini, "Ethnographic Grounding of the Asia-Pacific Imaginary," in *What Is*

144 • Notes to Pages 20–27

in a Rim? Critical Perspectives on the Pacific Region Idea, ed. A. Dirlik (Boulder, CO: Westview Press, 1993), 73–96.

64 Huang, *Transpacific Imaginations*, 2.

65 Huang, *Transpacific Imaginations*, 10.

66 Tina Y. Chen, "Emergent Cartographies and the Directions of Asian American Literary Studies," *American Literary History* 23, no. 4 (2011): 892.

Chapter 1 Mapping Experiences of De/Reterritorialization

1 Some of the discussion in this section has previously appeared in Melody Yunzi Li, "Home and Identity En Route in Chinese Diaspora—Reading Ha Jin's *A Free Life*," *Pacific Coast Philology* 49, no. 2 (October 1, 2014): 203–220.

2 See Lo Kwai-Cheung, "The Myth of 'Chinese' Literature: Ha Jin and the Globalization of 'National' Literary Writing," *Xiandai zhongwen wenxue xuebao* 現代中文文學學報 6, no. 2 (2005): 63–78.

3 Ha Jin, *The Writer as Migrant* (Chicago: University of Chicago Press, 2008), 21.

4 Ha Jin signed five book contracts with a Shanghai publisher to publish four volumes of his fiction and a collection of poems in 2005. Unfortunately, two of them, *The Crazed* and *War Trash*, were rejected because of their "sensitive subjects": the Tiananmen massacre and the Korean War. Later, *Under the Red Flag* was also banned by the Shanghai Censorship Office. For a detailed discussion about the censorship of Ha Jin's works, see Ha Jin, "The Censor in the Mirror: It's Not Only What the Chinese Propaganda Department Does to Artists, but What It Makes Artists Do to Their Own Work," *American Scholar* 77, no. 4 (2008): 26–32; and Eric Eckholm, "After an Attack, Chinese Won't Print Expatriate's Novel," *New York Times*, June 24, 2000, https://www.nytimes.com/2000/06/24/books/after-an-attack-chinese-won-t-print-expatriate-s-novel.html.

5 From my email exchanges with Ha Jin in 2010.

6 Gilles Deleuze, Félix Guattari, and Robert Brinkley, "What Is a Minor Literature?," *Mississippi Review* 11, no. 3 (1983): 16.

7 Ha Jin, *Between Silences: A Voice from China* (Chicago: University of Chicago Press, 1990), 2.

8 "Loyal Roads to Betrayal: An Interview with Ha Jin," Asian American Writers' Workshop, June 1, 2015, https://aaww.org/loyal-roads-to-betrayal-ha-jin/.

9 Deleuze, Guattari, and Brinkley, "What Is a Minor Literature?," 18.

10 "Self-Orientalism" means a play of the "other" by non-Westerners. It is often a derogatory term referring to someone using the Western portrayal of the East to gain popularity or recognition.

11 In the preface to his first collection of poems, *Between Silences*, Ha Jin writes: "As a fortunate one I speak for those unfortunate people who suffered, endured or perished at the bottom of life and who created the history and at the same time were fooled or ruined by it." Ha Jin, *Between Silences*, 1.

12 Ha Jin, *Writer as Migrant*, 3.

13 See Eckholm, "After an Attack." According to this report in the *New York Times*, Liu claims that Ha Jin's depiction of an extremely rustic peasant wife with bound feet is an anachronism intended "to emphasize the backwardness of China." The resistance of fellow villagers to Kong Ling's request for a divorce, she says, is meant to show that the Chinese do not appreciate love. Liu says the book's cover features a male pigtail, a symbol of the feudal era, and that all the critics and newspapers

who propelled *Waiting* to win big prizes did so not because of its supposedly elegant writing but because it meets their goal of portraying the Chinese as ignorant and repressed.

14 Sheng-mei Ma, *East-West Montage: Reflections on Asian Bodies in Diaspora* (Honolulu: University of Hawai'i Press, 2007), 91.

15 My discussion of this in my article "Home and Identity En Route in Chinese Diaspora" takes into consideration Ha Jin's background as a northeasterner, yet the peripheral state of Dongbei in China is not well established.

16 Ng Franklin, *The Asian American Encyclopedia* (Singapore: Marshall Cavendish, 1995), 223.

17 Some prominent ones include Qiu Xiaolong and Li Yiyun. More could be added to this list.

18 Earlier key anthologies in the field, like King-Kok Cheung's *An Interethnic Companion to Asian American Literature* (1997) and Xiao-huang Yin's *Chinese American Literature since the 1850s* (2000), do not include Ha Jin. Yet, some later references identify him as a Chinese American writer. For instance, Seiwoong Oh's *Encyclopedia of Asian-American Literature* (2007) includes a long section on Ha Jin. In 2013 he was introduced as a guest speaker at the University of Delaware as one of "the foremost and most respected Chinese-American writers of fiction, poetry and essays." See University of Delaware, "March 7, 8: Ha Jin," *UDaily*, February 26, 2013, http://www1.udel.edu/udaily/2013/feb/visiting-writers-ha-jin-022613.html.

19 This term is inspired by Salman Rushdie's construction of "imaginary homelands."

20 This analogy was pointed out in conversation with Noah Weber.

21 Ha Jin writes in his essay, "People often asked me, 'Why burn your bridges' or 'Why mess with success?' I would reply, 'My heart is no longer there.' In retrospect, I can see that my decision to leave contemporary China in my writing is a way to negate the role of the spokesmanship I used to envision for myself." See Ha Jin, *Writer as Migrant*, 28.

22 Ma, *East-West Montage*, 91.

23 Shuang Shen, "Time, Place, and Books in Ha Jin's *Waiting* 哈金作品中的時間、地點與書本," *Journal of Modern Literature in Chinese*, no. 6.2 and 7.1 (2005): 57. Her focus is more on the books in *Waiting* instead of places, but her suggested concept of "internal diaspora" (following James Clifford's description of diaspora's psychology of 'living here and remembering/desiring another place') to describe the temporal and spatial construction of the novel is useful and relevant to my study.

24 José Ramón Ibáñez Ibáñez, "Writing Short Fiction from Exile: An Interview with Ha Jin," *Odisea No. 15: Revista de Estudios Ingleses* (2014): 73–87.

25 For the local–global conjunctions and disruptions in cultural production during the late twentieth-century global capitalism in the Asia-Pacific regime, see Rob Wilson and Wimal Dissanayake, eds., *Global/Local: Cultural Production and the Transnational Imaginary* (Durham, NC: Duke University Press, 1996), which maps "a new world space" that is simultaneously more globalized and localized than before.

26 Kevin Nance, "Ha Jin on '*A Map of Betrayal*,'" *Chicago Tribune*. November 13, 2014, https://www.chicagotribune.com/entertainment/books/ct-prj-map-of-betrayal-ha-jin-20141113-story.html.

27 From the protagonist Nan's poem "A Contract" in Ha Jin, *A Free Life* (New York: Pantheon Books, 2007), 634.

28 James R. Akerman, "The Structuring of Political Territory in Early Printed Atlases," *Imago Mundi* 47, no. 1 (1995): 152.

146 • Notes to Pages 31–35

29 Anssi Paasi, "Territory," in *A Companion to Political Geography*, ed. John Agnew, Katharyne Mitchell, and Gerard Toal, 109–122 (Oxford: Blackwell Publishing, 2003), 112.

30 Edward W. Soja, *Postmodern Geographies: The Reassertion of Space in Critical Social Theory* (London: Verso, 1989), 150.

31 J. R. V. Prescott, "Electoral Studies in Political Geography," in *The Structure of Political Geography*, ed. Roger E. Kasperson and Julian V. Minghi, 376–383 (Chicago: Aldine Press, 1969); R. J. Johnston, *Geography and the State: An Essay in Political Geography* (New York: St. Martin's Press, 1982).

32 Stuart Elden, "Missing the Point: Globalization, Deterritorialization and the Space of the World," *Transactions of the Institute of British Geographers* 30, no. 1 (2005): 8–19.

33 They first used these terms to register the interplay of social forces in *Anti-Oedipus* (1972). Gilles Deleuze, *Anti-Oedipus: Capitalism and Schizophrenia* (Minneapolis: University of Minnesota Press, 1983).

34 Tom Conley, "Space," in *The Deleuze Dictionary*, ed. A. Parr (Edinburgh: Edinburgh University Press, 2010), 262.

35 Conley, "Space," 261.

36 Ha Jin, *A Free Life*, 660.

37 Virinder Kalra, Raminder Kaur, and John Hutnyk, *Diaspora and Hybridity* (Thousand Oaks, CA: SAGE Publications, 2005), 32.

38 Kalra, Kaur, and Hutnyk, *Diaspora and Hybridity*, 135.

39 Quoted in Steph Cha, "Ha Jin Roves U.S. and China, Charting 'A Map of Betrayal,'" *Orlando Sentinel*, accessed October 31, 2022, https://www.orlandosentinel.com /entertainment/la-ca-jc-ha-jin-20141109-story.html.

40 Sarah Fay, "Interviews: Ha Jin, The Art of Fiction," *Paris Review*, no. 191 (Winter 2009), https://www.theparisreview.org/interviews/5991/the-art-of-fiction-no-202 -ha-jin.

41 Fay, "Interviews."

42 In July 2020 the U.S. government abruptly ordered the closure of the Chinese consulate in Houston, accusing diplomats of aiding economic espionage. See Edward Wong, Lara Lakes, and Steven Lee Myers, "U.S. Orders China to Close Houston Consulate, Citing Efforts to Steal Trade Secrets," *New York Times*, July 22, 2020, https://www.nytimes.com/2020/07/22/world/asia/us-china-houston-consulate .html.

43 Chung-jen Chen, "A Portal to Transnational Communication: Problematizing Identity Politics in Ha Jin's *A Map of Betrayal*," *Textual Practice* 34, no. 10 (2020): 1671–1689.

44 For instance, Monica Chiu's analysis in *Scrutinized! Surveillance in Asian North American Literature* (2014) examines the literary responses to the surveillance of raced subjects, including internment, espionage, and post-9/11 surveillance.

45 Tina Chen defines "double agents" as those "who work both to establish their own claims to a U.S. American identity and to critique the American institutions that have designated them as 'aliens.'" Tina Chen, *Double Agency: Acts of Impersonation in Asian American Literature and Culture* (Stanford, CA: Stanford University Press, 2005), xix.

46 Ha Jin, *Map of Betrayal*, 260.

47 Fay, "Interviews."

48 Nicole Schroder, *Spaces and Places in Motion: Spatial Concepts in Contemporary American Literature* (Tubingen: Gunter Narr Velag, 2006), 11.

Notes to Pages 37–45 • 147

49 Interestingly, it seems that Ha Jin projects his own autobiographical experiences of confusing and shifting patriotism. In an interview with Sarah Fay in the *Paris Review*, he discusses his prior misconception of patriotism as a youth, admitting, "I couldn't imagine the world beyond the borders of China. . . . Like most young Chinese, I became very patriotic and believed in the righteousness of the revolution and the party." Fay, "Interviews."

50 Ha Jin, *Map of Betrayal*, 135.

51 Sara Ahmed, *Cultural Politics of Emotion* (New York: Routledge, 2004), 130.

52 Ha Jin, *Map of Betrayal*, 188.

53 This metaphor comes from George Orwell's 1936 essay "Shooting an Elephant."

54 Ha Jin, *Map of Betrayal*, 197.

55 Ha Jin, *Map of Betrayal*, 155.

56 Ha Jin, *Map of Betrayal*, 223.

57 Ha Jin, *Map of Betrayal*, 25.

58 Ha Jin, *Map of Betrayal*, 211.

59 Ha Jin, *Map of Betrayal*, 104.

60 When she runs into a man she is attracted to, Uncle Weifu, she moves away to avoid him, for example.

61 Ha Jin, *Map of Betrayal*, 25.

62 Ha Jin, *Map of Betrayal*, 61.

63 Ha Jin, *Map of Betrayal*, 211.

64 Ha Jin, *Map of Betrayal*, 211.

65 Ha Jin, *Map of Betrayal*, 211.

66 Ha Jin, *Map of Betrayal*, 139.

67 Ha Jin, *Map of Betrayal*, 140.

68 One typical example is Yu Dafu's "Sinking" (1921), where Yu describes a sexually repressed Chinese man's desires for women.

69 Ha Jin, *Map of Betrayal*, 91.

70 Ha Jin, *Map of Betrayal*, 134.

71 Ha Jin, *Map of Betrayal*, 134.

72 Ha Jin, *Map of Betrayal*, 177.

73 Chingyen Mayer, "Review of *A Map of Betrayal*, by Ha Jin," *Asiatic* 8, no. 2 (December 2014).

74 King-Kok Cheung, "Fate or State: The Double Life of a Composite Chinese Spy in *A Map of Betrayal*," in *Asia and the Historical Imagination*, ed. Jane Yeang Chui Wong (Singapore: Springer, 2018), 80.

75 Ha Jin, *Map of Betrayal*, 103.

76 Ha Jin, *Map of Betrayal*, 264.

77 Robert T. Tally, *Topophrenia: Place, Narrative, and the Spatial Imagination* (Bloomington: Indiana University Press, 2019), 55.

78 Ha Jin, *Map of Betrayal*, 151.

79 Ha Jin, *Map of Betrayal*, 273.

80 Ha Jin, *Map of Betrayal*, 279.

81 Ha Jin, *Map of Betrayal*, 129.

82 Ha Jin, *Map of Betrayal*, 132.

83 Ha Jin, *Map of Betrayal*, 159.

84 Virginia Woolf, "Literary Geography," in *Books and Portraits: Some Further Selections from the Literary and Biographical Writings of Virginia Woolf*, ed. Mary Lyon (New York: Harcourt, Brace, Jovanovich, 1977), 161.

Notes to Pages 46–50

Chapter 2   Cartographing Carceral Dystopia in the Mao Era

1   Zhang Xiaogang, *Bloodline: Big Family*, 1993, Opera Gallery DIFC, http://
hauteliving.com/2011/05/opera-gallery-difc-presents-lithographs-by-five
-contemporary-chinese-artists/153337/.

2   In Mao Zedong's "Talks at the Yenan Forum on Art and Literature," he states
the purpose of their meeting is "to make art and literature a component part of the
whole revolutionary machine." See Mao Tse-tung, *Talks at the Yenan Forum on
Art and Literature* (Peking: Foreign Languages Press, 1960), 2. In films set during
the Cultural Revolution, we often see portraits of Mao hanging in people's houses.
For instance, Jiang Wen's *In the Heat of the Sun* (1994) includes scenes of boys
gathering at a long table, with Chairman Mao's picture hanging on the wall in the
background. Similarly, in *Mao's Last Dancer* (2009), people dance while Mao's
portrait hangs in the middle of the room.

3   Zhang Fan, et al., *Lian'ai hunyin yu fufu shenghuo* 戀愛婚姻與夫婦生活 [*Love,
Marriage and Life as a Couple*] (Shanghai: Zhanwang zhoukan she, 1952), II.

4   Jianmei Liu, *Revolution Plus Love: Literary History, Women's Bodies, and Thematic
Repetition in Twentieth-Century Chinese Fiction* (Honolulu: University of Hawai'i
Press, 2003), 256.

5   Liu, *Revolution Plus Love*, 23.

6   According to Chen Sihe, "after the 90s, the representative of overseas themes is no
one but Yan Geling. Her series of works achieve great success in overseas Chinese
literary circles." Chen Sihe, *Zhongguo dangdai wenxue shi jiaocheng* (Shanghai:
Fudan daxue chubanshe, 1999), 351. Liu Denghan also points out the significance
of female writers in American Sinophone literary circle, and Yan Geling is the most
representative one. Liu Denghan, *Shuangchong jingyan de kuayu shuxie: 20 century
huamei wenxue shi lun* (Shanghai: Shanghai sanlian shudian, 2007), 221. Li Bin
considers the "writings of the Chinese immigrants in the U.S. by Yan Geling and
others show that overseas Chinese literature and Sinophone literature are of the
newest and also the utmost achievement." Li Bin 李檳, "'Ziyou Shen' Yu
'Manhadun'—Ba, jiushi niandai liuxuesheng wenxue chutan" '自由身'與'曼哈頓'—
八, 九十年代留學生文學初探, *Shijie huawen wenxue luntan* 世界華文文學論壇
[*Forum for Chinese Literature of the World*] (2002): 24–27.

7   Yan Geling, *Fusang* 扶桑 [*The Lost Daughter of Happiness*] (Beijing: Renmin
wenxue chubanshe, 2015), v.

8   Yan Geling, *Fusang*, v.

9   In the preface of *Fusang*, she argues that we should fairly look at immigrant
literature. Offering the examples of Milan Kundera and Isabel Allende, she claims
that their immigrant stories take their work beyond their own national boundaries. Yan Geling, *Fusang*, iii.

10   Many have written on Yan Geling's writings from gender perspectives, such as Meng
Xia, "Gender Myth and Disciplined Sexuality in Geling Yan's White Snake," *Journal
of Language, Literature and Culture* 67, nos. 2–3 (2020): 172–189; and Sally E.
McWilliams, "From a Distance of One Hundred and Twenty Years: Theorizing
Diasporic Chinese Female Subjectivities in Geling Yan's 'The Lost Daughter of
Happiness,'" *Meridians* 6, no. 1 (2005): 133–160. Some have focused on the historical
readings of her novels, such as Graham J. Matthews, "Chinese Historical Fiction
in the Wake of Postmodernism: Two Versions of Yan Geling's *The Flowers of War*,"
Modern Fiction Studies 62, no. 4 (2016): 659–677.

Notes to Pages 50–53 • 149

11　Shenshen Cai, "Scar Literature Reconsidered: Yan Geling's Novels *The Criminal Lu Yanshi* and *A Woman's Epic*." 327; and Shenshen Cai, "Zhang Yimou's Coming Home: A Depoliticized Melodrama Adapted from a Scar Literature Novel." *New Review of Film and Television Studies* 13, no. 3 (2015): 275–291.

12　Park argues that the protagonist Lu Yanshi is a survivor and witness of the Cultural Revolution and that the novel rejects oblivion of tragic events in China's modern history. The novel covers many important themes like discrimination of love, confession of life, and the pursuit of freedom. But at the same time, Park also points out the deficiency of the book: Yan does not reveal directly how to heal the pain or who is responsible for the lost lives, and how the perpetrators and victims reconciliate each other. He also says the novel does not mention conflicts between Han and minority ethnic groups in China. Namyong Park, "Narrative of Memory and Historical Trauma in Yan Geling's *Lu Fan Yanshi*" 옌거링(嚴歌苓)의 『죄수 루옌스(陸犯焉識)』에 나타난역사적 트라우마와 기억의, 세계문학비교연구 (CSWL) 제54집 no. 54 (2016): 107–133.

13　Pin-chia Feng, "Remapping Chinese American Literature: The Case of Yan Geling," in *Diasporic Representations: Reading Chinese American Women's Fiction* (Berlin: LIT Verlag Münster, 2010), 152.

14　Schwarcz borrows this concept from Leon and Rebecca Grinberg's analysis of exiles.

15　Quoted in Feng, "Remapping Chinese American Literature," 163.

16　Yan Geling 嚴歌苓, "Qing Ningmengse de niao" 青檸檬色的鳥 [Bird of Lime Color], https://www.kanunu8.com/files/chinese/201103/1974/45877.html.

17　Her novel *Youth* (*Fanghua* 芳華, 2017) is inspired by her experience as a dancer in the People's Liberation Army and narrates the story about the singing and dancing troupe in the 1970s.

18　Mary Lynn Babcock and Lynnette Young Overby, "Human Kind in the Apex of Borders: Artistic and Expressive Communication in Projected Images, Dance, and Narrative," in *Global Movements: Dance, Place, and Hybridity*, ed. Olaf Kuhke and Adam Pine (Lanham, MD: Lexington Books, 2015), 103.

19　John Pickles, *A History of Spaces: Cartographic Reason, Mapping and the Geo-Coded World* (London: Routledge, 2004), 12.

20　Wen Jin, "Transnational Criticism and Asian Immigrant Literature in the U.S.: Reading Yan Geling's *Fusang* and Its English Translation," *Contemporary Literature* 47, no. 4 (2006): 571.

21　David Der-wei Wang, "Cong 'luo ming' dao ziyou ren—Yan Geling de *Lufan Yanshi*" 從「裸命」到自由人—嚴歌苓的《陸犯焉識》 (From a "Naked Life" to a Freeman: Yan Geling's *The Criminal Lu Yanshi*) (Taipei: Maitian chubanshe, 2014), 3–17.

22　Lu Xinhua published his first story, "The Scar" (aka "The Wounded"), in *Wenhui Daily*, August 11, 1978, when he was a freshman at Fudan University in Shanghai. This story depicts a female Red Guard, Wang Xiaohua, who is cut off from her mother after the latter is denounced as "traitor." When her mother is proven innocent nine years later, Wang returns home only to find her mother dead with a scar on her forehead. This story became instantly famous, and has come to be thought of as a pure representation of scar literature.

23　Yibing Huang has elaborated on this topic. Particularly, Huang points out through the discussion of Li Jiangyun's stories that scar literature is overly simplistic, and may have covered up many more complex and perhaps darker human truths and unnamed historical traumas. See his *Contemporary Chinese*

150 • Notes to Pages 53-62

Literature: From the Cultural Revolution to the Future (New York: Palgrave Macmillan, 2007), 90.

24 Lingchei Letty Chen summarizes this in her study of memoirs of the Cultural Revolution. See Lingchei Letty Chen, "Translating Memory, Transforming Identity: Chinese Expatriates and Memoirs of the Cultural Revolution," *Tamkang Review* 38, no. 2 (June 2008): 25.

25 Michel Foucault, *Discipline and Punish: The Birth of the Prison* (New York: Pantheon Books, 1977), 293.

26 Ling Yuan, "Renjian diyu: Zhongguo wu da laogai ying" 人間地獄: 中國五大勞改營, Aboluowang 阿波羅新聞網, February 1, 2015, https://www.aboluowang.com/2015/0201/508429.html.

27 Yan Geling, *The Criminal Lu Yanshi (Lufan Yanshi* 陸犯焉識) (Taipei: Maitian chubanshe, 2014), 29.

28 Yan Geling, *Criminal Lu Yanshi*, 36.

29 Yan Geling, *Criminal Lu Yanshi*, 64.

30 Yan Geling, *Criminal Lu Yanshi*, 65.

31 Yan Geling, *Criminal Lu Yanshi*, 65.

32 Yan Geling, *Criminal Lu Yanshi*, 62.

33 Yan Geling, *Criminal Lu Yanshi*, 89.

34 Yan Geling, *Criminal Lu Yanshi*, 198.

35 Yan Geling, *Criminal Lu Yanshi*, 218.

36 Yan Geling, *Criminal Lu Yanshi*, 82–83.

37 Yan Geling, *Criminal Lu Yanshi*, 334.

38 Foucault, *Discipline and Punish*, 298.

39 Foucault, *Discipline and Punish*, 138.

40 Yan Geling, *Criminal Lu Yanshi*, 228.

41 Yan Geling, *Criminal Lu Yanshi*.

42 Yan Geling, *Criminal Lu Yanshi*, 123.

43 Yan Geling, *Criminal Lu Yanshi*, 123.

44 Under the Mao regime everyone must show loyalty to the state. If any member of the family commits an offense against the state, it's one's duty and legal obligation to expose that member to the government. See C. K. Yang, *The Chinese Family in the Communist Revolution* (Cambridge, MA: Harvard University Press, 1959), 174–175.

45 Yan Geling, *Criminal Lu Yanshi*, 285.

46 Yan Geling, *Criminal Lu Yanshi*, 402.

47 Yan Geling, *Criminal Lu Yanshi*, 27.

48 Yan Geling, *Criminal Lu Yanshi*, 301.

49 Yan Geling, *Criminal Lu Yanshi*, 305.

50 Yan Geling, *Criminal Lu Yanshi*, 305.

51 David Der-wei Wang, preface to *Criminal Lu Yanshi*.

52 Yan Geling, *Criminal Lu Yanshi*, 380.

53 David Der-wei Wang points out that the labor camp movement disobeys laws in the name of law. For further reference, see Ramin Pejan, "Laogai: 'Reform through Labor' in China," *Human Rights Brief: A Legal Resource for the International Rights Community* 7, no. 2 (2000 Winter): 23–27.

54 Yan Geling, *Criminal Lu Yanshi*, 270.

55 Yan Geling, *Criminal Lu Yanshi*, 98–99.

56 Yan Geling, *Criminal Lu Yanshi*, 445.

Notes to Pages 65–68 • 151

Chapter 3 Affective Mapping of Touristic Diasporic Experience

1 These writers are considered to be "new immigrants" (新移民), which largely refers to emigrants from mainland China after the Reform and Opening Up Policy began in 1978. But debates are still going on regarding the definition of this term.

2 Many of them first submitted their stories to magazines in China and then submitted them to Chinese journals overseas. For instance, Chen Qian first submitted to the magazine *Zhong shan* (鍾山) in China, and then subsequently submitted to *Guo feng* (國風). See http://www.chinawriter.com.cn/n1/2017/0517/c405057-29281756 .html.

3 Gilles Deleuze theorizes this as "reterritorialization," a notion on which I elaborated in my chapter on Ha Jin. Gilles Deleuze, *A Thousand Plateaus: Capitalism and Schizophrenia* (Minneapolis: University of Minnesota Press, 1987).

4 For detailed discussions of popular fiction, see Ken Gelder, *Popular Fiction: The Logics and Practices of a Literary Field* (Milton Park: Routledge, 2004). He proposes popular fiction "as a singular and definitive category, preferring this term to the more porous and generally open-to-definition notion of a bestseller" (3).

5 Zhang Zhen has offered a detailed discussion on the commercialization of literature in the post-Mao era on mainland China. See Zhang Zhen, "Commercialization of Literature in the Post-Mao Era: Yu Hua, Beauty Writers, and Youth Writers," in *The Columbia Companion to Modern Chinese Literature*, ed. Kirk A. Denton (New York: Columbia University Press, 2016), 386–393.

6 As chapter 2 has shown, Yan Geling avails herself of commercial tactics in her narratives and marketing. Her works are often adapted into TV series or movies, which makes her a successful popular writer. Her novel *The Lost Daughter of Happiness* (*Fusang* 扶桑,1996) successfully brings the "Yellow Peril" stories back to the Sinophone regions—Taiwan, Hong Kong, and China—at the time when such stories were popular in the United States.

7 Ken Gelder points out that the field of popular fiction is a "culture industry," which "was invested with negative connotations back in the 1940s by two influential, highbrow cultural critics, Theodor W. Adorno and Max Horkheimer." Cited in Gelder, *Popular Fiction*, 1.

8 Whether the act of drawing these tourist maps to Sinophone readers back home is Occidentalist is debatable. Still, it is quite clear that their privileged background and mobility are critical causes of these maps. Chen Xiaomei's concept of Occidentalism goes beyond Edward Said's notion of it by studying how Chinese writers "antiimperialistically" used the Occidental other to achieve their political aims back home. Though these Sinophone writers bring the stories of American life back home, they don't necessarily misinterpret the Occident. See Xiaomei Chen, *Occidentalism: A Theory of Counter-Discourse in Post-Mao China*, 2nd ed. (Lanham, MD: Rowman & Littlefield, 2003).

9 Elisa Giaccardi and Daniela Fogli define "affective geographies" as "the digital representation of space and place that is enabled by cartographic semantics capable to elicit and visualize affective meaning in collaborative web maps." Elisa Giaccardi and Daniela Fogli, "Affective Geographies: Toward a Richer Cartographic Semantics for the Geospatial Web," paper presented at the working conference on Advanced Visual Interfaces, Napoli, Italy, 2008.

10 I am indebted to Rob Tally's notion of literary cartography. One of the leading figures in geocriticism and spatial literary theories, he coined this notion in *Melville,*

152 • Notes to Pages 68–71

Mapping and Globalization: Literary Cartography in the American Baroque Writer (London: Bloomsbury Publishing, 2011), and later developed this idea in other books. See Robert T. Tally, *Literary Cartographies: Spatiality, Representation, and Narrative* (New York: Palgrave Macmillan, 2014).

11 I am indebted to Weijie Song's *Mapping Modern Beijing: Space, Emotion, Literary Topography* (Oxford: Oxford University Press, 2017) for the notion of "affective mapping," which he uses to explore how literary representations capture and shape urban transformations and social constructions in the worlds of emotional life. He used the term vaguely with "mapping" and "affective" as two critical approaches in his book.

12 For more elaborations on this, please see the introduction of this volume.

13 More examples are shown in the introduction.

14 Svetlana Boym, "Nostalgia and Its Discontents," *Hedgehog Review* 9, no. 2 (Summer 2007): 18.

15 For instance, Julia O'Connell Davidson, in her book on the global sex trade, calls attention to local place narratives so we do not "overlook the realities of many people's lived experience." She argues for more complicated stories to be told so as to portray a broader picture, including of those who are able to protect themselves and those who are subject to abuse and exploitation. Julia O'Connell Davidson, *Children in the Global Sex Trade* (Cambridge: Polity, 2005). 3.

16 Anthony Carrigan, *Postcolonial Tourism: Literature, Culture, and Environment* (New York: Routledge, 2011).

17 Anne-Marie d'Hauteserre, "Postcolonialism, Colonialism and Tourism," in *A Companion to Tourism*, ed. Alan A. Lew, C. Michael Hall, and Allan M. Williams (Malden, MA: Blackwell Publishing, 2004), 238.

18 Shi Yu graduated from Fujian Medical University in 1988 before moving to the United States in 1989. After earning a medical degree there, she worked at Dartmouth Medical School, the Southwest Medical Center in Texas College, and a New York downtown hospital for eleven years. This ambition follows the famous modern Chinese writer Lu Xun. Shi Yu, "'Haigui nü zuojia' de shiyi shenghuo yü chuangzuo xinzhi," 海歸女作家的詩意生活與創作新買 [The Poetic Life of the Woman Writer Returning from Overseas and the Novelty of Her Writings], interview by Wang Hongqi, China Female Culture Forum, accessed December 15, 2019, http://www.china.com.cn/opinion/female/index_3.htm

19 This is a very similar line of thinking to Lu Xun in his famous preface to *Call to Arms*, 吶喊, in which he writes of abandoning medicine for the arts (*wenyi*, 文藝) in order to save peoples' spirits (*jingshen* 精神).

20 Shi Yu 施雨, *Niuyue qingren* (紐約情人, *New York Lover*) (Tianjin: Baihua wenyi chubanshe, 2007), 276. All translations cited are my own.

21 Her other works include the collections of essays *American Son Chinese Mother* (*Meiguo erzi zhongguo niang* 美國兒子中國娘, 2003) and *Growing up in the U.S.* (*Meiguo de yizhong chengzhang* 美國的一種成長, 2003), and a collection of poetry, *Sleepless Shore* (*Wumian de an* 無眠的岸, 2004).

22 For her biographical information, see her speech at Emory University: https://www.youtube.com/watch?v=0-quDkUQdmY.

23 Online writers have become a popular phenomenon in China in the twenty-first century. The "Chinese online writer rich list," first released in 2012, keeps track of changes in Chinese writers' wealth and the reading trends in Chinese society. This shows that readership in China has been drawn to more popularized forms of writing.

Notes to Pages 71–76 • 153

24 This was aired on Shanghai People's Radio Station.

25 *Fan Zhi* won the 2012 People's Literature Prize; *Wang duan nan fei yan* won the 2009 People's Literature Award; *Theresa's Hooligan* won the first Yu Dafu novel award.

26 For a full list of her works, see http://www.overseaswindow.com/home/writer/149.

27 Some scholars divide Chinese emigrants from China to the United States, especially *liuxuesheng*, into three generations: the first group between 1978 and 1989, the second group from 1989 to 2001, and a third generation of students who came afterward. For this generational divide, see Amy Pei-ting Lum, "Liu Xuesheng: An Ethnography of the Socialization of Chinese Students Attending College in the United States," BA thesis, Wesleyan University, 2010, http://citeseerx.ist.psu.edu/viewdoc/download?doi=10.1.1.851.1547&rep=rep1&type=pdf.

28 Zhen Zhang, "The World Map of Haunting Dreams: Reading Post-1989 Chinese Women's Diaspora Writings," in *Spaces of Their Own: Women's Public Sphere in Transnational China*, ed. Mayfair Mei-hui Yang (Minneapolis: University of Minnesota Press, 1999), 317.

29 Shi Yu says, "No matter how far I am from home, my root is grounded in Fu Zhou," accessed 2021, https://www.sohu.com/a/125739162_349441.

30 Yanyan Wang, "Yi tuo bang, yi sheng shuxie, wenhua xieshang 異托邦·醫生書寫·文化協商[Heterotopia,·Doctor's Writing, Cultural Negotiation]," *Masterpieces Review*, no. 8 (2021): 38–41.

31 Han-ping Chen, "Kuayu de qingsu yu fuza de rentong—dui Shi Yu liangbu changpian de bijiao yuedu 跨域的情愫与复杂的认同—— 对施雨两部长篇的比较阅读," [A Comparative Study of Shi Yu's Two Novels], *Hainan shifan daxue xuebao: shehui kexueban* 海南师范大学学报: 社会科学版 25, no. 4 (2012): 111–115.

32 Both her *Branches* and *Listen to the Caged Bird Sing* were awarded an important literary prize in China—the Ren Min Literary Prize. Her other novel, *Teresa's Hooligan* (特蕾莎的流氓犯, *Teleisha de liumangfan*, 2008) was awarded the Yudafu Novel Prize.

33 Xiaoya Xu, "Personal Elegy under the Ruins of Soul—On Chen Qian's Novels about Trauma," *Xiaoshuo pinglun* 小說評論, no. 3 (2022): 196–202.

34 Liwang Wu 吳禮旺, "Nüxing geti qinggan zhigui yu shengming suqiu de biaoda 女性個體情感旨歸與生命訴求的表達—— 評陳謙《望斷南飞雁》" [Narratives of Female Individual Emotions and Life Pursuits—Discussion of Chen Qian's *Wang duan nan fei yan*], *Wenxuejie: xia xun*文學界: 下旬, no. 6 (2010): 10–11.

35 Ge Hu 胡格, "Liusan shijiao xia jiedu Chen Qian *Wang duan nan fei yan* zhong de Nanyan xingxiang 流散視角下解讀陳謙《望斷南飛雁》中的南雁形象" [Reading the Image of Nanyan in *Wang duan nan fei yan* from Diaspora Perspective], *Overseas English*, no. 3 (2020): 172–173.

36 All the quotes from the novels discussed in this chapter were translated by me.

37 Wendy Click, "Zoujin beimei yeshengquan de Shanghai nüzi—fang lümei zhuming nüzuojia Rongrong 走進北美野生圈的上海女子— 訪旅美著名女作家融融," *Chuguo* 出國 [*Going Abroad*], no. 4 (2012).

38 There are many more contemporary overseas Chinese student writers writing on the themes of love, affect, emotions, and migration in North America; for example, Zha Jianying (查建英), Zhang Ci (張慈), Yan Geling (嚴歌苓), Li Yan (李彥), and Zhang Ling (張翎).

39 Rong Rong. *Fuqi biji* 夫妻筆記 [Notes of a Couple] (Beijing: Shi jie zhishi chubanshe, 2005), 2.

154 • Notes to Pages 76–81

40 Boym, "Nostalgia and Its Discontents," 18.
41 For more on tourist experience, see Richard Sharpley and Philip R. Stone, *Tourist Experience Contemporary Perspectives* (London: Routledge, 2010). The book indicates that tourist experience is individual-based and defined by social fabrics surrounding them.
42 Shi Yu 施雨, *Niuyue qingren* 紐約情人 [*New York Lover*] (Tian Jin: Bai hua wen yi chubanshe, 2004), 1.
43 Shi Yu, *Niuyue qingren*, 29.
44 Shi Yu, *Niuyue qingren*, 30.
45 Shi Yu, *Niuyue qingren*, 30.
46 Shi Yu, *Niuyue qingren*, 70.
47 Shi Yu, *Niuyue qingren*, 98.
48 Shi Yu, *Niuyue qingren*, 188.
49 Shi Yu, *Niuyue qingren*, 95.
50 Shi Yu, *Niuyue qingren*, 145.
51 Shi Yu, *Niuyue qingren*, 233.
52 Shi Yu, *Niuyue qingren*, 19.
53 Shi Yu, *Niuyue qingren*, 95.
54 Psychologists point out the commonality between lovesickness and homesickness: "(1) strong affective reactions arise when the individual is separated from the place or person; (2) the home cq. person is not replaceable or exchangeable; and (3) the cognitive and somatic sensations show remarkable similarity: obsessive thoughts, rumination, idealization, stomach troubles, lack of appetite, and sleeplessness." See Miranda A.L. van Tilburg and Ad Vingerhoets, eds., *Psychological Aspects of Geographical Moves: Homesickness and Acculturation Stress*, ed. (Amsterdam: Amsterdam University Press, 2005), 8.
55 Shi Yu, *Niuyue qingren*, 94–95.
56 Shi Yu, *Niuyue qingren*, 182.
57 Boym, "Nostalgia and Its Discontents," 7.
58 Shi Yu, *Niuyue qingren*, 114.
59 Shi Yu, *Niuyue qingren*, 7.
60 Shi Yu, *Niuyue qingren*, 160.
61 Shi Yu, *Niuyue qingren*, 161.
62 Boym, "Nostalgia and Its Discontents," 7.
63 Marianne David and Muñoz-Basols, eds., *Defining and Re-Defining Diaspora: From Theory to Reality* (UK: Inter-Disciplinary Press, 2011), xi.
64 David and Muñoz-Basols point out that "etched in memory and idealized by nostalgia, the vanished home associated with the angst of exclusion, loss, abandonment would become a driving force, a relentless desire to recover one's emotional center against the unbearable pressure of an alien reality." David and Muñoz-Basols, *Defining and Re-Defining Diaspora*, xi.
65 Shi Yu, *Niuyue qingren*, 256.
66 Shi Yu, *Niuyue qingren*, 270.
67 Shi Yu, *Niuyue qingren*, 270.
68 Shi Yu, *Niuyue qingren*, 270.
69 Shi Yu, *Niuyue qingren*, 114.
70 Boym, "Nostalgia and Its Discontents," 7.
71 Boym, "Nostalgia and Its Discontents," 13.
72 Boym, "Nostalgia and Its Discontents," 13.

Notes to Pages 81–86 • 155

73 Boym, "Nostalgia and Its Discontents," 13.

74 Boym, "Nostalgia and Its Discontents," 9.

75 Boym, "Nostalgia and Its Discontents," 18.

76 This sense of connecting with homeland distantly and generating a sense of belonging from abroad aligns with the author Chen Qian's belief. To Chen, leaving is to achieve a "long-established dream," as she always desires to leave home for abroad. Nie Meng 聶夢, "Lun Chen Qian de ziwo shixian xushi jianji xin yimin wenxue de yanjiu zouxiang 論陳謙的自我實現敘事兼及新移民文學的 研究走向" [Chen Qian's Narrative of Self-Fulfillment and Research Direction for New Immigrant Literature], *Zhongguo xiandai wenxue yanjiu congkan*, no. 2 (2019):174–183.

77 Chen Qian, *Wang duan nan fei yan*, 40.

78 Chen Qian, *Wang duan nan fei yan*, 46.

79 Chen Qian, *Wang duan nan fei yan*, 40.

80 Chen Qian, *Wang duan nan fei yan*, 61.

81 *I Know Why the Caged Bird Sings* is a 1969 autobiography about the early years of African American writer and poet Maya Angelou. The first in a seven-volume series, it is a coming-of-age story that illustrates how strength of character and a love of literature can help overcome racism and trauma. According to my conversation with Chen Qian, her title is inspired by Angelou's book.

82 Quoted from Mao's poem *Qing Ping le liu pan shan* 清平樂. 六盤山.

83 Chen Qian, *Wang duan nan fei yan*, 8.

84 I have previously discussed elsewhere the multiple implications of "South" in the novella: nostalgia for her homeland, as well as her ambition and forever searching for her dream. Melody Yunzi Li, "Reorienting Sinophone America through 'Sinophone Orientalism,'" in *Orientalism and Reverse Orientalism in Literature and Film* (London: Routledge, 2021).

85 Chen Qian, *Wang duan nan fei yan*, 4.

86 Chen Qian, *Wang duan nan fei yan*, 16.

87 William Safran, "Diasporas in Modern Societies: Myths of Homeland and Return," *Diaspora* 1, no. 1 (1991): 84.

88 Rong Rong, *Fuqi biji*, 55.

89 Rong Rong, *Fuqi biji*, 64.

90 Li-Hsing Lisa Rosenlee argues that "the *nei* and the *wai*, just as the yin and the yang, are not two opposing, conflicting categories . . . they complement and complete each other." Li-Hsiang Lisa Rosenlee, *Confucianism and Women: A Philosophical Interpretation* (Ithaca: State University of New York Press, 2006), 71.

91 Rosenlee, in her *Confucianism and Women*, points out many examples where *nei–wai* distinction is not gender-specific. But when it is, *nei* "signifies the domestic realm wherein through occupying the role of daughter, wife, and mother" whereas *wai* "symbolizes the extended field beyond the centripetal domestic realm." Rosenlee, *Confucianism and Women*, 88.

92 Rong Rong, *Fuqi biji*, 200.

93 Rong Rong, *Fuqi biji*, 139.

94 Rong Rong, *Fuqi biji*, 79. In reality, voyeurism is prominent in the tradition of *qing* (affects) in Chinese literary tradition. For instance, in discussing Tang Xianzu's *Mudan Ting*, Martin W. Huang claims that Du Liniang's desire comes from her reading and dreaming, followed by an invention of an object to sustain that desire.

156 • Notes to Pages 86–95

Huang goes on to argue that Du Liniang's desire is sustained "by constantly inventing and reinventing both the object and the subject." See Martin W. Huang, *Desire and Fictional Narrative in Late Imperial China* (Boston: Harvard University Asia Center, 2001), 78–79.

95 Rong Rong, *Fuqi biji*, 47.

96 Rong Rong, *Fuqi biji*, 49.

Chapter 4   The Palimpsestic Map of the American and Chinese Dreams

1 Cao Guilin, *Beijinger in New York* (San Francisco: China Books & Periodicals, 1993), 214.

2 Lydia H. Liu, "Beijing Sojourners in New York: Postsocialism and the Question of Ideology in Global Media Culture," *Positions: East Asia Cultures Critique* 7, no. 3 (1999): 781, https://doi.org/10.1215/10679847-7-3-763.

3 Liu, "Beijing Sojourners," 764.

4 See Melanie E. L. Bush, *Tensions in the American Dream: Rhetoric, Reverie, or Reality* (Philadelphia: Temple University Press, 2015); Jim Cullen, *The American Dream: A Short History of an Idea That Shaped a Nation* (Oxford: Oxford University Press, 2003); Lawrence R. Samuel, *The American Dream: A Cultural History* (Syracuse, NY: Syracuse University Press, 2012); and Leslie K. Wang, *Chasing the American Dream in China: Chinese Americans in the Ancestral Homeland* (New Brunswick, NJ: Rutgers University Press, 2021).

5 James Truslow Adams, *The Epic of America* (Boston: Little, Brown, 1931), 404.

6 Jim Cullen, *American Dream*, 7.

7 Chen Yuanzhu, Song #59, 72, in Chen Yuanzhu, *Taishan geyao ji* [*A Collection of Taishan Folksongs*] (1929; reprint ed., Taibei, 1969), 128. Marlon Kau Hom, "Some Cantonese Folksongs on the American Experience," *Western Folklore* 42, no. 2 (1983): 126–139, https://doi.org/10.2307/1499969.

8 This term is used to describe the period of intervention of the Qing dynasty and the Republic of China by Western powers and Japan between 1839 and 1949.

9 For the detailed data, see Carlos Echeverria-Estrada and Jeanne Batalova, "Chinese Immigrants in the United States," Migration Policy Institute, January 15, 2020, https://www.migrationpolicy.org/article/chinese-immigrants-united -states; "2017 Sees Increase in Number of Chinese Students Studying Abroad and Returning after Overseas Studies," Ministry of Education, People's Republic of China, April 3, 2018, http://en.moe.gov.cn/News/Top_News/201804/t20180404 _332354.html.

10 Margaret Hillenbrand, "Letters of Penance: Writing America in Chinese and the Location of Chinese American Literature," *MELUS: The Society for the Study of the Multi-Ethnic Literature of the United States* 38, no. 3 (2013): 54.

11 Ning Shen, *Bieji xiaojie* (Nanjing: Jiangsu fenghuang wenyi chubanshe, 2016), 13.

12 Michael Berry, "The Absent American: Figuring the United States in Chinese Cinema of the Reform Era," in *A Companion to Chinese Cinema*, ed. Yingjin Zhang (West Sussex, UK: Wiley-Blackwell, 2012), 554, 569.

13 He specified his idea of the Chinese dream in a closed-door Chinese Communist Party anniversary meeting in June 2013: "Now the Party and the country are advancing toward completing the building of a moderately prosperous society in all respects and rejuvenation of the Chinese nation." "Xi Stresses Adherence to

Notes to Pages 95–113 • 157

Socialism, 'Serving the People,'" *Xinhua, People's Daily Online*, June 26, 2013, http://en.people.cn/90785/8300828.html.

14 Thomas Friedman, "China Needs Its Own Dream," *New York Times*, October 2, 2012, https://www.nytimes.com/2012/10/03/opinion/friedman-china-needs-its-own-dream.html.

15 For details on this topic, see Manoranjan Mohanty, "Xi Jinping and the 'Chinese Dream,'" *Economic and Political Weekly* 48, no. 38 (September 21, 2013): 35–36.

16 For example, see https://cn.nytimes.com/opinion/20130506/c06sebag/zh-hant/ (accessed December 10, 2022).

17 William A. Callahan, "Dreaming as a Critical Discourse of National Belonging: China Dream, American Dream and World Dream," *Nations and Nationalisms* 23, no. 2 (2017): 248–270.

18 André Corboz, "The Land as Palimpsest," trans. R. Scott Walker, Atlas of Places, 1983, accessed February 1, 2023, https://www.atlasofplaces.com/essays/the-land-as-palimpsest/.

19 Yiorgos D. Kalogeras, Johanna C. Kardux, Monika Mueller, and Jopi Nyman, *Palimpsests in Ethnic and Postcolonial Literature and Culture: Surfacing Histories* (Cham, Switzerland: Palgrave Macmillan, 2021), 7.

20 For more on the experience of indenture, see Lily Cho, "The Diasporic Turn: Diaspora as a Condition of Subjectivity," *Topia* 17 (2007): 11–30.

21 The song "Stars and Stripes Forever" is a patriotic American march written and composed by John Philip Sousa. A 1987 act of the U.S. Congress made it an official national march of the United States of America. Sousa composed this in 1896 when he sailed back home from a long European vacation. The song was "about the feeling of coming home to America," https://www.americaslibrary.gov/aa/sousa/aa_sousa_forever_3.html (accessed January 12, 2023).

22 The original poem by Tao Yuanming 陶淵明 in the Song dynasty. The line quoted here is 歸去來兮, 田園將胡不歸 [Why not go home, seeing that my field and garden with weeds are overgrown?]

23 See http://www.xinhuanet.com//zgjx/2013–04/10/c_132297333.htm (accessed January 13, 2023).

24 Fighting corruption is one of the major initiatives in Xi's regime. He mentioned it in several important meetings, particularly in his first meeting with the press in November 2012. A yearlong campaign was launched in 2013 to clean up the party. See Mohanty, "Xi Jinping," 35.

25 "歸去來兮, 田園將蕪胡不歸, 既自以心為形役, 奚惆悵而獨悲? 悟以往之不諫, 知來者之可追; 實迷途其未遠, 覺今是而昨非。" [*Gui qu lai xi, tianyuan jiang wu hu bu gui, ji zi yi xin wei xing yi, xi chouchang er du bei? Wu yiwang zhi bu jian, zhi laizhe zhi ke zhui; shi mitu qi weiyuan, jue jinshi er zuo fei*].

26 *Gui qu lai* 歸去來, Youku Video, 2018, https://v.youku.com/v_show/id_XMzU5OTkwMzQzNg==.html.

27 Xi Jinping first brought up this concept in his visit to "Road to Rejuvenation" exhibit in the National Museum.

28 *Gui qu lai*, 273.

29 *Gui qu lai*, 60.

30 *Waishengren* refers to Chinese coming from the mainland to Taiwan after 1945, distinctive from native Taiwanese. This term has been commonly used, though it is sensitive and controversial. For more information on this topic, see Hou Ruqi

侯如綺, *Shuang xiang zhijian* 雙鄉之間 [*Between Two Homelands*] (Taipei: Lianjing, 2014): 43–45.

31 For further discussion on the term *dalu* and its political implications, see Hui-Ching Chang and Richard Holt, "The Mainland (Dalu)—The Nostalgia Never Land," in *Language, Politics and Identity in Taiwan: Naming China* (New York: Routledge, 2015), 86–136.

32 Chang and Holt, "Mainland (Dalu)," 90.

33 David Der-wei Wang, *Ruhe xiandai zenyang wenxue shijiu ershi shiji zhongwen xiaoshuo xin lun* 如何現代, 怎樣文學? : 十九、二十世紀中文小說新論 [*The Making of the Modern, the Making of a Literature: New Perspectives on 19th- and 20th-Century Chinese Fiction*] (Taipei: Rye Field, 1998), 163.

34 From her most famous novel, *Again the Palm Trees* (*Youjian zonglü, youjian zonglü* 又見棕櫚, 又見棕櫚, 1967).

Coda

1 Rob Wilson's recent *Pacific beneath the Pavements: Worlding Poesis and Oceanic Becoming* uses a triadic approach of deworlding, worlding, and reworlding to activate such "worlding" modes of world-belonging critically and poetically to challenge and undermine capitalist globalization as dominating frame.

2 Terence Chong, "Bukit Brown Municipal Cemetery: Contesting Imaginations of the Good Life in Singapore," in *Worlding Multiculturalisms: The Politics of Inter-Asian Dwelling*, ed. Daniel P. S. Goh (London: Routledge, 2015), 178.

3 "Sinophone Worlding" can be a loosely organized entity or a network that implies the interconnectedness of the cultural heritage of "Sino" and renewal of the ideas of worlding. Pheng Cheah, *What Is a World?: On Postcolonial Literature as World Literature* (Durham, NC: Duke University Press, 2016), 192.

4 Loong Wong, "Belonging and Diaspora: The Chinese and the Internet," *First Monday* 8, no. 4 (April 7, 2003), https://firstmonday.org/ojs/index.php/fm/article /view/1045/966.

5 Wilson and Dissanayake define globalized as "unified around dynamics of capitalogic moving across borders" and localized as "fragmented into contestatory enclaves of difference, coalition and resistant." See Rob Wilson and Wimal Dissanayake, eds., *Global/Local: Cultural Production and the Transnational Imaginary* (Durham, NC: Duke University Press, 1996), 1.

6 Web 1.0 refers to the first stage of the internet's evolution, roughly from 1991 to 2004. Web 2.0, in contrast, is more accessible and interactive; Jessa Lingel, *An Internet for the People: The Politics and Promise of Craigslist* (Princeton, NJ: Princeton University Press, 2020), 2.

7 Sheng Lin 盛林, "Huoxian chuanyue 40 xiaoshi, huidao meiguo de jia 火線穿越 40小時, 回到美國的家" [Returning Home after Traversing 40 Hours in Danger]. *Peng Pai News* 澎湃新聞, April 13, 2020, https://www.thepaper.cn/newsDetail _forward_6943209.

8 Jonathan Rutherford, "The Third Space: An Interview with Homi Bhabha," in *Identity, Community, Culture, Difference* (London: Lawrence & Wishert. 1990), 211.

9 Chen Ruilin 陳瑞琳. *Haiwai xingxing shu bu qing: Chen Ruilin wenxue pinglun xuan* 海外星星數不清: 陳瑞琳文學評論選 [*Collection of Chen Ruilin's Literary Criticism*] (Beijing: Jiuzhou chubanshe, 2014), 15.

Notes to Pages 120–126 • 159

10 This is a common research technique in sociology and anthropology in which researchers get into a foreign culture or group to gain a comprehensive understanding of the society and culture they are studying.

11 This article introduced several overseas Chinese writers who wrote about the pandemic in Europe: "Xie zai fengcheng jinxingshi: yiqing xia de haiwai huaren zuojia 寫在封城進行時: 疫情下的海外華人作家" [Writing in the Lockdown Time: Overseas Chinese Writers during the Pandemic], accessed November 9, 2020, https://www.huxiu.com/article/349440.html.

12 Hongwei Bao, "The Use of Literature in a Global Pandemic," *Cha*, October 25, 2020, accessed January 25, 2021, https://chajournal.blog/2020/10/25/literature/?fbclid=IwAR1MknWdYmL8SJRISShCt6WW81gyxvJQyjLGHf0di21gucEvaSP7JiyJUh4.

13 Bao, "Use of Literature in a Global Pandemic."

14 An example of this is the Twitter journal @olicketysplit, edited by Chen.

15 Swati Khurana and Yi Wei, "Five Asian Diasporic Writers on the Pandemic Present and the Possibilities of Flash Fiction," Literary Hub, accessed July 19, 2022, https://lithub.com/five-asian-american-writers-on-the-pandemic-present-and-the-possibilities-of-flash-fiction/.

16 This section has drawn upon previous research including Ouyang Ting 歐陽婷. "Beimei huawen wangluo wenxue de lishi mailuo jiqi tedian he juxian 北美華文網絡文學的歷史脈絡及其特點和侷限" [Historical Contour of Chinese American Internet Literature and Its Characteristics and Limits], *Nanfang wentan* 南方文坛, no. 2 (2021): 73–78. See also Su Xiaofang, *Wangluo yu xinshiji wenxue* 網絡與新世紀文學 [*Internet and New Century Literature*] (Beijing: Zhongguo shehui kexue chubanshe, 2011).

17 For a detailed summary of this timeline, see Ouyang Ting, "Beimei huawen wanglo."

18 See https://www.rongshuxia.com.

19 Ouyang Youquan 歐陽友權, *Wangluo wenxue gailun* 網絡文學概論 [*Introduction of Internet Literature*] (Beijing: Beijing daxue chubanshe, 2008), 32.

20 Quoted in Ouyang Ting, "Beimei huawen wangluo," 76.

21 Ouyang Ting, "Beimei huawen wangluo," 75.

22 Rey Chow has argued that "diasporic consciousness" is an intellectualized way of conceiving oneself and a group of people. Rey Chow, *Writing Diaspora: Tactics of Intervention in Contemporary Critical Studies* (Bloomington: Indiana University Press, 1993), 15.

23 Sheng-mei Ma, *Immigrant Subjectivities in Asian American and Asian Diaspora Literatures* (New York: State University of New York Press, 1998), 110.

24 His article "Immigrant Subjectivities and Desires in Overseas Student Literature" examines Yu Lihua's *Again the Palm Trees*. He argues that Mou's view of his homeland is problematic because it is born from his elite status, and it speaks more about his bourgeois condition. Sheng-mei Ma, "Immigrant Subjectivities and Desires in Overseas Student Literature: Chinese, Postcolonial, or Minority Text?," *Positions: East Asia Cultures Critique* 4, no. 3 (Winter 1996): 421–458.

25 Xiao-huang Yin, *Chinese American Literature since the 1850s* (Urbana: University of Illinois Press, 2000).

26 See the full interview of Shao Jun at http://hsb.hspress.net/2009–09/13/content_7461799.htm.

27 Da Wei 大慰, "Wangluo wenxue chu yi 網絡文學刍議," *Yinhe yuedu*, April 9, 2021, accessed December 2, 2022, http://www.yinheyuedu.com/article/detail/28655.

160 • Notes to Pages 126–132

28 See http://www.chinesewritersusa.org.

29 See http://www.newworldpoetry.com/poemfile/.

30 See http://www.overseaswindow.com/.

31 The annual growth rate of the number of publications in MDPI has been over 50 percent since 2018. Christos Petrou, "Guest Post—MDPI's Remarkable Growth," *Scholarly Kitchen*, August 10, 2020, https://scholarlykitchen.sspnet.org/2020/08/10/guest-post-mdpis-remarkable-growth/.

32 Both of these articles are related to the pandemic. Particularly, my article "Rebuilding Home around Hardened Borders" (2020) is relevant to this coda. See Melody Yunzi Li, "Rebuilding Home around Hardened Borders," *British Journal of Chinese Studies* 10 (2020), https://bjocs.site/index.php/bjocs/article/view/77.

33 Wenxuecity.com, "About Us," last modified April 11, 2013, https://www.wenxuecity.com/aboutus/wenxuecity.shtml.

34 See, for instance, Feng Yun 豐雲, *Xin yimin wenxue: ronghe yu shuli* 新移民文學：融合與疏離 (Beijing: Zhongguo shehui kexue chubanshe, 2009).

35 Chen Ruilin 陳瑞琳, "Wang shang zou lai yi 'Shao Jun'—Jian lun Shao Jun de *Ren Sheng Ziyou* '網'上走來一'少君'—— 兼論少君的《人生自白》," *Shijie huawen wenxue luntan* 世界華文文學論壇, September 25, 2000, 64.

36 Chen, "Wang shang zou lai," 64.

37 Meng's arguments from this paragraph are from Meng Xingyu 蒙星宇, "Gexing yu yuwang de shenmei zhang li—Shao Jun wangluo wenxue de 'geti jingshen' 個性與慾望的審美張力— 少君網絡文學的 '個體精神' [The Aesthetic Tension between Individualism and Desire—the "Individualism" in Shao Jun's Internet Literature], *Masterpieces Review* 名作欣賞, May 1, 2011, 93–95.

38 He mentions this in his interview with Ling Yu: Shao Jin 少君 and Ling Yu 凌逾, "Wangluo shidai de kuajie xiezuo—Shao Jun fangtanlu" 網絡時代的跨界寫作—少君訪談錄 [The Cross-Border Writing in the Internet Age—Interview with Shao Jun], *Wangluo wenxue pinglun* 網絡文學評論, June 15, 2018, 88.

39 Shao Jun 少君, *Yinxiang Chengdu* 印象成都 (Chengdu: Zhongguo Chengdu shidai chubanshe, 2006), 85.

40 While studying urbanization in South African migration, Kihato writes of migrants occupying a "liminal space" within the city. See Caroline Wanjiku Kihato, "Migration, Gender and Urbanisation in Johannesburg" (PhD diss., University of South Africa, 2009).

41 Victor Turner, *The Ritual Process: Structure and Anti-Structure* (Chicago: Aldine Publishing, 1969). In 1967 he published his book *The Forest of Symbols*, which includes an essay entitled "Betwixt and Between: The Liminal Period in Rites of Passage."

42 For Su Wei's online works, see http://www.chinese-oversea-poet.org/HaiShi/AncientPoem/Su_Wei.htm.

43 Norris Brock Johnson, "Sex, Color, and Rites of Passage in Ethnographic Research," in *Ethnographic Fieldwork: An Anthropological Reader*, ed. Antonius C. G. M. Robben and Jeffrey A. Sluka (Oxford: Wiley-Blackwell, 2012), 76.

44 See http://chinesewritersna.com/review/?page_id=232.

45 This metaphor is inspired by an event with the blog *U.S. Studies Online*. See Melody Yunzi Li, "'We Are Not a Virus': Challenging Asian/Asian American Racism in the 21st Century," *U.S. Studies Online*, March 22, 2021, https://usso.uk/we-are-not-a-virus-challenging-asian-asian-american-racism-in-the-21st-century/?fbclid=IwAR3RYzeoxoT_k8JH4s9Z-gTyRoYy6rM8iQHIGFiIaY9Nzo8k2Z8FRGGcLLA.

46 Walter Benjamin, *The Work of Art in the Age of Its Technological Reproducibility, and Other Writings on Media* (Cambridge, MA: Harvard University Press, 2008).
47 Walter Benjamin, "The Task of the Translator," trans. Harry Zohn, Ricorso, accessed March 10, 2023, http://www.ricorso.net/rx/library/criticism/guest /Benjamin_W/Benjamin_W1.htm.

Bibliography

Adams, James Truslow. *The Epic of America*. Boston: Little, Brown, 1931.

Ahmed, Sara. *Cultural Politics of Emotion*. New York: Routledge, 2004.

Akerman, James R. "The Structuring of Political Territory in Early Printed Atlases." *Imago Mundi (Lympne)* 47, no. 1 (1995): 138–154. https://doi.org/10.1080/03085699508592817.

Amirthanayagam, Guy. *Asian and Western Writers in Dialogue: New Cultural Identities*. London: Palgrave Macmillan, 1982.

Babcock, Mary Lynn, and Lynnette Young Overby. "Human Kind in the Apex of Borders: Artistic and Expressive Communication in Projected Images, Dance, and Narrative." In *Global Movements: Dance, Place, and Hybridity*, edited by Olaf Kuhlke and Adam Pine, 77–104. Lanham, MD: Lexington Books, 2015.

Bai, Juyi. "Chu chucheng liubie" 初出城留別 [Parting with Friends outside the City]. *Bai Juyi ji* 白居易集, vol. 1. Beijing: Zhonghua shuju, 1999.

Bao, Hongwei. "The Use of Literature in a Global Pandemic," *Cha*, October 25, 2020. https://chajournal.blog/2020/10/25/literature/?fbclid=IwAR1MknWdYmL8SJRISShCt6WW81gyxvJQyjLGHfodi21gucEvaSP7JiyJUh4.

Barmé, Geremie. "On New Sinology." *Chinese Studies Association of Australia Newsletter*, no. 31 (May 2005): 5–9.

Beijinger in New York 北京人在紐約. January 1, 1994. YouTube Video. https://youtu.be/24_u6-FACjo?si=YF_VXVKzozk6mnu4.

Benjamin, Walter. "The Task of the Translator." Translated by Harry Zohn. *Ricorso*. Accessed March 10, 2023. http://www.ricorso.net/rx/library/criticism/guest/Benjamin_W/Benjamin_W1.htm.

Benjamin, Walter. *The Work of Art in the Age of Its Technological Reproducibility, and Other Writings on Media*. Cambridge, MA: Harvard University Press, 2008.

Berry, Michael. "The Absent American: Figuring the United States in Chinese Cinema of the Reform Era." In *A Companion to Chinese Cinema*, 552–574. West Sussex, UK: Wiley-Blackwell, 2012. https://doi.org/10.1002/9781444355994.ch30.

Blunt, Alison, and Robyn Dowling. *Home*. London: Routledge, 2006.

Boym, Svetlana. "Nostalgia and Its Discontents." *Hedgehog Review* 9, no. 2 (July 2007): 7–18.

Brah, Avtar. *Cartographies of Diaspora: Contesting Identities*. London: Routledge, 1996.

Bush, Melanie E. L. *Tensions in the American Dream: Rhetoric, Reverie, or Reality*. Philadelphia: Temple University Press, 2015.

Callahan, William A. "Dreaming as a Critical Discourse of National Belonging: China Dream, American Dream and World Dream." *Nation and Nationalism* 23, no. 2 (2017): 248–270.

Cai, Shenshen. "Scar Literature Reconsidered: Yan Geling's Novels *The Criminal Lu Yanshi* and *A Woman's Epic*." *Social Semiotics* 25, no. 3 (2015): 322–341.

Cai, Shenshen. "Zhang Yimou's Coming Home: A Depoliticized Melodrama Adapted from a Scar Literature Novel." *New Review of Film and Television Studies* 13, no. 3 (2015): 275–291.

Cao, Guilin. *Beijinger in New York*. San Francisco: China Books & Periodicals, 1993.

Carrigan, Anthony. *Postcolonial Tourism: Literature, Culture, and Environment*. New York: Routledge, 2011.

Cha, Steph. "Ha Jin Roves U.S. and China, Charting 'A Map of Betrayal.'" *Orlando Sentinel*, November 6, 2014.

Chang, Hui-Ching, and Richard Holt, "The Mainland (Dalu)—The Nostalgia Never Land." In *Language, Politics and Identity in Taiwan: Naming China*, 86–136. New York: Routledge, 2015.

Cheah, Pheng. *What Is a World?: On Postcolonial Literature as World Literature*. Durham, NC: Duke University Press, 2016.

Chen, Aimin. "Claim for Existence in Another Language: An Interview with Ha Jin." *Foreign Literature Studies* 3 (2008): 1–4.

Chen, Chung-jen. "A Portal to Transnational Communication: Problematizing Identity Politics in Ha Jin's A Map of Betrayal." *Textual Practice* 34, no. 10 (2020): 1671–1689.

Chen, Han-ping 陳涵平. "Kuayu de qingsu yu fuza de renting—dui Shi Yu liangbu changpian de bijiao yuedu 跨域的情愫与复杂的认同—— 對施雨兩部長篇的比較閱讀" [A Comparative Study of Shi Yu's Two Novels]. *Hainan shifan daxue xuebao* 社會科學版 25, no. 4 (2012): 111–115.

Chen, Lingchei Letty. "Translating Memory, Transforming Identity: Chinese Expatriates and Memoirs of the Cultural Revolution." *Tamkang Review* 38, no. 2 (June 2008): 25–40.

Chen, Lingchei Letty. "When Does 'Diaspora' End and 'Sinophone' Begin?" *Postcolonial Studies* 18, no. 1 (2015): 52–66.

Chen, Sihe 陳思和. *Zhongguo dangdai wenxue shi jiaocheng* 中國當代文學史教程 [Chinese Contemporary Literary History Textbook]. Shanghai: Fudan daxue chubanshe, 1999.

Chen, Tina. *Double Agency: Acts of Impersonation in Asian American Literature and Culture*. Stanford, CA: Stanford University Press, 2005.

Chen, Tina. "Global Asias: On the Structural Incoherence of Imaginable Ageography." In *Asian American Literature in Transition*, vol. 4, edited by Victor Román Mendoza and Betsy Huang, 311–330. Cambridge: Cambridge University Press, 2021.

Chen, Tina Y. "Emergent Cartographies and the Directions of Asian American Literary Studies." *American Literary History* 23, no. 4 (2011): 885–898.

Chen, Qian 陳謙. *Wang duan nan fei yan* 望斷南飛雁 [*Listen to the Caged Bird Sing*]. Beijing: Xinxing chubanshe, 2010.

Chen, Ruilin 陳瑞琳. *Haiwai xingxing shu bu qing: Chen Ruilin wenxue pinglun xuan* 海外星星數不清: 陳瑞琳文學評論選 [*Collection of Chen Ruilin's Literary Criticism*]. Beijing: Jiuzhou chubanshe, 2014.

Chen, Ruilin 陳瑞琳. "Wang shang zou lai yi 'Shao Jun'—Jian lun Shao Jun de *Ren Sheng Ziyou* '網'上走來一'少君'——兼論少君的《人生自白》," *Shijie huawen wenxue luntan* 世界華文文學論壇, September 25, 2000, 64.

Chen, Xianmao 陳賢茂. *Haiwai huawen wenxueshi* 海外華文文學史. Xiamen: Lujiang chubanshe, 1999.

Chen, Xiaomei. *Occidentalism: A Theory of Counter-Discourse in Post-Mao China* 2nd. ed. Lanham, MD: Rowman & Littlefield Publishers, 2003.

Chen, Xuechao 陳學超. "Ta xiang, gu xiang, jia yuan." In *Honeymoon Paris* "蜜月"巴黎: 走在地球經緯線上, 1–3. Tianjin: Bai hua wen yi chubanshe, 2003.

Chen, Yuanzhu. *Taishan geyao ji* 台山歌謠集 [*A Collection of Taishan Folksongs*]. Originally published 1929; reprint ed., Taibei, 1969.

Cheng, Wendy. "Transpacific Articulations: Student Migration and the Remaking of Asian America by Chih-Ming Wang (Review)." *Journal of Asian American Studies* 17, no. 3 (2014): 382–385.

Cheung, King-Kok. "Fate or State: The Double Life of a Composite Chinese Spy in *A Map of Betrayal*," in *Asia and the Historical Imagination*, ed. Jane Yeang Chui Wong. Singapore: Springer, 2018.

Cheung, King-Kok. *An Interethnic Companion to Asian American Literature*. Cambridge: Cambridge University Press, 1997.

Cho, Lily. "The Diasporic Turn: Diaspora as a Condition of Subjectivity." *Topia* 17 (2007): 11–30.

Chong, Terence. "Bukit Brown Municipal Cemetery: Contesting Imaginations of the Good Life in Singapore." In *Worlding Multiculturalisms: The Politics of Inter-Asian Dwelling*, edited by P. S. Goh, 161–182. London: Routledge, 2015.

Chow, Rey. *Writing Diaspora: Tactics of Intervention in Contemporary Cultural Studies*. Bloomington: Indiana University Press, 1993.

Click, Wendy. "Zoujin beimei yeshengquan de Shanghai nüzi—Fang Lümei zhuming nü zuojia rongrong 走進北美野生圈的上海女子— 方旅美著名女作家融融," *Chuguo* 出國 [*Going Abroad*], no. 4 (2012).

Clifford, James. *Routes: Travel and Translation in the Late Twentieth Century*. Cambridge, MA: Harvard University Press, 1997.

Conley, Tom. "Space." In *The Deleuze Dictionary*, edited by Adrian Parr, 260–262. Edinburgh: Edinburgh University Press, 2010.

Corboz, André. "The Land as Palimpsest." Translated by R. Scott Walker. Atlas of Places, 1983. https://www.atlasofplaces.com/essays/the-land-as-palimpsest/.

Cullen, Jim. *The American Dream: A Short History of an Idea That Shaped a Nation*. Oxford: Oxford University Press, 2003.

Da, Wei 大慰. "Wangluo wenxue chu yi 網絡文學刍議." *Yinhe Yuedu*, April 9, 2021. http://www.yinheyuedu.com/article/detail/28655.

David, Marianne, and Javier Munoz-Basols, eds. *Defining and Redefining Diaspora: From Theory to Reality*. Oxford: Inter-Disciplinary Press, 2011.

Deleuze, Gilles. *A Thousand Plateaus: Capitalism and Schizophrenia*. Minneapolis: University of Minnesota Press, 1983.

166 • Bibliography

Deleuze, Gilles, Félix Guattari, and Robert Brinkley. "What Is a Minor Literature?" *Mississippi Review* 11, no. 3 (1983): 13–33.

d'Hauteserre, Anne-Marie. "Postcolonialism, Colonialism and Tourism." In *A Companion to Tourism*, edited by Alan A. Lew, C. Michael Hall, and Allan M. Williams, 235–245. Malden, MA: Blackwell Publishing, 2004.

Echeverria-Estrada, Carlos, and Jeanne Batalova. "Chinese Immigrants in the United States." Migration Policy Institute, January 15, 2020. https://www.migrationpolicy.org/article/chinese-immigrants-united-states.

Eckholm, Eric. "After an Attack, Chinese Won't Print Expatriate's Novel," *New York Times*, June 24, 2000. https://www.nytimes.com/2000/06/24/books/after-an-attack-chinese-won-t-print-expatriate-s-novel.html.

Elden, Stuart. "Missing the Point: Globalization, Deterritorialization and the Space of the World." *Transactions of the Institute of British Geographers* 30, no. 1 (2005): 8–19.

Fay, Sarah. "Interviews: Ha Jin, The Art of Fiction." *Paris Review,* no. 191 (Winter 2009). https://www.theparisreview.org/interviews/5991/the-art-of-fiction-no-202-ha-jin.

Feng, Pin-chia. *Diasporic Representations: Reading Chinese American Women's Fiction.* Berlin: LIT Verlag Münster, 2010.

Feng, Yun 豐雲. *Xin yimin wenxue: ronghe yu shuli* 新移民文學: 融合與疏離. Beijing: Zhongguo shehui kexue chubanshe, 2009.

Foucault, Michel. *Discipline and Punish: The Birth of the Prison.* New York: Pantheon Books, 1977.

Friedman, Thomas. "China Needs Its Own Dream." *New York Times*, October 2, 2012. https://www.nytimes.com/2012/10/03/opinion/friedman-china-needs-its-own-dream.html.

Fusco, Serena. *Incorporations of Chineseness: Hybridity, Bodies, and Chinese American Literature.* Newcastle upon Tyne: Cambridge Scholars Publishing, 2016.

Gelder, Ken. *Popular Fiction: The Logics and Practices of a Literary Field.* Milton Park, UK: Routledge, 2004.

Giaccardi, Elisa, and Daniela Fogli. "Affective Geographies: Toward a Richer Cartographic Semantics for the Geospatial Web." Paper presented at the working conference on Advanced Visual Interfaces, Napoli, Italy, May 28–30, 2008. https://dl.acm.org/doi/abs/10.1145/1385569.1385598.

Gilroy, Paul. *The Black Atlantic: Modernity and Double Consciousness.* Cambridge, MA: Harvard University Press, 1993.

GoGwilt, Chris. "Writing without Borders." *Guernica*, January 14, 2007. Accessed March 26, 2024. http://www.guernicamag.com/interviews/post-2/.

Grice, Helena. "Homes and Homecomings." In *Negotiating Identities: An Introduction to Asian American Women's Writing*, 199–230. Manchester: Manchester University Press, 2002.

Gui qu lai 歸去來. Youku Video. 2018. https://v.youku.com/v_show/id_XMzU5OTkwMzQzNg==.html. Accessed March 1, 2023.

Hall, Stuart. "Cultural Identity and Diaspora." In *Identity: Community, Culture, Difference*, edited by Jonathan Rutherford, 222–237. London: Lawrence & Wishart, 1990.

Hamill, Sam. "Translator's Introduction." In *The Narrow Road to the Interior and Other Writings*, by Matsuo Bashō, ix–xxxi. Boston: Shambhala, 2000.

Heidegger, Martin. *Being and Time*. Translated by John Macquarrie and Edward Robinson. New York: Harper & Row, 1962.

Hillenbrand, Margaret. "Letters of Penance: Writing America in Chinese and the Location of Chinese American Literature." *MELUS: The Society for the Study of the Multi-Ethnic Literature of the United States* 38, no. 3 (2013): 44–66.

Hom, Marlon Kau. "Some Cantonese Folksongs on the American Experience." *Western Folklore* 42, no. 2 (1983): 126–139. https://doi.org/10.2307/1499969.

Hou, Ruqi 侯如綺. *Shuang xiang zhijian* 雙鄉之間 [*Between Two Homelands*]. Taipei: Lianjing, 2014.

Hsu, Madeline. *The Good Immigrants: How the Yellow Peril Became the Model Minority.* Princeton, NJ: Princeton University Press, 2015.

Hu, Ge 胡格, "Liusan shijiao xia jiedu Chen Qian Wangduan nan fei yan zhong de nanyan xingxiang 流散視角下解讀陳謙《望斷南飛雁》中的南雁形象" [Reading the Image of Nanyan in *Wangduan nan fei yan* from Diaspora Perspective]. *Overseas English*, no. 3 (2020): 172–173.

Huang, Martin W. *Desire and Fictional Narrative in Late Imperial China.* Boston: Harvard University Asia Center, 2001.

Huang, Wanhua. "20 shiji meihua wenxue de lishi lunkuo 20 世紀美華文學的歷史輪廓" [Historical Contour of Twentieth Century Chinese American Literature]. 華文文學 *Huawen wenxue* 4 (2000).

Huang, Yibing. *Contemporary Chinese Literature: From the Cultural Revolution to the Future.* New York: Palgrave Macmillan, 2008.

Huang, Yunte. *Transpacific Displacement Ethnography, Translation, and Intertextual Travel in Twentieth-Century American Literature.* Berkeley: University of California Press, 2002.

Huang, Yunte. *Transpacific Imaginations: History, Literature, Counterpoetics.* Cambridge, MA: Harvard University Press, 2008.

Jameson, Frederic. *Postmodernism, or, The Cultural Logic of Late Capitalism.* Durham, NC: Duke University Press, 1991.

Jin, Ha. *Between Silences: A Voice from China.* Chicago: University of Chicago Press, 1990.

Jin, Ha. "The Censor in the Mirror: It's Not Only What the Chinese Propaganda Department Does to Artists, but What It Makes Artists Do to Their Own Work." *American Scholar* 77, no. 4 (2008): 26–32.

Jin, Ha. *A Free Life.* New York: Pantheon Books, 2007.

Jin, Ha. "The Individual's Story in Historical Events." *Reflexion* 16 (2010): 1–24.

Jin, Ha. *A Map of Betrayal.* New York: Pantheon Books, 2014.

Jin, Ha. *The Writer as Migrant.* Chicago: University of Chicago Press, 2008.

Jin, Wen. "Transnational Criticism and Asian Immigrant Literature in the U.S.: Reading Yan Geling's Fusang and Its English Translation." *Contemporary Literature* 47, no. 4 (2006): 570–600.

Johnson, Ian. "Biden's Grand China Strategy: Eloquent but Inadequate." Council on Foreign Relations, May 27, 2022. https://www.cfr.org/in-brief/biden-china -blinken-speech-policy-grand-strategy.

Johnson, Norris Brock. "Sex, Color, and Rites of Passage in Ethnographic Research." In *Ethnographic Fieldwork: An Anthropological Reader,* edited by Antonius C. G. M. Robben and Jeffrey A. Sluka, 191–208. Oxford: Wiley-Blackwell, 2012.

Johnston, R. J. *Geography and the State: An Essay in Political Geography.* New York: St. Martin's Press, 1982.

Kalogeras, Yiorgos D., Johanna C. Kardux, Monika Mueller, and Jopi Nyman. *Palimpsests in Ethnic and Postcolonial Literature and Culture: Surfacing Histories.* Cham, Switzerland: Palgrave Macmillan, 2021.

Bibliography

Kalra, Virinder, Raminder Kaur, and John Hutnyk. *Diaspora and Hybridity*. Thousand Oaks, CA: SAGE Publications, 2005.

Keen, Ruth. "Information Is All That Counts: An Introduction to Chinese Women's Writing in German Translation." *Modern Chinese Literature* 4, no. 2 (1988): 225–234.

Kelsky, Karen. *Women on the Verge: Japanese Women, Western Dreams*. Durham, NC: Duke University Press, 2001.

Khurana, Swati, and Yi Wei. "Five Asian Diasporic Writers on the Pandemic Present and the Possibilities of Flash Fiction." *Literary Hub*. Accessed July 19, 2022. https://lithub.com/five-asian-american-writers-on-the-pandemic-present-and-the-possibilities-of-flash-fiction/.

Kihato, Caroline Wanjiku. "Migration, Gender and Urbanisation in Johannesburg." PhD diss., University of South Africa, 2009.

Kong, Belinda. *Tiananmen Fictions outside the Square: The Chinese Literary Diaspora and the Politics of Global Culture*. Philadelphia: Temple University Press, 2012.

Li, Bin 李檳. "'Ziyou Shen' Yu 'Manhadun'—Ba, jiushi niandai liuxuesheng wenxue chutan" '自由身'與'曼哈頓'— 八, 九十年代留學生文學初探. *Shijie huawen wenxue luntan* 世界華文文學論壇 [Forum for Chinese Literature of the World]. 2002.

Li, Melody Yunzi. "Home and Identity En Route in Chinese Diaspora—Reading Ha Jin's *A Free Life*." *Pacific Coast Philology* 49, no. 2 (2014): 203–220.

Li, Melody Yunzi. "Rebuilding Home around Hardened Borders." *British Journal of Chinese Studies*, July 12, 2020. https://bjocs.site/index.php/bjocs/article/view/77.

Li, Melody Yunzi. "Reorienting Sinophone America through 'Sinophone Orientalism.'" In *Orientalism and Reverse Orientalism in Literature and Film*, edited by Sharmani Patricia Gabriel and Bernard Wilson, 176–190. London: Routledge, 2021.

Li, Melody Yunzi. "'We Are Not a Virus': Challenging Asian/Asian American Racism in the 21st Century." *U.S. Studies Online* (blog), March 22, 2021. https://usso.uk/we-are-not-a-virus-challenging-asian-asian-american-racism-in-the-21st-century/.

Li, Yao, and Harvey L. Nicholson Jr. "When 'Model Minorities' Become 'Yellow Peril'—Othering and the Racialization of Asian Americans in the COVID-19 Pandemic." *Sociology Compass* 15, no. 2 (2021): e12849.

Lin, Sheng 林盛. "Yan Geling haiwai duanpian xiaoshuo nüxing xingxiang yanjiu 嚴歌苓海外短篇小說女性形象研究" [The Characterization of Women in Yan Geling's Short Stories]. MA thesis, University of Hong Kong, 2015.

Lingel, Jessa. *An Internet for the People: The Politics and Promise of Craigslist*. Princeton, NJ: Princeton University Press, 2020.

Liu, Denghan. 劉登翰 *Shuangchong jingyan de kuayu shuxie: 20 century huamei wenxue shi lun*. 雙重經驗的跨語書寫: 20世紀美華文學史論 Shanghai: Shanghai sanlian shudian, 2007.

Liu, Jianmei. *Revolution Plus Love: Literary History, Women's Bodies, and Thematic Repetition in Twentieth-Century Chinese Fiction*. Honolulu: University of Hawai'i Press, 2003.

Liu, Lydia H. "Beijing Sojourners in New York: Postsocialism and the Question of Ideology in Global Media Culture." *Positions: East Asia Cultures Critique* 7, no. 3 (1999): 763–798.

Lo, Kwai-Cheung. "The Myth of 'Chinese' Literature: Ha Jin and the Globalization of 'National' Literary Writing." *Xiandai zhongwen wenxue xuebao* 現代中文文學學報 6, no. 2 (2005): 63–78.

Lowe, Lisa. "The Trans-Pacific Migrant and Area Studies." In *The Trans-Pacific Imagination: Rethinking Boundary, Culture and Society*, edited by Naoki Sakai and Hyon Joo Yoo, 61–74. Singapore: World Scientific, 2012.

"Loyal Roads to Betrayal: An Interview with Ha Jin." Asian American Writers' Workshop, June 1, 2015. https://aaww.org/loyal-roads-to-betrayal-ha-jin/.

Lum, Amy Pei-ting. "Liu Xuesheng: An Ethnography of the Socialization of Chinese Students Attending College in the United States." BA thesis, Wesleyan University, 2010. http://citeseerx.ist.psu.edu/viewdoc/download?doi=10.1.1.851.1547&rep=rep1&type=pdf.

Ma, Sheng-mei. *East-West Montage: Reflections on Asian Bodies in Diaspora*. Honolulu: University of Hawai'i Press, 2007.

Ma, Sheng-mei. "Immigrant Subjectivities and Desires in Overseas Student Literature: Chinese, Postcolonial, or Minority Text?" *Positions: East Asia Cultures Critique* 4, no. 3 (Winter 1996): 421–458.

Ma, Sheng-mei. *Immigrant Subjectivities in Asian American and Asian Diaspora Literatures*. Albany: State University of New York Press, 1998.

Ma, Sheng-mei. *The Tao of S: America's Chinee and the Chinese Century in Literature and Film*. Columbia and Taipei: University of South Carolina Press and National Taiwan University Press, 2022.

Mao, Tse-tung. *Talks at the Yen'an Forum on Art and Literature*. Peking: Foreign Languages Press, 1960.

Matthews, Graham J. "Chinese Historical Fiction in the Wake of Postmodernism: Two Versions of Yan Geling's *The Flowers of War*." *Modern Fiction Studies* 62, no. 4 (2016): 659–677.

Mayer, Chingyen. "Review of *A Map of Betrayal*, by Ha Jin." *Asiatic* 8, no. 2 (December 2014): 247–250.

McLeod, John. *Beginning Postcolonialism*. Manchester: Manchester University Press, 2000.

McWilliams, Sally E. "From a Distance of One Hundred and Twenty Years: Theorizing Diasporic Chinese Female Subjectivities in Geling Yan's 'The Lost Daughter of Happiness.'" *Meridians* 6, no. 1 (2005): 133–160.

Meiners, William. "Geling Yan MFA '99: Novelist. Screenwriter. Luminary." *Columbia College Chicago*. Accessed March 26, 2024. http://www.colum.edu/academics/alumni/geling-yan.html.

Meng, Nie 聶夢. "Lun Chen Qian de ziwo shixian xushi jianji xin yimin wenxue de yanjiu zouxiang 論陳謙的自我實現敘事兼及新移民文學的研究走向" [Chen Qian's Narrative of Self-Fulfillment and Research Direction for New Immigrant Literature]. *Zhongguo xiandai wenxue yanjiu congkan*, no. 2 (2019): 174–183.

Meng, Xingyu 蒙星宇. "Gexing yu yuwang de shenmei zhang li—Shao Jun wangluo wenxue de 'geti jingshen.' 個性與慾望的審美張力— 少君網絡文學的 '個體精神'" [The Aesthetic Tension between Individualism and Desire—the "Individualism" in Shao Jun's Internet Literature]. *Masterpieces Review* 名作欣賞, May 1 (2011): 93–95.

Mohanty, Manoranjan. "Xi Jinping and the 'Chinese Dream.'" *Economic and Political Weekly* 48, no. 38 (2013): 35–36.

Nance, Kevin. "Ha Jin on 'A Map of Betrayal.'" *Chicago Tribune*, November 13, 2014. https://www.chicagotribune.com/entertainment/books/ct-prj-map-of-betrayal-ha-jin-20141113-story.html.

Ng, Franklin. *The Asian American Encyclopedia*. New York: Marshall Cavendish, 1995.

Bibliography

Ng, Maria, and Philip Holden. *Reading Chinese Transnationalisms: Society, Literature, Film*. Hong Kong: Hong Kong University Press, 2006.

Nonini, Donald M. "Ethnographic Grounding of the Asia-Pacific Imaginary." In *What Is in a Rim? Critical Perspectives on the Pacific Region Idea*, edited by Arif Dirlik, 73–96. Boulder, CO: Westview Press, 1993.

Ni, Liqiu 倪立秋. *Xin yimin xiaoshuo yanjiu* 新移民小說研究 [*Research of New Immigrant Novel*]. Shanghai: Shanghai Jiaotong daxue chubanshe, 2009.

O'Connell Davidson, Julia. *Children in the Global Sex Trade*. Cambridge: Polity, 2005.

Ouyang, Ting 歐陽婷. "Beimei huawen wangluo wenxue de lishi mailuo jiqi tedian he juxian 北美華文網絡文學的歷史脈絡及其特點和侷限" [Historical Contour of Chinese American Internet Literature and Its Characteristics and Limits]. *Nanfang wentan*, no. 2 (2021): 73–78. https://doi.org/10.14065/j.cnki.nfwt.2021.02.015.

Ouyang, Youquan 歐陽友權. *Wangluo wenxue gailun* 網絡文學概論 [*Introduction of Internet Literature*]. Beijing: Beijing daxue chubanshe, 2008.

Paasi, Anssi. "Territory." In *A Companion to Political Geography*, edited by John Agnew, Katharyne Mitchell, and Gerard Toal, 109–122. Oxford: Blackwell Publishing, 2003.

Park, Namyong. "Narrative of Memory and Historical Trauma in Yan Geling's *Lu Fan Yanshi*" 옌거링(嚴歌苓)의 『죄수 루옌스(陸犯焉識)』에 나타난역사적 트라우마와 기억의. 세계문학비교연구 (CSWL) 제54집 no. 54 (2016): 107–133.

Pejan, Ramin. "Laogai: 'Reform through Labor' in China." *Human Rights Brief: A Legal Resource for the International Rights Community* 7, no. 2 (2000 Winter): 23–27.

Pickles, John. *A History of Spaces: Cartographic Reason, Mapping, and the Geo-Coded World*. London: Routledge, 2004.

Pratt, Mary Louise. "Arts of the Contact Zone." *Profession*, 1991, 33–40.

Prescott, J. R. V. "Electoral Studies in Political Geography." In *The Structure of Political Geography*, edited by Roger E. Kasperson and Julian V. Minghi, 376–383. Chicago: Aldine Press, 1969.

Ramón Ibáñez Ibáñez, José. "Writing Short Fiction from Exile: An Interview with Ha Jin." *Odisea No. 15: Revista de Estudios Ingleses* (2014): 73–87.

Rong, Rong 融融. *Fuqi biji* 夫妻筆記 [*Notes of a Couple*]. Beijing: Shijie zhishi chubanshe, 2005.

Rosenlee, Li-Hsiang Lisa. *Confucianism and Women: A Philosophical Interpretation*. Ithaca: State University of New York Press, 2006.

Rushdie, Salman. *Imaginary Homelands: Essays and Criticism, 1981–1991*. New York: Viking, 1991.

Rutherford, Jonathan. "The Third Space: Interview with Homi Bhabha." In *Identity: Community, Culture, Difference*, edited by Jonathan Rutherford, 207–221. London: Lawrence & Wishart, 1990.

Safran, William. "Diasporas in Modern Societies: Myths of Homeland and Return." *Diaspora* 1, no. 1 (1991): 83–99.

Samuel, Lawrence R. *The American Dream: A Cultural History*. Syracuse, NY: University Press, 2012.

Schroder, Nicole. *Spaces and Places in Motion: Spatial Concepts in Contemporary American Literature*. Tubingen: Gunter Narr Velag, 2006.

Shao, Jun 少君. *Yinxiang Chengdu* 印象成都. Chengdu: Zhongguo Chengdu shidai chubanshe, 2006.

Shao, Jun 少君 and Yu Ling 凌逾. "Wangluo shidai de kuajie xiezuo—Shao Jun fangtanlu" 網絡時代的跨界寫作— 少君訪談錄" [The Cross-Border Writing in the Internet Age—Interview with Shao Jun]. *Wangluo wenxue pinglun* 網絡文學評論 (June 15, 2018): 88.

Shen, Ning 潘寧. *Bieji xiaojie* 別基小姐. Nanjing: Jiangsu fenghuang wenyi chubanshe, 2016.

Shan, Te-hsing 單德興. "Maoxian de wenxue/yanjiu: Taiwan de Yamei wenxue yanjiu—jian lun meiguo yuanzhumin wenxue yanjiu 冒現的文學/研究: 台灣的亞美文學研究—兼論美國原住民文學研究" [An Emerging Literature/Research: Taiwan's Asian American Literature and the Literature of Native American Residents]. *Chung-Wai Literary Monthly* 中外文學 29, no. 11 (2001): 11–28.

Shen, Shuang. "Time, Place, and Books in Ha Jin's *Waiting* 哈金作品中的時間、地點與書本." *Journal of Modern Literature in Chinese*, no. 6.2 and 7.1 (2005): 53–62.

Sheng, Lin 盛林. "Huoxian chuanyue 40 xiaoshi, huidao meiguo de Jia 火線穿越40小時, 回到美國的家" [Returning Home after Traversing 40 Hours in Danger]. *Peng Pai News* 澎湃新聞, April 13, 2020. https://www.thepaper.cn/newsDetail_forward _6943209.

Shi, Flair Donglai. "Reconsidering Sinophone Studies: The Chinese Cold War, Multiple Sinocentrisms, and Theoretical Generalisation." *International Journal of Taiwan Studies* 4, no. 2 (2021): 311–344.

Shi, Yu 施雨. "'Haigui nü zuojia' de shiyi shenghuo yu chuangzuo xinzhi" "海歸"女作家的詩意生活與創作新質 [The Poetic Life of the Woman Writer Returning from Overseas and the Novelty of Her Writings]. Interview by Wang Hongqi, China Female Culture Forum. Accessed November 10, 2021. http://www.lianghui.org.cn /blog/zhuanti/female/node_7117250.htm.

Shi, Yu 施雨. *Niuyue qingren* 紐約情人 [*New York Lover*]. Tianjin: Baihua wenyi chubanshe, 2007.

Shih, Shu-mei. *Visuality and Identity: Sinophone Articulations across the Pacific.* Berkeley: University of California Press, 2007.

Shih, Shu-mei, Chien-hsin Tsai, and Brian Bernards, eds. *Sinophone Studies: A Critical Reader. Global Chinese Culture.* New York: Columbia University Press, 2013.

Smith, I. C. *Inside: A Top G-Man Exposes Spies, Lies, and Bureaucratic Bungling inside the FBI.* New York: Nelson Current, 2004.

Soja, Edward W. *Postmodern Geographies: The Reassertion of Space in Critical Social Theory.* London: Verso, 1989.

Song, Weijie. *Mapping Modern Beijing: Space, Emotion, Literary Topography.* Oxford: Oxford University Press, 2017.

Su, Xiaofang. *Wangluo yu xinshiji wenxue* 網絡與新世紀文學 [*Internet and New Century Literature*]. Beijing: Zhongguo shehui kexue chubanshe, 2011.

Tally, Robert T. *Literary Cartographies: Spatiality, Representation, and Narrative.* New York: Palgrave Macmillan, 2014.

Tally, Robert T. *Melville, Mapping and Globalization: Literary Cartography in the American Baroque Writer.* London: Bloomsbury Publishing, 2011.

Tally, Robert T. "On Literary Cartography: Narrative as a Spatially Symbolic Act." *New American Notes Online*, no. 1 (January 2021). https://nanocrit.com/issues/issue1 /literary-cartography-narrative-spatially-symbolic-act.

Tally, Robert T. *Spatiality.* London: Routledge, 2013.

Tally, Robert T. *Topophrenia: Place, Narrative, and the Spatial Imagination.* Bloomington: Indiana University Press, 2019.

Tsai, Chien-hsin. "At the Crossroads: *Orphan of Asia*, Postloyalism, and Sinophone Studies." *Sun Yat-Sen Journal of Humanities* 35 (2013): 27–46.

172 • Bibliography

Turchi, Peter. *Maps of the Imagination: The Writer as Cartographer*. San Antonio, TX: Trinity University Press, 2004.

Turner, Victor. *The Ritual Process: Structure and Anti-Structure*. Chicago: Aldine Publishing, 1969.

van Tilburg, Miranda, and Ad Vingerhoets. *Psychological Aspects of Geographical Moves: Homesickness and Acculturation Stress*. Amsterdam: Leiden University Press, 2007.

Walters, Wendy W. *At Home in Diaspora: Black International Writing*. Minneapolis: University of Minnesota Press, 2005.

Wang, Chih-ming. "Huayu yuxi (yu) yijiusijiu: Chongxin biaoshu zhongguo meng '華語語系 (與) 一九四九: 重新表述中國夢'" [The Sinophone [and] 1949: The Chinese Dream Rearticulated]. *Sun Yat-Sen Journal of Humanities* 中山人文學報 42 (2017): 1–27.

Wang, Chih-ming. *Transpacific Articulations: Student Migration and the Remaking of Asian America*. Honolulu: University of Hawai'i Press, 2013.

Wang, David Der-wei. "Cong 'luo ming' dao ziyou ren—Yan Geling de *Lufan Yanshi*" 從「裸命」到自由人—嚴歌苓的《陸犯焉識》 [From a "Naked Life" to a Free Man: Yan Geling's *The Criminal Lu Yanshi*]. Taipei: Maitian chubanshe, 2014, 3–17.

Wang, David Der-wei. *Ruhe xiandai zenyang wenxue shijiu ershi shiji zhongwen xiaoshuo xin lun* 如何現代, 怎樣文學?：十九、二十世紀中文小說新論 [*The Making of the Modern, the Making of a Literature: New Perspectives on Nineteenth- and Twentieth-Century Chinese Fiction*]. Taipei: Rye Field, 1998.

Wang, Leslie K. *Chasing the American Dream in China: Chinese Americans in the Ancestral Homeland*. New Brunswick, NJ: Rutgers University Press, 2021.

Wang, Ling-chi. "The Structure of Dual Domination: Toward a Paradigm for the Study of the Chinese Diaspora in the United States." *Amerasia Journal* 33, no. 1 (January 1, 2007): 144–166.

Wang, Yanyan 王彥彥. "Yi tuo bang, yi sheng shuxie, wenhua xieshang 異托邦·醫生書寫·文化協商" [Heterotopia, Doctor's Writing, Cultural Negotiation]. *Masterpieces Review*, no. 8 (2021): 38–41.

Wang, Yuechan. "An Experience of In-Betweenness: Translation as Border Writing in Gene Luen Yang's *American Born Chinese*." *Neohelicon* 48 (2021): 161–178.

Wenxuecity.com. "About Us." Last modified April 11, 2013. https://www.wenxuecity .com/aboutus/wenxuecity.shtml.

Wilson, Rob. *Reimagining the American Pacific: From South Pacific to Bamboo Ridge and Beyond*. Durham, NC: Duke University Press, 2000.

Wilson, Rob, and Wimal Dissanayake. *Global/Local: Cultural Production and the Transnational Imaginary*. Durham, NC: Duke University Press, 1996.

Wong, Cynthia. "Chinese American Literature." In *An Interethnic Companion to Asian American Literature*, edited by King-Kok Cheung, 39–61. Cambridge: University of Cambridge Press, 1997).

Wong, Edward, Lara Lakes, and Steven Lee Myers. "U.S. Orders China to Close Houston Consulate, Citing Efforts to Steal Trade Secrets." *New York Times*, July 22, 2020. https://www.nytimes.com/2020/07/22/world/asia/us-china-houston -consulate.html.

Wong, Loong. "Belonging and Diaspora: The Chinese and the Internet." *First Monday* 8, no. 4 (April 7, 2003).

Wong, Sau-ling Cynthia. "Global Vision and Locatedness: World Literature in Chinese/by Chinese from a Chinese American Perspective." In *Global Chinese*

Literature: Critical Essays, edited by Jing Tsu and David Der-wei Wang, 49–76. Leiden: Brill, 2010.

Woolf, Virginia. "Literary Geography." In *Books and Portraits: Some Further Selections from the Literary and Biographical Writings of Virginia Woolf*, edited by Mary Lyon, 158–161. New York: Harcourt, Brace, Jovanovich, 1977.

Wu, Liwang 吳禮旺. "Nüxing geti qinggan zhigui yu shengming suqiu de biaoda 女性個體情感旨歸與生命訴求的表達—— 評陳謙《望断南飞雁》" [Narratives of Female Individual Emotions and Life Pursuits—Discussion of Chen Qian's *Wang duan nan fei yan*]. *Wenxuejie: Xiaxun*, no. 6 (2010): 10–11.

Xia, Meng. "Gender Myth and Disciplined Sexuality in Geling Yan's White Snake." *Journal of Language, Literature and Culture* 67, no. 2–3 (2020): 172–189.

Xu, Xiaoya. "Personal Elegy under the Ruins of Soul—On Chen Qian's Novels about Trauma." *Xiaoshuo pinglun* 小說評論, no. 3 (2022): 196–202.

Yan, Geling 严歌苓. *Fusang* 扶桑 [*The Lost Daughter of Happiness*]. Beijing: Renmin wenxue chubanshe, 2015.

Yan, Geling. *Lu Fan Yanshi* 陸犯焉識 [*The Criminal Lu Yanshi*]. Taipei: Maitian chubanshe, 2014.

Yang, C. K. *The Chinese Family in the Communist Revolution*. Cambridge, MA: Harvard University Press, 1959.

Yin, Xiao-huang. *Chinese American Literature since the 1850s*. Urbana: University of Illinois Press, 2000.

Yuan, Ling 袁凌. "Renjian diyu: Zhongguo wu da laogai ying 人間地獄: 中國五大勞改營" [Hells on the Earth: Five Labor Camps in China]. February 1, 2015. https://www.aboluowang.com/2015/0201/508429.html.

Zhang, Fan, et al. *Lian'ai hunyin yu fufu shenghuo* 戀愛婚姻與夫婦生活 [*Love, Marriage and Life as a Couple*]. Shanghai: Zhanwang zhoukan she, 1952.

Zhang, Lei. "The Chinese Student Protection Act of 1992: Student Immigration and the Transpacific Neoliberal Model Minority." *Journal of Asian American Studies* 24, no. 3 (October 2021): 443–470.

Zhang, Xiaogang. *Bloodline: Big Family*, 1993, Opera Gallery DIFC. Accessed March 22, 2024. https://hauteliving.com/2011/05/opera-gallery-difc-presents-lithographs-by-five-contemporary-chinese-artists/153337/

Zhang, Zhen. "Commercialization of Literature in the Post-Mao Era: Yu Hua, Beauty Writers, and Youth Writers." In *The Columbia Companion to Modern Chinese Literature*, edited by Kirk A. Denton, 386–393. New York: Columbia University Press, 2016.

Zhang, Zhen. "The World Map of Haunting Dreams: Reading Post-1989 Chinese Women's Diaspora Writings." In *Spaces of Their Own: Women's Public Sphere in Transnational China*, edited by Mayfair Mei-hui Yang, 308–336. Minneapolis: University of Minnesota Press, 1999.

Index

Figures indicated by page numbers in italics

Adams, Truslow, 92
Adorno, Theodor W., 151n7
affective geographies, 67, 151n9
affective home, 67, 68
affective mapping, 68, 69–70, 88–89,
   152n11. See also *Listen to the Caged
   Bird Sing* (*Wang duan nan fei yan;*
   Chen); *New York Lover* (*Niuyue
   qingren;* Shi); *Notes of a Couple* (*Fuqi
   biji;* Rong)
After Separation (*Da sa ba*; film), 7, 94
Ahmed, Sara, 37
Ai zai Biexiang de Jijie (*Farewell China;*
   film), 94
American dream: about, 91–92; and
   Chinese immigrants and Chinese
   diasporic literature and film, 92–94;
   comparison to Chinese dream, 95;
   deconstructed in *Beijinger in New York*,
   6, 90–91, 94–95, 97–105; palimpsestic
   maps of, 96–97; as stepping stone to
   Chinese dream in *The Way We Were*, 96,
   107–109, 112–113, 114–116
Angelou, Maya: *I Know Why the Caged
   Bird Sings*, 155n81
anti-Asian racism, 4, 119, 139n8
anti-corruption, 109–110, 157n24
The Asian American Encyclopedia
   (Ng), 28

Asian Americans, 4, 13, 20, 34, 121–122.
   See also Chinese Americans; Chinese
   diaspora
Asian American studies, 18, 34

Bai Juyi, 14
Bao, Hongwei, 23, 121
Barmé, Geremie, 143n54
Bashō, 14
Beijinger in New York (*Beijingren zai
   Niuyue;* Cao), 90–91, 97
Beijinger in New York (*Beijingren zai
   Niuyue;* TV show), 97–105; about, 6, 23,
   91–92, 116; American dream decon-
   structed, 6, 91, 94–95, 97–105, *99*, *101*;
   background and synopsis, 97; capitalism
   critiqued, 102–103, *103*; casino, 91, 98,
   103–104, *104*; comparison to *The Way
   We Were*, 105, 107, 109, 112, 114; dance
   hall, 6, 130, 132; palimpsestic maps and,
   94–95, 96–97, 98, *99*–100, 102, 104–105,
   116; popularity and spin-offs, 91; textile
   factory, 98, 101–102
belonging, 11, 45, 82, 88, 141n30. *See also* home
Benjamin, Walter, 133
Berry, Michael, 94
Be There or Be Square (*Bujianbusan*; film),
   7, 94
Bhabha, Homi, 120

176 • Index

Biden, Joe, 3
Blinken, Anthony, 3
Bloodline: Big Family (Zhang), 46–47
Blunt, Alison, 13
Book of Love (*Finding Mr. Right 2;* film), 91
boundaries, 31–32
Boym, Svetlana, 70, 79, 81, 88
Brah, Avtar, 12, 141n27
Bruno, Giuliana, 69
Bu jian bu san (*Be There or Be Square;* film), 7, 94

Cai, Shenshen, 50, 52
Cai Zhiheng: *Diyici qinmi jiechu*, 123
Cao Guilin: *Beijinger in New York* (*Beijingren zai Niuyue*), 90–91, 97. See also *Beijinger in New York* (*Beijingren zai Niuyue;* TV show)
capitalism, 23, 102–103, 118
carceral geography, 53–57, 63
Carrigan, Anthony, 70
cartography. *See* literary cartography
Chen, Chung-jen, 34
Chen, Han-ping, 73
Chen, Lingchei Letty, 10, 141n28, 150n24
Chen, Tina, 17, 20, 34, 146n45
Chen, Xianmao, 140n15
Chen, Xiaomei, 151n8
Chen Cun, 123
Chen Qian: about, 2, 5–6, 65, 72, 151nn1–2; awards and reception in China, 71, 73–74, 153n25, 153n32; background, 71; on leaving home, 155n76; PRC–Sinophone binary and, 19; **works**: *Branches*, 153n32; *Fan Zhi*, 153n25; *Gone as Falling Water* (*Fushui*), 71; *Infinity Mirror* (*Wuqiong jing*), 71; *Love in Loveless Silicon Valley* (*Ai zai wu'ai de guigu*), 71; *Teresa's Hooligan* (*Teleisha de liumangfan*), 73, 153n25, 153n32. See also *Listen to the Caged Bird Sing* (*Wang duan nan fei yan;* Chen)
Chen Ruilin, 120, 123, 129; *Honeymoon Paris*, 14
Chen Sihe, 148n6
Chen Xuechao, 14
Cheung, King-Kok: *An Interethnic Companion to Asian American Literature*, 145n18; "Fate or State," 42

Chin, Larry, 42
China: anti-corruption, 109–110, 157n24; Cultural Revolution, 25, 27, 48, 49, 50, 52–53, 62–63, 74; early reform era and Tiananmen incident, 72; national humiliation, 93, 156n8; nationalists (*waishengren*) on, 113–114; students and emigration to U.S., 7–8, 93; tensions with U.S., 3, 5, 11, 119, 146n42. See also Chinese diaspora; Chinese diasporic writers and literature; Chinese dream; Mao era
Chinese American literature, 6, 28, 140n13. *See also* Chinese diasporic writers and literature
Chinese Americans, 7, 9, 64, 140n14. *See also* Asian Americans; Chinese diaspora
Chinese diaspora: American dream and, 92–94; author within, 140n9; categories and labels, 6–7; and COVID-19 pandemic and anti-Asian racism, 3–4, 119, 139n8; generational divide, 153n27; immigration and students to U.S., 7–8, 93; "in-between" immigrant stories, 111–112; and "in-betweenness," "hybridity," and "Chineseness" concepts, 3, 139n5; precarious sense of home, 5; Sinophone and, 141n28; Sino-U.S. tensions and, 3, 5, 11, 119; vulnerability of, 8–9. *See also* Chinese Americans; Chinese diasporic writers and literature; new immigrants (*xinyimin*); overseas Chinese students (*liuxuesheng*)
Chinese diasporic writers and literature: approach to, 2–3, 5, 10–11, 21–23; American dream and, 93–94; commercialization of, 65–67, 72, 123; COVID-19 pandemic and, 4, 119–122; elitism and, 124–125; global Asias and, 17; home and, 11–12, 13–15; mapping in, 15–16, 68; overseas Chinese students (*liuxuesheng*) literature vs. and new immigrant literature, 73–74, 114, 127; palimpsestic maps and, 96–97; scholarship and terminology, 9–10; Sinophone and, 17–19; transpacific and, 5–6, 19–21. *See also* Sinophone and Sinophone literature; *specific authors and works*
Chinese dream: about, 95, 156n13; American dream as stepping stone to in *The Way*

We Were, 96, 107–109, 112–113, 114–116, *115*; elements of in *The Way We Were*, 109–111; palimpsestic maps of, 96–97
Chinese immigrant, use of term, 6
Chinese in Tokyo (Shanghairen zai dongjing; TV show), 91
Chineseness, 3, 139n5
Chinese Student Protection Act (1992), 7
Chinese Writers Association of America, 123, 125, 126, 131
Chiu, Monica: *Scrutinized!*, 146n44
Chong, Terence, 118
Chow, Rey, 13, 159n22
Clifford, James, 12, 141n27, 145n23
cognitive mapping, 15. *See also* literary cartography
commercialization, of literature, 65–67, 72, 123
communism. *See* Mao era
contact zone, 19, 143n57
Corboz, André, 96
corruption, anti-, 109–110, 157n24
COVID-19 pandemic, 3–4, 119–122, 131–132
The Criminal Lu Yanshi (Lufan Yanshi; Yan): about, 22, 48–49, 52, 63–64; carceral geography in, 53–57; comparison to *A Map of Betrayal* (Ha Jin), 49, 50, 63; distorted love and personal spaces of confinement, 60–63; film adaptations, 64; hierarchical observation and, 57, 58; normalizing judgment and, 57, 58–60; scar literature and, 52–53, 62; scholarship on, 50, 149n12; synopsis, 52
Cullen, Jim, 92
Cultural Revolution, 25, 27, 48, 49, 50, 52–53, 62–63, 74
cyberspace. *See* internet; internet-based writing

dancing, 51
Da sa ba (After Separation; film), 7, 94
David, Marianne, 80, 154n64
Da Wei, 125
Deleuze, Gilles, 25, 26, 32, 146n33, 151n3
Deng, Jireh, 121
Deng Xiaoping, 7, 33, 93
deterritorialization, 25, 30, 31–33, 36, 37–38, 146n33

d'Hauteserre, Anne-Marie, 70
diaspora: affective home and, 67; COVID-19 pandemic and, 131–132; cyberspace and, 118; definition, 10; de-/reterritorialization and, 32; dichotomous relationship between security/home and adventure/diaspora, 81–82, 82–84, 88; gender and, 82; home and, 12–13, 68–69, 80, 82, 84, 117–118, 130, 133, 141n30, 154n64; internal diaspora, 145n23; nostalgia and, 79–81; romantic love and, 67; scholarship on, 12–13, 142nn32–33; touristic experiences, 66–67, 88–89. *See also* Chinese diaspora; Chinese diasporic writers and literature; Sinophone and Sinophone literature
diasporic consciousness, 159n22
Dissanayake, Wimal: *Global/Local* (with Wilson), 118, 145n25, 158n5
diversification, 127–128
double agents, 34, 42, 146n45
Dowling, Robyn, 13

Elden, Stuart, 31
elitism, 124–125
espionage, 34, 37, 42, 44
exile, use of term, 7
expatriate, use of term, 7
extraterritorial domination, 6, 140n11

family: Mao era and, 46–48, 52, 56–57, 58–60, 63, 150n44; nation and, 22, 47; *nei–wai* dynamic and, 85, 87, 155nn90–91
Fang Fang, 120
Fang Zhouzi, 122
Farewell China (Ai zai Biexiang de Jijie; film), 94
Feng Pin-chia, 50
Feng Xiaogang: *Be There or Be Square (Bujianbusan;* film), 7, 94
Finding Mr. Right (Beijing yusheng Xiyatu; film), 91
flash fiction, 121–122
Fogli, Daniela, 151n9
Foucault, Michel, 52, 54, 57, 58
Friedman, Thomas, 95
Fuqi biji (Rong). See *Notes of a Couple (Fuqi biji;* Rong)

178 • Index

Gan lan shu (internet poetry journal), 122
Gao Xuan, 105. See also *The Way We Were*
 (*TWWW, Gui qu lai*; TV show)
Ge Fei, 48
Gelder, Ken, 151n4, 151n7
gender, 82. *See also* women, female
 characters
A Generation of Flying Swans (*Yidai
 feihong*), 74
Giaccardi, Elisa, 151n9
Gilroy, Paul, 12, 142n32
global Asias, 17
globalization, 118–119, 145n25, 158n1, 158n5
Grice, Helena, 13
Grinberg, Leon and Rebecca, 149n14
Guattari, Félix, 25, 26, 32, 146n33
Gui qu lai (TV show). See *The Way We
 Were* (*TWWW, Gui qu lai*; TV show)
Guofeng (National Styles) website, 71
guojia, 22, 47

haiwai huaren wenxue (literature by
 overseas Chinese [writers]), 9, 10
haiwai huawen wenxue (overseas Chinese
 [language] literature), 9, 10, 141n23
Haiwai Wenxuan, 123, 126
Hai Yun, 123
Ha Jin: about, 2, 5, 24; background, 8,
 25–26, 27, 145n15; challenges categoriz-
 ing, 25–29; Chinese American literature
 and, 10, 28, 145n18; Chinese translations
 of, 26; de-/reterritorialization and,
 32–33; as literary cartographer, 28–29,
 29–30, 31; localism and place names,
 29–30; minor literature and, 26; on
 patriotism, 147n49; pen name, 29;
 realism and, 27; reception in China,
 26–27, 28, 144n4; Sinophone and, 19;
 works: *The Bridgegroom*, 27, 30; *The
 Crazed*, 26, 144n4; "Exiled to English,"
 28; *A Free Life*, 1–2, 29, 31, 32, 142n34; *A
 Good Fall*, 26, 94; *Ocean of Words*, 26, 27,
 30; *Under the Red Flag*, 27, 30, 144n4;
 Between Silences, 26, 144n11; "The
 Spokesman and the Tribe," 27; *Waiting*,
 26, 27, 29–30, 144n13; *War Trash*, 26,
 144n4; *Writer as Migrant*, 145n21.
 See also *A Map of Betrayal* (Ha Jin)
Hall, Stuart, 12

Hamill, Sam, 14
Han Shaogong: "Gui qu lai," 111
Harvard Girl Liu Yiting (*Hafo nühai Liu
 Yiting*; Liu and Zhang), 8–9, 94
Heidegger, Martin, 15
heteroglossia, 19
hierarchical observation, 57, 58
Hillenbrand, Margaret, 93–94
home: affective home, 67, 68; in Chinese
 diasporic literature, 11–12, 13–15;
 Chinese women as metaphor for, 40,
 147n68; COVID-19 pandemic and,
 131–132; definition, 11; diaspora and,
 12–13, 68–69, 80, 82, 84, 117–118, 130, 133,
 141n30, 154n64; in *A Free Life* (Ha Jin),
 1–2; homesickness, 14, 37, 66–67, 68, 70,
 78–79, 88, 154n54; in online spaces, 118,
 132–133; precarious sense of among
 Chinese diaspora, 5; prison and, 57–60,
 63; touristic diasporic experiences and,
 66–67
Horkheimer, Max, 151n7
Hoskins, Janet, 143n59
Huang, Martin W., 155n94
Huang, Wanhau, 140n15
Huang, Yibing, 149n23
Huang, Yunte, 20, 143n59
Huaxia wenzhai (internet journal), 122
Hu Xueyang: *Those Left Behind* (*Liushou
 nüshi*; film), 94
hybridity, 3, 139n5

identities, split, 34–35, 40
immigrants and immigration: Chinese
 students and immigration to U.S., 7–8,
 93; gender and, 82; "in-between"
 immigrant stories, 111–112; Shi Yu on, 124;
 Yan Geling on, 49–50, 148n9. *See also*
 American dream; Chinese diaspora;
 diaspora; new immigrants (*xinyimin*);
 overseas Chinese students (*liuxuesheng*)
imprisonment. *See* carceral geography
in-betweenness, 3, 139n5
internal diaspora, 145n23
internet (cyberspace), 23, 118, 158n6
internet-based writing: about, 6, 23,
 118–119; Chinese diasporic writers
 during COVID-19 pandemic, 119–122;
 genres, themes, and diversification, 124,

127–128; history of, 122–123; home and, 118, 132–133; as liminal spaces, 131; literary mapping and, 118, 128; popularity in China, 152n23; Shao Jun's experience, 128–130; technological advantages, 124, 125–127

Jameson, Fredric, 15
Japanese Americans, 139n7
Jiang Wen: *In the Heat of the Sun* (film), 148n2
Jin, Wen, 51
Jin Liang, 26
journals, open-access, 126, 160n31

Kafka, Franz, 65
Keen, Ruth, 143n54
Kelsky, Karen: *Women on the Verge*, 16
Kihato, Caroline Wanjiku, 160n40
Kingston, Maxine Hong, 28, 140n14
Kong, Belinda, 8

labor camp movement, 54–56, 60, 63, 64, 150n53
Lao She, 68
Law, Clara: *Farewell China* (*Ai zai Biexiang de Jijie;* film), 94
Li Bin, 148n6
liminality and liminal spaces, 43, 131, 160n40
Lingel, Jessa, 118
Listen to the Caged Bird Sing (*Wang duan nan fei yan;* Chen), 82–84; about, 22–23, 67–68, 71, 74–75, 87–88; awards and reception in China, 73, 74, 153n25, 153n32; comparison to *Notes of a Couple* (Rong), 85; dichotomous relationship between security/home and adventure/diaspora, 82–84; and gender and migration, 82; "South" in, 155n84; synopsis, 75–76; title, 83, 155n81; touristic, affective maps in, 69–70
literary cartography: about, 15–16, 68, 151n10; affective mapping, 68, 69–70, 88–89, 152n11; carceral geography, 53–57; by Ha Jin, 28–29, 29–30, 31
Liu, Jianmei, 48
Liu, Lydia, 91
Liu Denghan, 148n6

Liu Jiang, 105. See also *The Way We Were* (*TWWW, Gui qu lai;* TV show)
Liushou nüshi (*Those Left Behind;* film), 94
Liu Weihua: *Harvard Girl Liu Yiting* (*Hafo nühai Liu Yiting;* with Zhang), 8–9, 94
liuxuesheng. *See* overseas Chinese students
Liu Yiqing, 27, 144n13
Li Yan, 153n38
Li Yiyun, 145n17
localism, 29–30
Lo Kwai-Cheung, 25
love: lovesickness, 67, 70, 78–79, 88, 154n54; in Mao era and prison confines, 48, 60–63; power of, 37; romantic love, 22–23, 66, 67, 69–70, 72, 74–75, 78–79, 88–89
Lowe, Lisa, 19
Lufan Yanshi (Yan). See *The Criminal Lu Yanshi* (*Lufan Yanshi;* Yan)
Lukács, György, 15
lümei zuojia (sojourning writers in the States), 9, 10
Lu Xinhua: "The Scar," 53, 149n22
Lu Xun, 152nn18–19; "What Happens after Nora Leaves Home," 83

Ma, Sheng-mei, 27, 29, 125, 139n7, 159n24
Mao era: carceral geography, 53–57; family and love in, 46–48, 52, 56–57, 57–60, 60–63, 150n44
Mao's Last Dancer (film), 148n2
Mao Zedong, 47, 83, 148n2
A Map of Betrayal (Ha Jin): about, 21–22, 24–25; comparison to *The Criminal Lu Yanshi* (Yan), 49, 50, 63; contemporary Sino-U.S. relations and, 34; de-/reterritorialization and, 25, 30, 31–33, 36, 37–38; on home and nation, 43–45; Lillian (narrator) as cartographer, 35–36, 43–45; national map of betrayal, 36–38, 42; personal map of betrayal, 38–42; split immigrant subjectivities, 34–35, 42–43; synopsis, 33–34
mapping, 15–16, 51. *See also* literary cartography
Matsuo Bashō, 14
McLeod, John, 141n30
MDPI, 126, 160n31

180 • Index

Meiguo huaren wenxue (American Chinese [writers'] literature), 9

Meiguo huaren zuojia (Chinese American writers), 10

Meiguo huawen wenxue (American Chinese [language] literature), 9

Meng Xingyu, 129–130

minor literature, 26

model minority, 4, 8–9, 139n8

Mo Yan, 48

Muir, John, 132

Muñoz-Basols, Javier, 80, 154n64

nation: family and, 22, 47; *A Map of Betrayal* (Ha Jin) on, 43–45

national humiliation, 93, 156n8

nationalists (*waishengren*), 113–114, 157n30

nei–wai dynamic, 85, 87, 155nn90–91

new immigrants (*xinyimin*): about, 7, 140n15, 151n1; America as stepping stone, 112–113; comparison to overseas Chinese students (*liuxuesheng*) literature, 73–74, 114, 127; home and, 14; literature of, 6, 9, 124; palimpsest maps and, 96–97

new media. *See* internet-based writing

New World Poetry (website), 126

New York Lover (*Niuyue qingren;* Shi), 76–82; about, 22–23, 67–68, 74–75, 87–88; comparison to *Notes of a Couple* (Rong), 85; diasporic nostalgia and, 79–81; dichotomous relationship between security/home and adventure/diaspora, 81–82; and homesickness and lovesickness, 78–79; reception in China, 72–73; synopsis, 75; touristic, affective mapping, 69–70, 76–78

Ng, Franklin: *The Asian American Encyclopedia*, 28

Nguyen, Viet, 143n59

Nieh Hualing, 114, 125; *Mulberry and Peach* (*Sangqing yu Taohong*), 41

Niuyue qingren (Shi). *See New York Lover* (*Niuyue qingren;* Shi)

Nonini, D., 143n63

normalizing judgment, 57, 58–60

nostalgia, 40, 66, 68, 70, 78, 79–81, 88

Notes of a Couple (*Fuqi biji;* Rong), 84–87; about, 22–23, 67–68, 74–75, 87–88; American household setting, 84–85, 87,

130; self-discovery and sexual awakening through Western bodies, 74, 85–87; synopsis, 76; touristic, affective maps in, 69–70, 85

Occidentalism, 151n8

O'Connell Davidson, Julia, 152n15

Oh, Seiwoong: *Encyclopedia of Asian-American Literature*, 145n18

One Second (*Yi miao zhong;* film), 64

online writing. *See* internet-based writing

Ouyang Ting, 122, 127

overseas Chinese students (*liuxuesheng*): about, 6–7, 93, 114, 153n27; comparison to new immigrant literature, 73–74, 114, 127; elitism and, 124–125; home and, 8; scholarship on, 140n12

Overseas Window (*Haiwai wenxuan;* website), 126

Paasi, Anssi, 31

Pacific Rim discourse, 20, 143n63

Pai Hsien-yung, 8, 114, 125; *Taipei People* (*Taibei ren*), 141n16

palimpsestic maps, 96–97. See also *Beijinger in New York* (*Beijingren zai Niuyue;* TV show); *The Way We Were* (*TWWW, Gui qu lai;* TV show)

Park, Namyong, 50, 149n12

participant observation, 120, 159n10

Pelosi, Nancy, 3

Pickles, John, 51

popular fiction, 65–66, 151n4, 151n7

postcolonialism, 96

Pratt, Mary Louise, 143n57

prison. *See* carceral geography

Qiu Xiaolong, 145n17

racism, anti-Asian, 4, 119, 139n8

realism, 27

Ren Baoru, 105. See also *The Way We Were* (*TWWW, Gui qu lai;* TV show)

reterritorialization, 25, 30, 31–33, 36, 37–38, 146n33, 151n3

romantic love, 22–23, 66, 67, 69–70, 72, 74–75, 78–79, 88–89. *See also* love

Rong Rong: about, 2, 5–6, 65, 72, 151nn1–2; background, 71–72; categorization of,

10; reception in China, 74; **works:** *Journey (Yuan xing)*, 71–72; *Morning, Mr. Wild Bear (Zao'an, Yexiong Xiansheng)*, 71; *Su Su's American Romance (Su Su de Meiguo lian'qing)*, 72; *Touring North America in an RV (Kaizhe fangche zou Beimei)*, 74. See also *Notes of a Couple (Fuqi biji;* Rong)

Rongshuxia (online literary journal), 123

Rosenlee, Li-Hsing Lisa, 155nn90–91

routed identity, 12, 141n27

Rushdie, Salman, 2

Safran, William, 12, 84

Said, Edward, 151n8

Sakai, Naoki, 143n59

Sartre, Jean-Paul, 15

scar literature (*shanghen wenxue*), 52–53, 62, 149nn22–23

Schwarcz, Vera, 50, 149n14

self-orientalism, 26–27, 144n10

Shanghairen zai dongjing (Chinese in Tokyo; TV show), 91

Shan Te-hsing, 140n13

Shao Jun (Qian Jianjun), 23, 125, 128–130; *Impression of Chengdu (Yinxiang Chengdu)*, 130; *Life Portrait (Rensheng zibai)*, 129; *Struggles and Equality (Fendou yu pingdeng)*, 122, 129

Shen Fuyu: *Lockdown Paris (Fengcheng Bali)*, 121

Sheng Lin, 119–120

Shen Ning: *Miss Bieji*, 94

Shen Shuang, 30, 145n23

Shi, Flair Donglai, 18

Shih, Shu-mei, 18–19; *Sinophone Studies*, 28

shijie huaren wenxue (global Chinese literature), 10

shijie huawen wenxue (global Chinese literature), 10

Shi Yu: about, 2, 5–6, 65, 72, 151nn1–2; background, 8, 70–71, 152n18, 153n29; categorization of, 10; on immigrants, 124; internet-based writing and, 131; PRC–Sinophone binary and, 19; reception in China, 72–73; **works:** *American Son Chinese Mother (Meiguo erzi zhongguo niang)*, 152n21; *Blind Spot under the Blade (Daofeng xia de Mangdian)*, 71, 131; *Growing up in the U.S. (Meiguo de yizhong chengzhang)*, 152n21; *Inside the City Emergency Room (Xiacheng jizhenshi)*, 71; *Sleepless Shore (Wumian de an)*, 152n21. See also *New York Lover (Niuyue qingren;* Shi)

Sinophone and Sinophone literature: Chinese American literature and, 140n13; Chinese diasporic writers and, 17–19; commercialization of, 65–66; definitions, 143n54; diaspora and, 141n28; Ha Jin and, 28; Occidentalism and, 151n8; Sinophone Worlding, 118, 158n3. *See also* Chinese diasporic writers and literature

sojourner, use of term, 7

Song, Weijie, 68, 152n11

space, 51

split identities, 34–35, 40

Stalling, Jonathan, 143n59

"Stars and Stripes Forever" (song), 98, 157n21

Su Tong, 48

Su Wei, 131; *Traveler (Yuanxingren)*, 9

Suzuki, Erin, 143n59

Tally, Robert J., 15, 43, 151n10

Tan, Amy, 28

Tang Xianzu: *Mudan Ting*, 155n94

Tao Yuanming, 110, 112

territory and territorialization, 31. *See also* deterritorialization; reterritorialization

third space, 120

Those Left Behind (Liushou nüshi; film), 94

Tiananmen incident, 26, 72, 144n4

touristic diasporic experiences, 66–67, 70, 76–78, 82, 84, 87, 88–89

transitional space, 50

transpacific, 5–6, 16, 19–21, 23, 118, 133, 143n59

Trump, Donald, 3–4, 119

Tsai Chien-hsin, 18

Turchi, Peter, 16

Turner, Victor, 131

United States of America: students and immigration from China, 7–8, 93; tensions with China, 3, 5, 11, 119, 146n42

182 • Index

Van Gennep, Arnold, 131
voyeurism, 86, 155n94

wai–nei dynamic, 85, 87, 155nn90–91
waishengren (nationalists), 113–114, 157n30
Walters, Wendy, 12
Wang, Chih-ming, 8–9, 18, 20, 140n12, 143n59
Wang, David Der-wei, 52, 114, 150n53
Wang, Ling-chi, 6
Wang, Yanyan, 73
Wang duan nan fei yan (Chen). See *Listen to the Caged Bird Sing* (*Wang duan nan fei yan;* Chen)
Wang Qinbo, 121
The Way We Were (*TWWW, Gui qu lai;* TV show), 105–116; about, 6, 23, 91, 92, 116; American dream as stepping stone to Chinese dream, 96, 107–109, 112–113, 114–116, *115*; Chinese dream and, 95, 109–111; on comparison between America and China, 107, *108*; comparison to *Beijinger in New York,* 105, 107, 109, 112, 114; "in-between" diasporic characters, 111–112; palimpsestic maps and, 95, 96–97, 106–107, 110–111, 112, 116; popularity of, 105; synopsis, 105–106; title, 106, 111, 112
Wenxuecity (website), 127
Wilson, Rob: *Global/Local* (with Dissanayake), 118, 145n25, 158n5; on heteroglossia, 19; *Pacific beneath the Pavements,* 158n1
women, female characters, 41, 56–57, 61–62, 147n68
Wong, Lily, 143n59
Wong, Loong, 118
Wong, Sau-ling Cynthia, 10, 140n13
Woolf, Virgina: "Literary Geography," 45
writer, use of term, 139n4

Xia Gang: *After Separation* (*Da sa ba;* film), 7, 94
Xi Jinping, 3, 95, 110–111, 114, 156n13, 157n24, 157n27
xinyimin. See new immigrants
Xin yusi (internet literary journal), 122
Xue Haixiang: *Morning, America* (*Zao'an, Meilijian*), 9
Xu Xiaoya, 73

Yan Geling: about, 2, 5, 63–64, 153n38; background, 8, 49–50, 51; categorization of, 10; Chinese censorship of, 64; commercial tactics, 151n6; on immigrant experience, 49–50, 148n9; internet-based writing and, 123; as literary cartographer, 50–52; scar literature and, 52–53; scholarship on, 50, 148n6; **works:** "Bird of a Lime Color" (Qing Ningmeng se de niao), 51; *The Lost Daughter of Happiness* (*Fusang*), 49, 51–52, 94, 148n9, 151n6; "Riddles in Las Vegas" (La si wei jia si de miyü), 50–51; *A Woman's Epic* (*Yige nüren de shishi*), 50, 52; *The World of Man* (*Ren huan*), 50; *Youth* (*Fanghua*), 149n17. See also *The Criminal Lu Yanshi* (*Lufan Yanshi;* Yan)
Yao, Steven, 143n59
"Yellow Peril" stereotype, 4, 139n8, 151n6
Yidai feihong (*A Generation of Flying Swans*), 74
Yi miao zhong (*One Second;* film), 64
Yin, Xiao-huang: *Chinese American Literature since the 1850s,* 125, 145n18
Yu Dafu: "Sinking," 147n68
Yu Lihua, 8, 114, 124; *Again the Palm Trees* (*Youjian zonglü, youjian zonglü*), 41, 73, 141n16, 159n24

Zha Jianying, 153n38
Zhang, Lei, 8
Zhang Ci, 153n38
Zhang Langlang: *Not Willing to Be Small Emperor* (*Buyuan zuo erhuangdi*), 122
Zhang Ling, 153n38
Zhang Xiaogang: *Bloodline: Big Family* (painting), 46–47
Zhang Xinwu: *Harvard Girl Liu Yiting* (*Hafo nühai Liu Yiting;* with Liu), 8–9, 94
Zhang Yimou: *Coming Home* (*Gui lai;* film), 64
Zhang Zhen, 72, 151n5
Zhong Yilin: *Zhong Yilin's London Talk Show,* 121
Zhou Li: *Manhattan's China Lady* (*Manhadun de Zhongguo nüren*), 9, 94

About the Author

MELODY YUNZI LI is an assistant professor in Chinese studies at the University of Houston. She holds a PhD in comparative literature from Washington University in St. Louis, an MPhil degree in translation studies from the School of Chinese at the University of Hong Kong, and a BA in English/translation studies from Sun Yat-sen University, China. Her research interests include Asian diaspora literature and culture, modern Chinese literature, media, dance and culture, migration studies, translation studies, and cultural identities. She has published in *Pacific Coast Philology*, *Telos*, and other journals. She is the co-editor of *Affective Geographies and Narratives of Chinese Diaspora* (Palgrave Macmillan, 2022).